A. N Homer

Only Flesh and Blood

A. N Homer

Only Flesh and Blood

ISBN/EAN: 9783743324909

Manufactured in Europe, USA, Canada, Australia, Japa

Cover: Foto ©ninafisch / pixelio.de

Manufactured and distributed by brebook publishing software (www.brebook.com)

A. N Homer

Only Flesh and Blood

Only Flesh and Blood

BY
THE AUTHOR OF
"HERNANI THE JEW"

LONDON
HUTCHINSON & CO.
PATERNOSTER ROW
1898

To

R. D. BLACKMORE, Esq.,

WITH RESPECT, ADMIRATION, AND FRIENDSHIP.

Only Flesh and Blood.

CHAPTER I.

In the Province of Champagne, mid-way, or thereabouts, between Fumay and Mezieres, the sinuous course of the river Meuse described a wider and more pronounced curve. On the right bank it was bounded by silvery osiers, rich meadows and corn land; on the left towered a rocky height, which, after frowning for a brief distance, melted into a well-wooded hill. In the space which separated the grim rock and the leafy recesses of the wooded hill from the bold encroachments of the river, nestled a village; a few red roofs, a thin and quaintly-shaped church-spire, a grey-walled château, starting up from amidst smiling gardens and blossoming orchards. Conceive that, and you have the French village of La Jonquières before you.

A woman stood in the doorway of one of the red-roofed cottages, and, shading her eyes from the glare of the sunlight, gazed up the street in the direction of the château.

"Lisette, Lisette!" she called excitedly. "Do you not hear me? How deaf you are!"

"What is it, mother?" replied a voice from within.

"The new curé, Father Bernard, is coming down the street."

"And what of that? I shall see him time enough."

"Do as I tell you; come and look. Ah! he has

stopped to talk to the Widow Lemaitre; she always has her nose poking out of her door."

"Then take yours in, mother, and you won't see it," laughed Lisette.

"Give me no sauce, child. *Mon Dieu!* there's more of that in you than anything else. As for the Widow Lemaitre, she's a busy-body—you know that—and I never liked her. Now, he has left her, and is coming this way," she continued, still shading her eyes, and staring intently at the approaching figure.

"Now for a sight of the good Father," said Lisette, who had come to the door, "though, as I said, I shall see him time enough."

"How young he is!" said the elder woman.

"*Ma foi!* too young to hear all the ills we shall have to tell him. How I should laugh to myself, were I in his place, if only for once, to hear old Brunot whine through his sins, and say how much he'd envied, robbed, and made love. And then the Count himself, what fun it would be to hear him confess. He should tell me everything, but I should never be able to keep it to myself. I've often wondered how priests can."

"Hush, child, you are impious," said Mère Chotard sternly.

"Why, mother, there's no harm in wondering," retorted Lisette, a shadow of temper crossing her face, as she deftly arranged a bright-coloured bow which ornamented her bodice.

"I tell you there is. Holy men *are* holy men, and to talk of them, ignorant as we are, won't help us. Besides, you were laughing. How pale he is. That's from study. A young life given to pouring over books, and fasting, and trying to understand *le bon Dieu.*"

"If he's pale, he's beautiful," said Lisette, her eyes

sparkling, and her voice betraying the admiration which, as a young girl, she entertained for good looks. Then lowering her voice, for Father Bernard was nearly opposite, she added, " Shall I tell you what his face reminds me of, mother?"

"What, child?"

"The little ivory Christ in the *petit sanctuaire* yonder."

"Hush!"

Both women curtsied profoundly, as with a bow, a kindly smile, and a "bon-jour, mesdames," Louis Bernard passed them. Mère Chotard looked after him, whilst an ugly cloud settled upon her face.

"Well, there," she said, "I'd like to know why he can find time to talk to Madame Lemaitre, and yet sees fit to pass me by."

"Perhaps he's tired," suggested Lisette—" and then —his parents."

"Tired—bah! His parents! Is he a child?"

"He has gone into his house, anyhow, mother, and I'm sure he might easily be tired on a day like this. Why, the sun just scorches one."

"Well, well, child, you may be right, we shall see; but I never liked the Widow Lemaitre."

Lisette allowed her full red lips to part sufficiently to show two rows of perfectly sound white teeth. She could not help smiling thus, for she knew why her mother disliked the Widow Lemaitre. They had been girl rivals, and that fact, to her mind, supplied a reason for hatred infinitely deep and durable.

"And now, since there's nothing more to be seen," observed Lisette, after a brief pause, "if you don't want me I'll go upstairs again. I feel so terribly hot. These stockings are too thick, and for that matter, so is this bodice. I was just going to change them when you called me down. Have you found your knitting?"

Mère Chotard nodded, and, without saying anything more Lisette ascended the little wooden staircase, and shut herself up in her bedroom.

It was furnished much like most humble cottage chambers, with merely a bed, a chest of drawers, a table, and a couple of chairs; but the wood of which these necessaries were made, though old and worn, was polished till it shone like a mirror, and like the white window-curtains and coarse counterpane, as spotlessly clean as hands could achieve.

To free herself of the offending bodice, or more properly speaking blouse, and the equally obnoxious stockings, was only momentary employment for Lisette's nimble fingers; but as though not content with the freedom and coolness she had thus acquired, she hastily removed the pins which confined her hair, and let it fall about her shoulders in thick, silky masses. At that instant, Lisette presented the most perfect picture of health and shapeliness possible to conceive—a type of French peasant beauty. True, to some she might not have been altogether attractive, for her hair and eyes were as black as a gipsy's; but the rich bloom in her cheeks, and the whiteness of her skin, must have awakened admiration, whilst the most hypercritical could scarcely have failed to be struck by the compactness of her frame, the roundness of her well-turned limbs and bosom.

"There," she said, with an irritable exclamation of annoyance at the closeness of the room, "if I don't feel cooler now, I don't know what I shall do, for I've got to finish my sewing. That must be done, and then—then for a walk with André. André," she repeated softly to herself; "well, if André could have a peep at me now, he would be in love with me. Lucky he can't, though, at least for him," and with a glance at her white shoulders in a small painted looking-glass which stood on the chest of drawers, Lisette gave vent to a wicked little laugh of conceit and contentment at the reflection she saw, and sat herself down to her sewing.

Her needle sped with the regularity of a machine, and there was not a sound to be heard but that which was made by piercing the material she was at work upon. The glare of the sunlight disappeared, and Lisette rose and drew up the blind. Then she returned to her work and laboured on, unconscious of the soft cool wind which came to her through the open casement, sweet with the scent of the roses which clustered about it. What did she care for roses and their fragrance? Just then she only wanted to feel cool and to finish her task. The completion of it meant André and a couple of hours' freedom, which was a sufficient inducement to cause her to work her hardest. Curiosity got the better of her at length, however, and she laid it aside to see what was going on in the street below. She glanced to the right towards the château. There was not a soul to be seen, so she turned her head, and her eyes encountered the figure of a man with a gun over his shoulder and a brace of spaniels trotting soberly at his heels.

"Monsieur le Comte!" she exclaimed, craning her head to see to greater advantage. "What can have brought him back? Love of Madame la Comtesse? I think not. But yet she is very beautiful. Ah, if he were *my* husband, I'd make him love me."

Lisette supported herself upon her elbows, resting her face upon her hands in such a position that the symmetry of her arms could be seen to advantage, and in that way, her black hair falling about her, she peeped from amidst the clustering roses, never taking her eyes off the advancing figure of the man with the gun and the dogs. She was right when she had exclaimed "Monsieur le Comte," for Rudolph, Comte de la Jonquières, owner of the land for miles round, was the personage upon whom she had fixed her eyes, and fixed them so pertinaciously that it seemed as though she meant to compel him to look at her. If such was her object, it was attained with ease, for when within a few yards, the Count raised his eyes and encountered her gaze, slackened his pace, and ceased humming to himself the strains of a song which just then happened to be the rage in Paris. That he had all his wits about him, and was by no means blind to such charms as Lisette displayed, was soon manifested by his conduct, for when exactly under the window he stopped, whistled to one of the spaniels which had lagged behind, and, twirling his moustache with one hand whilst he bestowed a glance of unconcealed admiration upon her, he said:

"The roses don't equal your cheeks, mademoiselle, but next to your cheeks come the roses. Will you give me one?"

He looked swiftly about him, as much as to say, "Be quick, I don't want to be noticed."

Lisette never hesitated an instant. The warm blood mounted to her face, and she felt her pulse quicken; but with a steady hand she plucked one of the roses, and, with all the meaning she could convey lurking in the depths of her eyes, she flung it to him. She did not attempt to speak, she might have been overheard; besides, there was no time, for the Count caught it, fixed it in his buttonhole, and darting an amorous glance that was without doubt meant to repay Lisette's with interest, he strode away up the street towards the château gates.

Lisette watched him with parted lips and an expression of undisguised satisfaction until he was no longer to be seen, and then she gave vent to her feelings.

"Now, who would have thought that Monsieur le Comte de la Jonquières would have condescended to notice me, would have deigned to ask me for a rose, to say nothing of paying me a pretty compliment? Why, he must know that I'm only the daughter of Pierre Chotard the ferryman. But there, if I've got no place in the world, and not a franc besides what mother gives me and I can earn by sewing, I've got a face that even Monsieur le Comte, with all his knowledge must pay some attention to, when I will it so. I've got *that*, and a little foot and ankle that no one would say are not shapely. It's all I possess, but it is not to be despised, and I'm disposed to be thankful for small mercies. Now, brother Pierre would tell me over again that I'm wicked. I daresay I am, but I can't help it. Let Madame la Comtesse look after her husband herself. I shall not help her."

Lisette paused, pulled on the thinner stockings, gartered them tightly to her liking, slipped on a loose blue-striped blouse, and, with a few dexterous touches got ready to go out, but at length added, before opening the door, "I must be careful not to let André suspect, for he's got such a diabolical temper when he's roused, and he does love me, I know. Ah! I'm afraid Paris has changed me, as he says, in more ways than one," and Lisette laughed.

CHAPTER II.

THE Count had scarcely passed the house in which Louis Bernard had come to live as Abbé of La Jonquières, and paused under Lisette's window as described, than it so happened that Louis Bernard, disturbed and restless in mind owing to the newness of his surroundings, quitted his door, and bent his steps in the direction pursued by the Count. Being thus close at hand, he was a witness of what passed. He had not made the Count's acquaintance, as his arrival in La Jonquières was a question of hours only; still, the Count's dress and bearing caused him to notice the circumstance more than he otherwise would have done. When, following in the Count's footsteps, he saw him enter the château gates, there no longer remained a doubt in his mind, he felt sure that the man who had walked before him, with his gun over his shoulder, and his dogs at his heels, was the most important personage in the place. Yet, so ignorant was he of the world and its ways, that the little episode which had been enacted before him was without significance for him. With the resolve to call at the château on the morrow, he dismissed the circumstance from his mind.

That he should be a prey to a sensation of restlessness entirely foreign to him, was not singular. From the early age of thirteen his existence had been made over, as it were, to those men whose age, piety, and learning were such, as, in the eyes of the Church, fitted them to mould the minds of those who were to go forth and preach her doctrines. Before a man can do this, he must undergo long years of the most rigid discipline. From this protracted and trying ordeal Louis Bernard had just been released.

He had quitted *le Grand Seminaire*, and had become Abbé of La Jonquières. He had held scarcely any intercourse with men. He had been suddenly set to advise them. With the exception of his mother, it might be said he had never spoken to a woman. Full of the fire, the passion of youth, he had been suddenly set to counsel, to admonish, to listen to, and to even hear confessions of weaknesses and sins, of the existence of which no other mortal was aware. In such a position were there not pitfalls cunningly concealed, snares on all sides, grave dangers which Louis might or might not elude? He was young—but little over four-and-twenty. Lisette had poetically compared his face to that of the ivory Christ in the *petit sanctuaire*. If a casual glance could discover so much, might not other women become aware of the existence of much more, after a careful scrutiny? Possessing this knowledge, would they keep their feelings to themselves? Would they do this, would they consider him in the light of a holy man, and not as mortal, or would they be carried away by some strange power perhaps possessed by him, perhaps imagined, and then would they wield their strength, would they show themselves in witchery of word and glance, would they display the charms which might well tempt anything mortal? Ah, there was danger for Louis. Danger of the substance of which he was as ignorant as is the newly-born child of the source of its daily nourishment.

With Louis Bernard just then, as he set forth for his walk, dwelt no very deep thoughts. He was mainly possessed with the desire to explore the recesses and windings of the place, where he had good reason to think much of his life would be spent.

The existence of La Jonquières began, as it were, with the château, and following the simple village street until the houses ceased to be, ended in the *petit sanctuaire*, a deep niche hewn out of the solid rock, guarded with an iron grating, and within, the little ivory figure of Christ, of which Lisette had spoken.

When he had arrived at the head of the street, he struck to the left, skirting the château wall, and, leaving it behind, penetrated a narrow gorge, which, when rain was plentiful, was merely the channel for a small hill torrent. Lessened by warmth it was reduced to the dimensions of a streamlet, and by artifice it had been diverted from its course, so that it entered the château grounds, and flowed through them in a succession of cascades, thence dipped under the road, which a few yards further became the main, the one street, of La Jonquières, and blended with the Meuse itself. On the left of this gorge was the rocky, though partially verdure-clad, cliff, which formed a background to the village; on the right the wooded height, which, further afield, melted away into pleasant slopes and waving plantations of fir, larch, and oak. It was the summit of this hill that Louis set himself to gain, his object being to see the ruins which crowned it, which, he had been told, were the remnants of the ancient and once magnificent château of the old Counts of La Jonquières.

The way he had chosen led him amidst the stems of gnarled and twisted thorn trees of great age, yet healthy and white with bloom, wild cherries, covered with delicate falling blossoms, which whitened the path, and detached specimens of larch and fir, whose summits were yet gilded with the rays of the departing sunlight. The near recesses of shadow were wondrously painted with softly-blending greens, and when the eye dropped from the foliage to the ground, there, too, the Great Artist had done His work magnificently. Mosses and lichens of all shapes and fineness of texture were bedecked with wood anemones, bright purple violets, hyacinths, and cowslips. Wild strawberries gleamed in scarlet ripeness from amidst the leaves, and even the dark stems of the sloe bushes, to which he clung to prevent himself from slipping backwards, had put forth a covering of blossoms which nearly hid their nakedness.

To a man of Louis' temperament—sensitive in the extreme, an intense lover of Nature in all her quiet beauty—such a scramble was a pleasure so great that even while he breathed hard and scratched his hands in clutching for support, a quiet, a peace, as soothing as the sound of the wind rustling through the bright green foliage of the larches, stole upon his mind. He gained the ruin, and stood in what he conceived might have been the banqueting hall. Some partridges rose at his approach, and whirred into space like spectral birds of bronze. A cherry tree of great size grew in the very middle of what at least must have been a stately apartment. The only roof now was the sky. He climbed to the jagged edge of one of the windows. It might have lighted the very chamber of some lovely Countess of La Jonquières. Here was food for reflection; but his thoughts were interrupted by some distant sounds. Two other people had approached and entered the ruin; but since their presence was of no interest to him, Louis speedily forgot their entrance, and remained where he was at the window, hidden from sight by some large blocks of fallen masonry, being thus quite out of earshot of a little love-scene between André and Lisette.

"*You* accuse me of having changed towards you. Nonsense, Lisette! You know better. You say it to tease me, and why do it? Come, don't spoil a moment of our time together, it's short enough. If there is a change at all, it is on your side."

"I suppose you mean since I went to Paris. You are always saying that," broke forth a woman's voice in answer to the remark made to her.

"Assuredly yes, and you know there is truth in what I say; but don't let us quarrel."

"My dear André, when I quarrel with you there'll be no mistake about it."

"Then I hope you never will. But all this comes of my telling you, as I could not help doing, that there seems to me to have been a time when we understood each other better. To get to you when the work was done, and I could slip away, was the joy of my life—"

"And isn't it now? Ah, André."

"You know. A woman does. But you interrupted me. In those days you seemed to like to meet me better. You never objected; you *would* come. You never failed, in the face of any obstacles, and now—"

"Now you want to find fault."

"I don't, Lisette. *Mon Dieu*, I love you so much that all I want is to make you care for me as devotedly, ah, as desperately as I do for you. Yonder is the farm, and I want you in it as mistress. I am honest towards you. The old people can't live long, and what's to become of me if you change as all things seem to; if you pass away from me, as they soon must, and I am left alone—all alone?"

There was a quiver of intense feeling in the speaker's voice, but with a merry, thoughtless laugh, Lisette replied:

"Don't get sentimental. Bah! I can't bear it. Wait a little, and perhaps I'll come to the farm."

"Why not now? They won't interfere. You shall be mistress."

"No; can't make up my mind. Kiss me, André, kiss me again, and don't talk stuff."

There were the sounds of an embrace and broken expressions of affection accompanying it, then once again the ruin was empty, save for Louis Bernard, and the grey and green lizards that darted and lived midst the stones that had once sheltered men. Sobered by the silence, the loneliness—for the thought had come to him that he was very solitary—Louis descended the hill, and by a slightly different path into which he had turned inadvertently, arrived at the back of the château, within a few yards of a summer arbour, fashioned and painted like a Turkish kiosk. He paused, for he was out of breath. Two squirrels were cracking nuts overhead. He discovered them by the noise they made, and was amused at the adroitness with which they extracted the kernels. But for those squirrels, he would have gone straight homewards, and would never have heard the sound of voices in the kiosk, over the fence in the grounds of the château. They were those of a man and woman who were apparently in hot altercation. Since their conversation was not audible he did not trouble himself to move. He liked watching the squirrels. At length he shook the lower branches of the tree they were in. A panic ensued, a series of bounds of astonishing agility followed, and the woodland acrobats had vanished.

Louis Bernard laughed at the antics he had witnessed, remembered it was getting late, and set off again. When immediately behind the kiosk he stopped dead, for a woman's sobs were plainly audible. Grieved, and wondering what misfortune had occasioned such unhappiness, and whether he could alleviate it, he stood still. The sounds ceased at length, and, after some moments of profound silence, a white dress gleamed, a woman's head and shoulders were outlined against the sky for an instant, and then were lost amongst the leaves.

If he lacked knowledge of the world, of mental suffering and the anguish of it, Louis Bernard was not ignorant. He had witnessed it in its most appalling form. He had seen young minds absolutely unhinged by the persistency with which religious doctrines they could not grasp, and were intellectually too sensitively strung to receive, were thundered into their terror-stricken ears. Amidst such scenes, where stern religious discipline was prescribed for one temperament as for another, he had been bred. The effect upon him had been distinctly beneficial rather than the reverse, for the existence of sorrow, in whatever shape it might appear before him, was an ill to which it was impossible for him to be deaf.

When he reached his own door the sounds of distress he had heard were still ringing in his ears. Who could have given vent to them? Somehow he thought he should be able to recognise the head and shoulders he had caught so fleeting a glimpse of, should he come upon them again. Still musing, and in an absent frame of mind, he hung up his hat in the lobby. Had he been less preoccupied, he would have remarked that there was a discussion going on between his father and mother, that they were talking rapidly, and with raised voices. He turned the handle of the door where he knew he should find them, gently, because of his mood. These words, in his father's voice, struck upon his ear:

"Ah, well, you have gained your ends, wife, Louis is a priest; our bread is assured now, but—"

He was in the midst of them. A dead silence ensued. He glanced fixedly and inquiringly at each in turn, then sat down without a word, but full of wonderment at the strangeness of what he had heard, for to his quick wit, the brief sentence, cropped in its expansion, teemed with a variety of meanings.

CHAPTER III.

THE Château de la Jonquières, architecturally, could scarcely be said to belong to any distinct period. One wing enclosed a considerable portion of the remains of a hunting lodge, said to have been built during the reign of Charles IV., surnamed the Fair, and to have been the result of a whim of the then existing Comte de la Jonquières.

Some said that he had ridden forth to meet the daughter of a neighbouring noble, and that upon that spot they had first exchanged greetings. Captivated by her great beauty he had speedily offered his hand in marriage, was accepted, and in memory of the happiness he found in her, had shortly after caused the lodge to be built where her soft eyes had first met his. Others—and here the romance vanishes—related that, being an enthusiastic sportsman, but a martyr to a disease of the nature of gout, he had ordered its erection simply because its position facilitated a descent into the more open country beyond the river. In any case, there stood the ancient remnants, enclosed in the more modern masonry, which, with the central building and remaining wing, was, without doubt, of Louis XIII. style. White stone, dressed with red brick, the two wings supporting pointed roofs, the rooms beneath which were ventilated by quaintly characteristic sculptured chimney-stacks.

A terrace—as is so common in France—with a stone balustrade, extended the whole length of the château, and with the steps approaching it from the garden below, was ornamented by richly-carved vases containing brightly-flowering plants. In the rear of the building were the stables and domestic offices, and these, joined to the wings, enclosed a court-yard in which were walnut trees, whose roots were nourished by the moisture they derived from a pond, large and deep enough to contain some venerable carp. This pond was in the middle of the court-yard, and, overshadowed by the delightful green of the walnut trees, seemed ever cool and refreshing.

Blanche, Comtesse de la Jonquières, was in the drawing-room, the long French windows of which opened on to the terrace. Alone and seated in a softly-padded *bergère*, which she had drawn before one of the windows, her eyes strayed over the landscape, steeped in the languorous warmth of an unclouded noontide sun. Not a breath ruffled the surface of the river, which gleamed like burnished steel under the hot rays. Save an occasional fish which leapt clear of the water, and returned to it again with a splash, old Pierre Chotard alone seemed to be endowed with energy. He plied his punt-pole, and cracked jokes with the dusty, coarse-featured farm women, who were returning homewards with empty baskets, having been up with the lark, the earlier because it was market-day. Never a word did his sallies provoke beyond common courtesy. They knew the temper of his wit, and being too tired to enter into the lists, blinked contentedly in the sunlight, seeming to be as much inclined to sleep and reflection as the cattle, who chewed the cud in the shadow of the trees, or stood knee-deep amidst the soft murmur of the stream as it swept past them. Madame la Comtesse was not unconscious of the beauty and peace of the scene, as she sat looking forth upon it; and yet, somehow, it found no reflection in the expression of her face.

Her cheeks were as fair as—as the petals of the rose which Lisette had flung to the Count, her husband. Too probably in the very heart of that rose there were symptoms of decay. Had something markedly cankerous asserted its existence in the very centre of her being? It was just possible, for the face is no bad indicator of the mind; in which case Madame la Comtesse had a most sensitive and sympathetic one. Just the mind to be so afflicted. Yet a headache or the weather might have much to account for. Certainly the Count himself looked contented enough. He was on the terrace with his spaniels, courting the sunshine and smoking a cigar.

The heavy gilded doors of the salon were flung open by a servant. Madame had heard the noise, and turned in her chair.

"Monsieur L'Abbé Bernard, Madame la Comtesse,' announced the domestic.

Louis Bernard had not forgotten his resolution to call at the château, and as he entered between the great white gilded doors, the panels of which were ornamented by paintings of fruit and flowers by Mignard, Madame la Comtesse looked upon a man of more than middle height, broad-shouldered and spare, but well-knit; and though the face was pale, as Lisette had said, the features were straight and good, and the eyes were grey, deep, and fearless, whilst above them was a forehead already seamed by thought, from which the dark-brown hair was drawn backwards. Madame la Comtesse was prepossessed at a glance; but while she was examining him, Louis Bernard's eyes were not idle. He was nervous, and unaccustomed to society of any kind; yet, in a moment, the face and form of the woman before him were photographed upon his mind. Keen powers of perception are given to some. Once having seen, they never forget. Louis Bernard was of this sort. As he looked at her, he saw that she was tall and gracefully formed, that the slim waist supported a well-rounded bust, and that the shoulders and arms were in perfect proportion. Advancing, he bowed with all the studied politeness of French etiquette; but she held out her hand frankly. Retaining it in his for an instant, he glanced swiftly at her face, and encountered the steady gaze of eyes that seemed as blue as the sky on a summer day.

"Madame la Comtesse, I am the new vicar of La Jonquières," he said falteringly, for he was ill at ease.

"The Abbé Bernard," she said smilingly. "Monsieur, I do assure you your name was familiar to me before you were announced."

"But I have never had the pleasure of seeing you before, Madame la Comtesse," he answered, still with apparent nervousness of manner, and he added, "I am not known."

"Indeed you are, monsieur, far better than you think, and I myself have quite looked forward to your coming. Welcome to the château, monsieur, and I am sure I may add with as much safety, to La Jonquières."

The shyness began to vanish. Louis no longer felt as though he scarcely knew what to do with himself.

"I cannot thank you sufficiently for your kind words, Madame la Comtesse," he replied, and then after a few trifling remarks he added ceremoniously, "and now, allow me to take my leave, Madame la Comtesse, for you will understand that a new vicar has many calls to pay."

"Very well, my dear Abbé; but if you must leave me so quickly, you must not go without promising to come back soon to *déjeuner*, for I want you to meet the Count."

Delighted with the kind reception he had met with,

Louis slipped away. Having made the numerous visits he had alluded to, and almost without an exception won the good approval of his parishioners, after the lapse of a week or so, he again called at the château.

"Ah, now you have taken me at my word, and I am delighted to see you," exclaimed Blanche, with the utmost affability.

"You overwhelm me, Madame la Comtesse. But you are not French, I think?" answered Louis, who could no longer find it in his heart to be shy.

Blanche laughed good-temperedly.

"Ah, have you found me out so soon, monsieur?"

"You speak very perfectly, but there is a *something*."

"If I merit so much praise, monsieur, I owe a deep debt of gratitude to those who taught me. I am English."

"I thought so, madame."

"As a kind of basis upon which to build what will, I trust, be friendship, I will give you an outline of my life. Come nearer the window though, we shall get the cool breeze from the river. There." Blanche seated herself in the *bergère*, and Louis drew close to her. "Well, let me see!" she began.

"Madame, what is that?" interrupted Louis.

The broad terrace and the gay *parterre* lay before them. Louis pointed to a long thin shadow which was suddenly flung across the glare of sunlight. It altered in shape while the words were leaving his lips.

"That, monsieur, why, that must be the Count's shadow," replied Blanche, bending forward to glance sideways from the window; "he is smoking outside I know. Rudolf! Rudolf! come here, I want you! Come and be introduced to Monsieur L'Abbé Bernard. Ah, he does not hear," she added, "but you will see him presently, monsieur."

The shadow changed in form, then faded and vanished.

As she leant to call, a shaft of sunlight touched her hair, and it shone in the brilliant gleam like burnished gold. She seated herself more comfortably, and shook the folds of her dress so that it covered a high instep and foot hidden in a black embroidered stocking and satin shoe. Was there a trace as of annoyance or sadness marking her face; had the delicate tinge of pink faded as though the shadow outside on the terrace had left its shade? When she looked at him, Louis thought so.

"How odd it was of me to notice so trifling a circumstance, Madame la Comtesse," he said, to cover a brief pause.

"Perhaps; but yet, no; as perfection is made up of trifles, so trifles become great with significance at times. We notice them acutely, we do not know why. It must be the mood one is in. Are you superstitious, monsieur?"

"All nervous people are to a certain extent, Madame la Comtesse."

"Does that mean that you are nervous?"

"Yes, I think so."

"But education destroys superstition."

"Perhaps, in its crude forms, but it sharpens the senses, and makes one more keenly alive to all things mystical and incomprehensible."

The Count's entrance interrupted them. Advancing he said:

"I am very glad to see you, Monsieur L'Abbé, and to know that you are our guest to-day. Well, what do you think of your parish? Already I hear that you are a favourite."

Talking in this strain they sat down to *déjeuner*, which, after the French fashion, was quickly discussed.

Not an hour after, the Count strode away with his dogs, remarking as he went:

"You must excuse me, Monsieur L'Abbé, for a little while, but Madame la Comtesse will take my place."

After a few trivial remarks exchanged with Blanche, with whom Louis now found himself alone, he ventured to say:

"May I remind you that you were going to tell me about yourself, Madame la Comtesse."

"Or we shall have a passage of arms, you would add."

"I think not, because we should agree," replied Louis quietly.

"Well, be it known unto you," began Blanche playfully, "that my maiden name was Fox, that my father is a colonel in the English army, and at this present moment in India. There are only two of us—my sister and myself. I am the elder. My mother died when I was fifteen."

"Then, madame, you sustained an irreparable loss, when you were ill able to bear it."

"Indeed, monsieur, you speak truly. It would have been impossible for me to have met with a greater misfortune. I thought then that rather than have lost mother—" the low, sweet voice shook, the blue eyes were for a moment bright with moisture— "I may tell you, monsieur, *you* will understand. I would have done anything, given up anything. But it was to be as it is. She has gone, and I know now that her going has changed my whole existence."

"But, madame, it was for the best. It was God's will."

"So is everything. I admit it; but the strange windings of that Will are inexplicable and very appalling. I once heard of a man who loved his wife so much that, when she was torn from him, he ceased to believe in the existence of a God."

"How terrible," said Louis gently.

"He said that he had been taught to think of God, as a Being, Omnipotent, but all loving, all merciful. There was no love, and not a spark of mercy, he said, in the chastisement he had received. But do you think it possible that deep down in his heart a man *could* think as I have said?"

"I doubt it; I cannot believe it possible, Madame la Comtesse. Buried within, though partially benumbed, there must be a belief in the Creator."

"Surely so. Monsieur, that is a likeness of my mother, painted when she was nineteen, and just before she was married. Do you think I am like her?"

Louis examined the picture minutely.

"I do," he said abruptly. "There are the same features and fair complexion, the same blue eyes and golden hair. I think you are the living image of what she must have been, madame."

"I love to think so. But I shall weary you. Let me finish my story. Soon after she was taken from me, I was sent to a convent in Paris. My sister went to live with an aunt who had always been fond of her. I saw nothing of her, though as children, we were devoted to each other. It was considered best that I should remain at the convent; so there I stayed until I was nineteen, at which age my father returned from India on sick leave. He came to Paris, brought Amy, my sister, with him, and we three lived together there and in other places for some months. Finally I met my husband, the Count, and, monsieur, here I am."

"With a long, happy, and useful life before you, Madame la Comtesse, I trust. A young and handsome husband, and a home at once lovely and luxurious, leave little to be desired that earth can give. Is it not so?"

Blanche merely inclined her head as though acquiescing; but it would seem that having weighed the suggestions, she found them wanting, for at length she said:

"With a few bold touches you have outlined a brilliant picture, monsieur; yet mere pigment fades. Good looks and wealth alone cannot satisfy a thinking person; but a mind, mental riches, are like a work by an old master. Time increases the value, and you never grow weary of admiring."

Through this web of innuendos, Louis thought he perceived the ideas they were intended to convey, but he was not sure. Did the Countess mean that mentally the Count was a disappointment to her; that the man as a man was not all she would have wished? It was clear that he was treading upon dangerous ground, so dexterously he reverted to her former remarks.

"But you have not finished your story, madame. You tell me that the colonel, your father, is in India. May I inquire what has become of your sister? Is she here?"

"No!"

"Has she, like you, a husband?"

"No!"

"Ah, then she is with the lady who is fond of her. Her aunt, I think you said?"

"Yes, you have guessed rightly."

"But I should have thought you would have liked to have her with you, madame, or have years and separation estranged you? You see, instead of wearying me, you have told me so much that I am becoming very much interested."

"She will soon be here, monsieur, and when she

comes, you shall judge for yourself whether it would be possible for me to become estranged."

"Ah, you dote on her, madame?"

"Yes, I think I do."

"Is she, too, like you?"

"Not in the least, unless, indeed, there is a family likeness which exists unknown to me. We are the very essence of opposition in every way."

"I have heard of the most devoted love existing between people so constituted," replied Louis dreamily.

"I can well believe it. In our case I'm sure it is so. Amy is a veritable little hoyden. Like a butterfly she revels in the sunshine. She does not seem to be conscious of the gloom; she is the very personification of innocence and goodness, and if you were to ask her why she laughs so lightly, she will tell you that *le bon Dieu* meant one to be happy. Not to do harm, but to enjoy all things. The lurking shadows, the gravity, the grand mystery of which one is a particle, an atom, she seems to think little about. Tax her with this and she will answer naïvely, 'Why do you think of things you cannot understand?'"

"There is something essentially philosophical in her reply, madame."

"Yes; but how can one help thinking?"

"Our temperaments are accountable for much, yet we cannot do as we please. We are mere instruments, dear madame, upon which a master hand plays. But you have drawn such a lively picture of your sister that I am quite anxious to know her. Tell me more plainly though, wherein does the contrast between you lie?"

Blanche smiled pleasantly.

"Ah, you must discover that for yourself. But you are not alone in La Jonquières, monsieur; I hear that your father and mother are with you."

Louis bowed assent, but asked, a moment later:
"How did you learn that, madame?"

"Oh, you have no idea how much we gossip here. The place is so tiny, and there is so little communication with the great world. Everyone thinks of his neighbour's doings, and their doings constitute the daily news. If you want to know everything that is happening, you have only to ask Pierre Chotard, who extracts all the information from those who use his ferry. He sucks them as dry as a bee does a flower. I must lose no time in becoming acquainted with your relatives, monsieur. The advent of anyone, is like a fresh drop of pleasure in a cup by no means full. Our immediate neighbours are limited to Monsieur le Baron de Courcelles, whose estate joins my husband's, but who is seldom here, since this one is the least of his possessions; Monsieur Brunot, a rich wine merchant; and a number of lesser bourgeois, whose forefathers have farmed the soil for generations."

"And you do not find it dull, madame?"

"I? no. I manage my household, read, play, and ride. Oh, no, the place is charming—all that one could wish. You must admit that naturally it is very beautiful; but perhaps you do not care for Nature?"

"Madame, I love it."

"So do I," replied Blanche pensively. "Monsieur, Nature never deceives one. It is true always—true as the Eternal, and fortunately, the capacity to enjoy its silent delights cannot be taken from one. But are you sure that a mass of busy people, and the distractions they afford, the turmoil of a great city, are not more to your mind? In Paris, for instance, there would be more scope for intellect, for doing good than here."

"Madame, I know nothing of great cities, I might

say with truth, of people. This house is a magnificent palace to me. I have never entered such an abode before. Bred honestly, but simply, in this province of Champagne, at thirteen I was sent to the seminary of Rheims, and practically I remained there until I came here. I am ignorant of the world. What chance have I had of knowing it? Were I to tell you my life, you would be astonished at its monotony, and—and what I have felt, perhaps in consequence."

Louis' face became suddenly very pale—pale with the pallor of old and painful recollections recalled, and very grave, too, as he finished speaking.

"I must tempt you to tell me more when you know me better, monsieur," said Blanche kindly, and in a lower voice, for she had noticed the signs of emotion.

At this moment the Count entered the salon through one of the terrace windows, and the two spaniels, with their tongues distended, were at his heels.

"Go down, Fidele; down, Philos, I tell you," he said, scolding his pets, as they capered about him; "it won't do for you to follow me here, my fine fellows. Go and wait for me."

From wagging vigorously, both tails flagged and hung disconsolately. Fidele, with beaming eyes, attempted a feeble remonstrance; then, recognising to the full a despotic will, both dogs shambled off, and stationed themselves on the terrace, occasionally peering into the room to see what was going on.

"Why do you turn them out?" inquired Blanche.

"To teach them to obey," said the Count curtly.

The tone in which he spoke startled Louis. Instantly he remembered watching the squirrels, and the voices coming to him from the kiosk. The thought made him examine the Count.

c

Two ideas were apt to strike one at once on regarding him attentively. First he was, or had been, a soldier; secondly, there was that indescribable *something*, which betrayed in every action, no matter how insignificant, a certain good breeding. He looked a gentleman—to use a word which, alas! is so often misapplied, and as oft made ludicrous by being so. A gentleman, but in the same breath, a *viveur*, even a *roué*. Small, lean, and muscular, with strongly marked, though delicately formed, features; a thick, pointed moustache, and above it a slightly hooked nose, set between brown eyes, which might fairly be described as brown eyes with a wild light in them; the whole face, though bronzed, bearing traces of many a night converted into day. He was attired in an irreproachably cut velveteen shooting suit, brown leather leggings, and boots in keeping. Altogether, Count Rudolf once seen was not to be forgotten.

" Have you been giving Monsieur L'Abbé a sketch of the peculiarities of the place ? " he said, addressing his wife.

" There is little to tell, but I think I have interested him."

" Madame la Comtesse has treated me to one of the pleasantest half-hour's chat I have ever had, Monsieur le Comte," said Louis ingenuously. " As for the place, I shall soon fall into its ways. You see, I look forward to spending many years of my life here."

" Who knows, you may soon become a bishop," replied the Count gaily.

" No, I shall be content as I am,"

" Ah, you will find us dull and unimpressionable, then you will want to leave us."

" On the contrary, monsieur, I am convinced that the more I know you all, the more I shall desire to remain," replied Louis, thus extricating himself gracefully from the corner into which he had been hemmed.

"Oh, I forgot, I have some news for you," suddenly remarked the Count, addressing Blanche. "When I was out a couple of hours ago, I met one of De Courcelles' keepers, and the man told me that this year they expect him earlier than usual. Of course the fellow was full of regrets that Monsieur le Baron did not come oftener and stay later. I listened to him; but I thought, my fine fellow, you will fatten better in your master's absence. There is no one to look after you, you are doing well."

"But the château is desolate, and Monsieur Turgot will keep a sharp enough eye on the accounts. Monsieur Turgot is the Baron's notary," continued Blanche, addressing Louis, "Monsieur le Baron de Courcelles, of whom I spoke to you."

"Monsieur Turgot, like his underlings, will thrive best with the least supervision," retorted the Count sarcastically.

"How terribly cynical you are," said Blanche; "don't you think so, monsieur?" she inquired of Louis.

"I know so little of these matters, madame," he answered evasively. Since the Count's entrance, he had again felt nervous and uneasy, and the sensation seemed to increase.

"When you do, believe me, you will agree with me. The more one knows of human beings, the more cynical one becomes."

"There is something morbidly unhealthy in such a statement," asserted Blanche; and then, feeling that the remarks the Count would insist upon making were not calculated to leave a good impression upon Louis, she added apologetically, "the Count does not really think as he speaks."

"Indeed he does," persisted the Count, "but let me tell you something that will amuse you more than discussing the merits or demerits of poor humanity. Monsieur Brunot is seeking to become a Deputy."

" For where ? "

" For the Department, of course, for the Ardennes," replied the Count, with marked irony.

" But he is the most ignorant of old men, is he not ? "

" Without doubt, but he is rich."

" But that does not qualify him to represent the people," said Louis, entering into the conversation.

" It probably will, in their eyes, and should they elect him, his ends will have been gained. My dear Abbé, you must not forget that the possession of riches covers a multitude of sins. The people worship wealth, and even the old aristocracy of France, like that of other countries, are to be found at those tables where their stomachs are best attended to. If birth cannot supply a good cook, wealth can. Have the famous *chef*, and make the money to pay him out of wine, anything you like. It does not matter. People will turn up their noses, but they will eat the dinner. Ah, to be poor is a crime, I assure you."

" You might be poor yourself, Rudolf, from the way you speak."

" So I am. However, Monsieur Brunot is not, and accordingly he is like an army flushed with success, he is confident of carrying all before him. I encountered him rolling along on the road to Mezieres seated in a yellow-painted barouche, emblazoned with armorial bearings. His attire was in keeping. He was dressed in a lavender-coloured coat, a drab waistcoat, and wore gloves of the hue of your cockatoo's crest. Three other men—parasites of some kind, probably—were with him ; but my dear Abbé, forgive me. How terribly *gauche* I must appear in your eyes, to monopolize the whole conversation, and to forget that it could be of no interest to you."

"But it has interested me, monsieur, and I entreat you to proceed."

"Well, as soon as Monsieur Brunot saw me approaching, he stopped his carriage, and engaged me in conversation whether I would or no. 'Monsieur le Comte,' said he, 'you are the very man of all others whom I most wished to behold.' I felt very much inclined to laugh outright, since we have scarcely met before."

"But you didn't?" interrupted Blanche.

"Why do you ask me? No, I was more scrupulously polite than I should probably have been to a prince of the blood; but I need scarcely add, that to see a man who would have been in his place at the head of a factory, masquerading *en prince*, exasperated me to no small extent. After a preamble, which I did my best to cut short, he said, without a blush, 'Monsieur le Comte, I am here on an electioneering campaign. Your influence in the Department is of the first importance to me; may I count upon it?' I fancy I astonished him, for after deliberating an instant, I replied: 'My dear monsieur, I know nothing of your views. I have never been tempted to dabble in politics, and in confidence, I am willing to admit to you that I am a better judge of a pretty woman'—my dear Abbé, I fear I shall shock you—'than of what constitutes a suitable Deputy.' From that moment Monsieur Brunot despaired, ceased to importune me further, and we parted."

"Poor man, you were rather hard on him."

"I said what I felt, and—witness the truth of my assertion, monsieur—behold my wife."

The colour deepened in Blanche's cheeks. She attempted to smile in acknowledgment of the compliment, but the effort subsided into doubt and veiled annoyance, and this expression, coupled with an awkward pause, induced Louis to take his leave. So terminated his second memorable visit to the château; but as he wended his way homewards in the soft summer light, amidst the blossoms and the hum of children's voices playing, more than one idea was agitating him.

He was sure that Madame la Comtesse was not happy, though she had a beautiful home; sure that hers were the white shoulders he had seen disappearing through the foliage. It was unfortunate; but what could he do? It might be in his power to lighten her burden, and if so, he would try his best. She was so beautiful and so kind, and the recollection of the friendly reception he had received, did something towards deadening the words which were constantly recurring to him: "Ah, well, you have gained your ends, wife. Louis is a priest, our bread is assured now, but—" How would the sentence have ended but for his entrance? What did it mean? He was too proud to seek to know, since he was not intended to hear; but he could not forget, and so full was he of these thoughts, that he was scarcely conscious of the marks of respect paid to him by those he passed, and failed altogether to notice the figure of André Moriseau leaning against the Widow Lemaitre's door talking to her earnestly. For that matter, he did not know André Moriseau, or that the Widow Lemaitre was a sworn enemy of the Chotard family, and of Lisette in particular.

CHAPTER IV.

LA JONQUIÈRES was wrapped in profound silence. Not a voice was to be heard, not a trace of a human being to be seen in the rough stone-paved street. Even the shaggy-haired, keen-scented dogs of the shepherd breed, which, as a rule, were reposing placidly at the entrances of their masters' humble dwellings, were no longer to be found at their respective coigns of vantage. The moon alone seemed to hold complete sway, and having risen laboriously from behind the hills, to be content to linger in the airy regions from which she looked and flung her silver radiance prodigally. With the exception of her light, the scintillating gems about her and two others, La Jonquières was in darkness.

One of these twinkled behind the roses in Lisette's window, the other flung strong gleams upon the terrace in front of the château. In the rooms from which those lights proceeded, the prelude to a little life-play was being enacted. Madame la Comtesse and the whole body of domestics had retired to sleep *en masse*. Why was the Count up alone, with restless steps and restless eyes, the latter gleaming as though they would never need repose? Old Pierre Chotard had retired to bed with the birds, for he meant to get up with them, so had his wife, and so had Lisette, virtually. She had taken off her clothes for coolness, and had lain down, blowing the candle out as though for the night. In reality that light was extinguished by her for effect, for she lay with a sheet over her, and never tried to close her eyes, stared rather into the darkness, and did her best to listen for the old clock of the church to chime forth the hour. What hour was she listening for, and why, when it came, did she cast the sheet from her, come to a sitting posture on the edge of her bed, and grope for the match she had placed at hand? Why, when the candle was lit, did she rise to her feet, and with every care to avoid a sound or a creak of the boards she trod upon, dress herself quickly? Why, too, while she was about it, did her eyes sparkle, her bosom heave, and her fingers tremble as one in excitement? Her cheeks, warm with rich blood, and her lips, scarlet with health, contrasted powerfully with the whiteness of her skin and her glossy black hair. Occasionally, as she proceeded with her simple and hurried toilet, the ruddy lips moved, as though some form of inward communing was in progress.

At length she had finished, and with stockings only on the feet she was proud of, her shoes in her hand, she leant and blew out the candle. With the darkness she paused, standing in the little room half-way to the door. Did the absence of the light bring fear? Surely not to one of her temperament; but a rush of thoughts—yes. To be truthful, not the darkness, but the nearer approach of what she was about, brought those thoughts, some of them too hard to fling aside. On the brink of her purpose, her head became the battle-ground of a spirited *melée* of contending ideas.

"Shall I go?" she thought, and hesitated. "What would André Moriseau think, and father and mother? Is it right, is it right?"

A sharp conflict ensued over this, and the "noes" had it clearly; but, on the opposing side, counteracting the effect, came a din of screeching, impish voices.

"It may not be quite right; but there's not much harm, and you'll never have any fun in your life if you are so silly. Besides, no one will know, and you'll have all your pleasure without anyone being the wiser. Why, of course, go, and don't make such a fuss about it. You promised. Keep your word, you can't back out of it now; you promised, so it's too late. What, promised to meet another woman's husband! yes—but. Bother the but's—to the devil with them. It's only for a chat in the moonlight, that's all."

So clamoured the imps and the angels, and while the fight was still fierce, Lisette, wishing hard to go, went.

Within the spacious walls of the château, in one of the stately apartments looking out on to the trim, flower-decked terrace, and the stretch of smooth tree-dotted turf, the Count paced, fidgetted, and was supremely restless; but good voices, though they still made themselves heard, were weak within him. They had fought often. He had stifled them much. His restlessness came of his desire that his schemes should succeed. There could be little new to him, and a general weariness was the result; but the charmingly unsophisticated person of Lisette had administered a fillip. Her rustic beauty had allured him as no other type would have done. He thought he understood the fashionable world and its feminine disciples so well; but this simple wood-land nymph, this creature of the village and its strong fresh air, he was blasé enough to think, would amuse him, act as a sort of tonic, and kill time, in fact. So he had sought and encouraged, not resisted. He was too great a man to be seen talking to Lisette as often as he might wish, before the little world even of La Jonquières, besides—the Countess—it would not do; but to meet her at night was romantic, what he wished, and attended, in his opinion, with little risk of discovery.

The people of La Jonquières were so wooden, and slept like their own cattle, soundly, because they had worked. Of course, if anything did come out, it would be annoying decidedly. The very devil, in fact; for madame was not of a sort to be trifled with. But—well, he would risk that. It was a good deal to do, yet he was enamoured, and risk, after all, was a salt, without which there would have been little savour.

For him, the time appointed had come, and he was about to step on to the terrace, through one of the long French windows, when he discovered, to his annoyance, that his cigar-case was empty. None of the household would be surprised if they knew him to be stirring at any hour. His constant and protracted visits to Paris, had accustomed him to retire when the nightingale's clear full warble was hushed by the joyous carol of the lark.

The great staircase, with its handsome but gloomy panelling, its military relics and battle-piece by Meissonier, was quickly ascended, his private sanctum gained, and case filled; but, in the act of returning, it occurred to him to see whether his wife slept. He passed on into her room.

There had been a time when to be free to enter where she was at the dead of night, to stand by and gaze upon her beauty unchecked, would have aroused as much feeling as he was capable of, struck a chord as deep as any in his nature. He had pursued her, hunted her down, would take no denial, and married her with the most violent protestations of sincere attachment. Now he could look upon her unmoved, or nearly so, certainly with little sentiment that was substantial or genuine Yet his conscience smote him as she stirred and muttered restlessly. He knew that he had done much to fill the blue eyes with tears, to hasten the inevitable coming of grey hairs, to wrinkle the fair skin, and cause the delicate complexion to fade prematurely. Why did he not stop? There was yet time. She was very forgiving, and susceptible to kindness. Ah, to tread one track long, is to become accustomed to it, so that its windings could almost be followed with closed eyes. Did she deserve ill at his hands? Not unless goodness and truth, a conduct which he knew to be above blame, merited chastisement. She had never wronged him in the smallest matter intentionally. He could not say the same, either in great or small things. A shudder passed over him; a spasm caused by self-acknowledged guilt. His conscience, compass-like, though subject to no variations, still indicated the straight, the right course. He chose to neglect its promptings. It pleased him to shut his eyes and shrug his shoulders, to ignore good, to meet Lisette at all hazards, and with a stifled exclamation of anger at his own weakness he turned his back upon the château to do so.

At the head of the village, and running at right angles to the main street, was a thin copse composed of an oak or two and some willows and alders, where the ground became moister as it sloped to the river. Lisette gained its shelter by leaving her home at the back, traversing the little garden, climbing the fence at the bottom of it, and running swiftly over a piece of ground which, stretching at the rear of the village was the common property of its inhabitants, and was bounded by the Meuse itself. This copse grew right down to the water's edge, and in its shadow, where some of the longer branches waved to and fro in the stream, she stood and waited.

"Perhaps, after all, he won't come," she said to

herself, looking about for a sign of the Count, and seeing none. "I've a good mind to go back, and if he doesn't appear soon I will. This comes of meeting a great man. Poor old André would have been waiting for me an hour ago. Ah," she sighed, "I wonder whether I'm foolish not to take him and his farm. He loves me, and is good enough for me. I couldn't expect a better husband, but—Pierre was right. I am changed. Paris has spoilt me—spoilt me at least for a life of drudgery in the country. I like excitement—love it, I ought to say. The Count is so rich and so handsome." Lisette laid great emphasis upon the words "so handsome," and clasped her hands together with a gesture expressive of the blindest adoration. "So handsome," she repeated, "and André, with his old farm amongst the trees yonder, will keep. *Ma foi*, I might be speaking of last year's apples." She burst into a peal of laughter at the queer comparison, and in the midst of her merriment a voice said:

"You laugh—ah! then you are not cross with me?"

"Oh, how you startled me!" exclaimed Lisette, putting her hand to her side.

"Did I?" returned the Count. "Is the little heart beating too fast? Let me feel."

"Take your arm away. I'm cross," retorted Lisette, pouting her red lips.

"But you were laughing a moment ago."

"Yes, but it was at my own thoughts, and not because I was glad you had kept me waiting ever so long, and in the cold, too."

"Why, it's not cold; but if it is, let me kiss the cold away."

"Don't. It's the middle of the night, and ought to be cold if it isn't."

"Not in these parts at this time of year, sweet Lisette."

"You are not half sorry enough, Monsieur le Comte. Why, you are trying to make fun of me."

"Indeed I'm not. Fun of you? Lisette, just think what you're saying. Sorry enough? I'm not sorry I'm here, that is if you'll be sweet to me as I know you can be."

"You don't know anything of the kind."

"As sweet as the roses which grow so near to you, that when I think of it, I become envious."

"How absurd you are, monsieur."

"Not at all. Hear me. I tell you I envy the roses that have climbed so near to you that the softest breath of wind can turn their faces, so that they can peer at you through that sweet little chamber window of yours, whenever they chance to be so pleasantly caressed. Ah, Lisette, the roses are more fortunate than I am. Come, let us make it up. I had to get some cigars, and that made me late."

"Had to get some cigars? How droll! Then the cigars were of more consequence than—"

"Of first consequence."

"Really?"

"Yes, because I knew you would come to me, and I had to go and fetch them."

"Don't talk in riddles. How could you tell that I should come?"

"Instinct."

"Well, it nearly deceived you. I had half a mind not to, and should have gone away again but for my own thoughts, which made me laugh."

"Exactly; but made you wait for me."

"Indeed, I'd forgotten all about you."

"Ah, you say that. You affect nonchalance. A little trick common to your sex. You shall speak the truth to me, you shall own, and it will be a different tale you will have to confess, my dear girl."

"How conceited you men are."

"You make us so, by the attentions you can't help paying us."

"Can't help paying you? How absurd! Do you suppose we have no control over ourselves?"

"None, when you meet the man you like. Then you are, as a woman in love, what that man makes you. Lisette, as a woman in love, come into my arms."

"Suppose anyone sees us," replied Lisette, posing coquettishly before the Count, who had seated himself on a convenient bough, which swayed with the weight of his small but well-formed figure. He lighted a cigar, and spoke between his efforts to make it burn smoothly.

"How can anyone see us?"

"If they happened to be prowling about in the village. Madame la Comtesse—"

"Do you suppose Madame la Comtesse is likely to be prowling about in the village?"

"She might follow you. Whatever would she say?"

"Don't talk nonsense."

"Or André."

"Who is André, pray?"

"He would kill me."

"Confound him. Who is he?"

"André Moriseau, Monsieur le Comte."

"What, who has the farm up on the hill?"

"Yes, monsieur."

"And why should he kill you? Ridiculous idea. But what power has he over you?"

"None."

"None? Then why did you allude to him?"

"Because he loves me."

"Is that all?"

"*All*, monsieur? If you only heard the way he speaks. He loves me madly."

"I daresay. He'd be a fool if he didn't."

"And is always pestering me by his offers of marriage."

"Well, why don't you tell him his attentions are distasteful?"

"Because I'm not sure."

"How droll! You can scarcely love him, and at the same time consent to meet me here at midnight."

"Why not? This place is so dull, and it amuses one."

"Oh, it amuses you? Meeting one here is a source of amusement, eh? Let me see. André, then, is the real, the acknowledged lover; but you don't mind filling up your spare time with me. So, if that is it, it strikes me that Monsieur André and I have an account to settle."

"Oh, he can take good care of himself," laughed Lisette, in the same bantering tones.

"Can he? He may want all his wits to do it. You little wretch, you shall not annoy me any further. I'll make you admit that you love me and only me, or I'll know why," and the Count suddenly sprang from his seat.

By an agile movement Lisette contrived to elude him. There was a moment's chase, but the Count was too quick for her, and she was in his arms.

"Now then, mademoiselle," he said, as he led her back, panting from the exertion, "you shall satisfy me as I have said. First, that plump white arm would rather be round my neck than anyone else's. I know it, so I shall place it there."

The Count suited the action to the word.

Lisette was passive.

"Secondly, that small round waist, so symmetrical, so firm, so altogether charming, would rather be encircled by my arm than anyone else's. I know it, so behold." He did as he said. "Thirdly—"

"Let me go."

"There is nothing further from my intentions."

"Let me go. If you don't, and at once, too, I'll never meet you again. And what would Father Bernard or anyone say, if they knew that I had done so?"

"Ah, you should have thought of that before. Now, the fact being known to us only remains a secret, the more sacred because of its sweetness. But why allude to Father Bernard?"

"Because I shall have to tell him how wicked it was of me to come here. If I don't I shall never feel happy."

"Tell him if you like, and let him be the judge of the extent of the evil committed by two people who desire to talk, at the hour when the nightingales claim the silence as their right. Tell him, of course, and you'll be forgiven. But, my dear Lisette, do you suppose that priests never do wrong; have no passions, in fact, like the rest of us?"

"Of course they haven't. But then they are different."

"Different, my poor, simple, little child—different! They are mortals, I suppose you will admit, and as such, subject to the weaknesses of flesh and blood. Can the leopard change his spots or the Ethiopian his skin, do you fancy, my darling little Lisette?"

"Oh, well, I don't know anything at all about it," replied Lisette, yawning, and showing her white teeth in the act.

"And you don't want to," answered the Count quickly, seeing that he was carrying her out of her depth. "Why should you? You were made for love, made to be loved, and that's all you want to be told or to know. Put your arms round me and kiss me."

Lisette brushed the Count's moustache aside with

her moist lips, and he, surprised at her acquiescence, returned the caress till it palled upon him.

"Do you know, Lisette," he said, "that the sight of you looking down upon me from amongst the roses, was the loveliest picture I've ever seen. I must have you painted like that."

"Yes, and madame would trample upon the picture. No, I shall not be painted, not even to please you," retorted Lisette.

"Not even to please me? Then you would do a good deal if I asked you—if I were to entreat you?"

"I have come here to-night," said Lisette simply.

"And that is much, that is a great deal."

"More—a great deal more—than you deserve. But I must go, I *must*. The thought that father or mother might have heard me stirring, by some evil chance, makes me tremble."

"No one has heard you, and you can't go yet. Why, we have not arranged when to meet again."

"Oh, I can't promise now."

"What! that pretty little foot, that has brought you here, will carry you away doubtful of when it shall bear you to me again."

"Yes; I can't stay another moment."

"But I haven't admired it half enough. Let me see, you could wear Cinderella's famous slipper, you are simply—"

But with a swift turn, and the exertion of her country strength, Lisette slipped from the Count's embrace, and sped away amidst the stems of the trees too swiftly to be followed. The Count looked after her until she had disappeared over the low fence of the garden, which was just visible in the uncertain light and then, when she was no longer to be seen, turned in the direction of the château grounds, saying to himself:

D

"I don't know when I've seen as pretty a woman. But she's not to be caught like a *grisette*. Really, this becomes interesting," and he strolled leisurely back to the terrace and to bed, pondering upon what had happened, while Blanche slept in ignorance, and Louis Bernard slumbered in the little home he had made for himself, unconscious even by the warning of a dream, that in the night, dark and quiet, webs were being spun which should affect him.

As for Lisette, of whom André Moriseau was dreaming on his rough couch under the thatch, away upon the hill amongst the poplars—as for Lisette, she closed her black eyes contentedly, thinking the Count "so handsome," and thinking also that she might acquire power over him.

CHAPTER V.

THE home in which Louis Bernard had come to live was as simple as could be conceived. So plain in its exterior, that there was absolutely nothing in its gray stone walls to please the eye. Merely a cottage, with a couple of windows on each side of the door, on either hand of which again grew an old and knotted pear tree, trained to conceal much of the bare stonework. A little garden cut in terraces as it encroached on the rocky heights already described, and rising at the extreme end, so that a view of the village and the grounds of the château could be had from it. These terraces fringed with espaliers of carefully cultured fruit trees, and marked by patches of herbs and old-fashioned flowers.

The interior of the cottage was likewise stamped with a plainness amounting to severity. A few pieces of old and treasured china, heirlooms from Madame Bernard's side of the house. Two or three prints, upon which the same value was set, and a scanty stock of old furniture in mahogany and cracked rosewood—much thought of, much polished.

Madame Bernard herself was not altogether out of keeping with her surroundings. Tall, bony, wrinkled, yet pink upon the cheeks; religiously, as severe as her appearance suggested. Beneath the harsh exterior, a love of her son, though this, alas, almost buried under a veneer of religious enthusiasm and deepest ambition that he should rise to eminence in the Church. Le Père Bernard, the reverse of her in all things, sleek, good-tempered, content to let his wife rule where he had not the brains, and, except for a bursting bubble of disapproval which rose to his tongue as if by mistake, quiescent in all things.

So it will be seen that so far as his parents were concerned, Louis fell between two stools. The mother, incapable of drawing forth love and confidence by kindness, and an effort to understand and sympathize. The father, mentally so inferior to his child, that Louis' quick and cultivated intellect shrank unsatisfied from any sustained intercourse. The two old people had chanced to split upon a life-long rock of contention—Louis, and his pursuit in life. Madame's religious fervour and dogged vigour of mind had carried the day. Le Père Bernard, beaten, looked on and occasionally lamented. Beyond this solitary disagreement, husband and wife were strangely happy for so ill-sorted a pair.

As a boy, Louis had uttered his complaints, vented his feelings of dislike, both of the life he then led and of the outlook it presented. Madame Bernard, in her strength, had chided and turned him back to the course she had chalked out for him. As a man, he had sought to find the consolation naturally needed by a sensitive, speculative, and somewhat restless disposition, sought for this where he should have discovered it—in his mother. He had found her barren, beyond holding up before him the skeleton of religion, and telling him to take comfort by clothing it with his daily acts. Being human, and therefore requiring human support, he had been driven back upon himself, and although unknown to him, this accident of birth, this parental want, coupled with a boyhood and youth immersed in study, had stored within him a torrent composed of all human passions and weaknesses, which were pent up only to burst their bonds with greater fury, when the ripe time should come.

CHAPTER VI.

At the château, the change, of which Blanche had spoken to Louis, had come. Amy had arrived, and like the butterfly to which Blanche had laughingly compared her, she flitted about the old place enraptured with everything. The court-yard, with its shimmering pond stocked with carp, and shaded with walnut trees, sent her into a reverie. The outlying woods of the park, the shady alleys, the broad terrace, the brilliant *parterre*, and view of the slowly gliding river, transported her into an ecstasy.

Loving Nature best, and the day of her arrival being propitious, she inspected the exterior first, her arm through Blanche's, her remaining hand full of the gay blossoms she could not resist the temptation of gathering *en route*. Once within doors again, she insisted upon being shown all the vast rooms—some of which were never used and seldom opened, except for dusting purposes—and would have poked into every hole and corner, carried away by the novelty the exploration afforded her, had she been left to herself. Finally, however, drawn by Blanche, she concentrated her attention and admiration upon the reception rooms, and there, though she was no connoisseur, the art treasures collected by generations of the Count's ancestors, came in for very honest, if uneducated, praise.

Common sense told her what labour the short-stitch tapestry of the Louis Quatorze furniture had cost, and her own innate taste caused her to detect the delicate workmanship and colouring of the old Dresden *bonbonnieres*. Gilded chairs of rare design upholstered in stately Genoa velvet, Gobelins tapestry, Venetian mirrors, and clocks of brass and ebony executed in Boule's well-known style, could not be seen even by her uncultured eyes without awakening their meed of praise. Besides, when Blanche witnessed her delight, her own love of the beautiful and artistic was thoroughly aroused, and in the most approved bric-à-brac parlance she discussed the merits of the wonders of which she was mistress. She even sifted her memory, and in examining the portraits of the Count's ancestors, of which he was justly proud, tried to recall the legends he had told her and the remarks he had made concerning them. Then, when Amy had looked, wondered, commented in her own fashion, and in short filled her mind, sponge-like, with as much as it would hold, the two sisters sat down to a cup of tea and a chat.

"Let's pull the table nearer to the window and then we can see the river," exclaimed Amy, waiting for no answer, but doing as she suggested. "Well, Blanche, you ought to be happy in such a lovely home. I suppose I shall get used to the grandeur of it in time. After aunt's unpretentious substantialness, it seems to me like a palace. And to think that you've been here all this time, and yet I've never seen it before."

"Not long after all, dear. You must remember we travelled about a good deal, and were in Paris some months before we settled down here."

"True, so you were."

"Then, too, you mustn't forget that after I was married, and papa went abroad again, I was incessantly begging you to come to me."

"But poor aunt couldn't spare me."

"That was why I ceased asking you. I thought she might think me unkind."

"Oh, she never thought that. She knew how we loved each other, and it never entered into her head to think anything bad of *you*. She always used to say to me, 'Amy, you are pretty, but Blanche is beautiful.' She admired you so much, you know, dear," added Amy naïvely, and by way of explanation.

"Did she?" replied Blanche, in a voice which seemed to imply her disbelief in the genuineness of anyone's admiration or regard.

"Did she?—of course she did," retorted Amy emphatically; "and how could she help it, I should like to know? Look at your beautiful broad shoulders and golden hair. Then you are tall and in proportion, while I am small, and my hair's—"

"Auburn," interrupted Blanche affectionately; "and you mustn't flatter, me, dear, or I shall become quite vain, and then you won't like me."

"No, I never shall; but I shall love you as long as I live, and you won't get me away from you again in a hurry. Can't I stay altogether, Blanche?"

"We'll see how it can be managed."

"I needn't be any expense, for we've both got ample to live on now. I often think how kind it was of aunt. Blanche, I wish she could have lived always."

"Whatever is, is best," replied Blanche, unconsciously quoting a line of Pope's, and with far more meaning in her voice than the subject demanded, for, in reality, she had seen little of the relative in question.

"I suppose so, if one stops to think, but how seldom one does; still, it has often occurred to me that when some terrible railway accident happens and scores of people are killed, or a vessel is wrecked and the crew and passengers lost, it becomes difficult to understand how that can be for the best."

"There are many things beyond our comprehension, dear. It would be better perhaps to say that there are few things we understand rightly, yet, in any case, we must accept them as being for the best. But what has come over you, Amy dear? I was only telling the Abbé, a little while ago, when we chanced to talk of you, that you were so mercurial, laughing always, and without a gloomy thought ever."

"Oh, I have them sometimes," said Amy demurely.

"The Abbé will accuse me of having given him false impressions if sometimes means often."

"But it doesn't."

"Certainly there can be no foundation for gloom with you. Healthy, pretty, and sweet seventeen."

"Eighteen nearly."

"Well, eighteen."

Amy nodded, leant back in her chair, and seemed ill-disposed to quarrel with her condition in life just then, while an expression, the very embodiment of innocent mischief, came into her eyes—eyes, by the way, of a much darker colour than Blanche's, but full of honesty, simplicity, and understanding. Her features were such as together constituted a very happy whole, but separately, would bear no comparison with the delicacy and beauty of Blanche's. In each case there was the same wide sensitive mouth, but Amy's complexion, instead of being perfectly fair, and tinged with warm colour like her sister's, was rosier and plentifully besprinkled over the bridge of the slightly retroussé nose with minute brown freckles. She wore her hair, which Blanche had justly called auburn, plaited into a long pigtail, which was thick, reached below her waist, and was tied with blue ribbon. In a few words, such is as faithful a sketch of her as can be given.

"Blanche," she said, at the end of a pause, setting down her empty cup, "give me some more tea, please, and plenty of cream. It's delicious. Who did you say was coming to dinner to-night? Someone with a most imposing title, if I recollect."

"The Baron de Courcelles."

"How intimidating, so very grand, but nice. Fox sounds horrid after it, and I feel quite small, though papa is a colonel, and of good family. You know I've never dined with a live Baron before, Blanche. Is he very awe-inspiring, with a dark bronzed face, huge curled moustachios, and great brown eyes? because I shall simply shrink up into a little round ball, and say nothing. Does he speak English? Tell me at once. What is he like?"

Blanche enjoyed a good laugh at the picture Amy had drawn, and highly amused at her simple impetuous manner, said:

"Well, give me a moment to think. Yes, certainly he speaks English."

"That's satisfactory, as I would much rather not air my French."

"Oh, but you must, you used to speak quite nicely; besides Rudolf detests English, as you know, and I don't believe the Abbé Bernard knows a word of it."

"Poor me. I suppose I'm in for it. What horrid blunders I shall make. I shall keep close to you, and you must come to the rescue. But finish about the Baron. He speaks English, you say?"

"Yes, and is not at all like the picture you have imagined. He is slight and thin, but well built. Fair-skinned, fair-haired, and with nice grey eyes. Much more likely to shrink and say nothing, than you are, Miss Amy, with all due deference to you."

"Oh, then if he's like that, we shall get on nicely.

I hate to feel myself so horribly small. But you know I'm still quite afraid of Rudolf."

"Nonsense! Rudolf likes you," replied Blanche gravely.

"Perhaps he does, but I'm quite afraid of him, though he used to kiss me tremendously. Why don't you laugh, Blanche, or have I made you cross? It wasn't my fault. I couldn't stop him. I used to try to look very severe, you know, then he used to seize me, hold me tightly, and I used to laugh. Why, you're not listening, I declare."

"Yes, I am, dear."

"Are you cross?"

"Not in the least. How could I be with you?"

"Oh, I don't know. Those blue eyes of yours can flash."

"But not at you," said Blanche, with amusement.

"And who else is coming did you say?" asked Amy, ignoring the last remark.

"The Abbé of La Jonquières, Monsieur Louis Bernard."

"What pretty names these Frenchmen have."

"He is constantly here. We like him, and he knows so much, though he has scarcely been anywhere."

"Learned and religious. You shall talk to him."

"Very well," laughed Blanche; "and you shall monopolize the Baron, though, when you have rubbed up your French, you'll like the Abbé, or I'm mistaken."

"Of course I shall, if you do. You must come and inspect my frocks, and help me to look nice, will you?"

Blanche nodded good-humouredly, and Amy strayed into a lengthy description of the things she had bought and wished to buy for her visit, suddenly stopping in the middle of it to dart from her seat at the sight of the two spaniels, who, with pretty hanging ears and gently waving tails, had trotted along the terrace and thrust their noses in through the window inquiringly.

"I'm wildly in love with all dogs," she said enthusiastically with a curly head secured under each arm.

"And I with horses, though I'm very fond of dogs, I confess," said Blanche, as she watched Amy's proceedings from her seat in the window.

"What's that about dogs and horses?" said the Count, for the spaniels were never very far from their master if they could help it.

"Why, we love them both."

"So I should imagine; then you shall ride with me sometimes."

"Oh, but I'm no good on a horse; I've never had any practice."

"But I'll teach you."

"Yes, Rudolf taught me—but you are wet and muddy," added Blanche, addressing the Count, whose dress was much stained. "Wherever have you been?"

"Only fishing, strolling along the river bank with a rod. I'm glad I was, too."

"Why? Have you had good sport?"

"No."

"Then why do you say you are glad, so energetically?"

"Because I had the opportunity of seeing that Abbé of yours prove—"

"Why do you speak of him in that way?" interrupted Blanche.

"Well, dear, he's more your friend than mine. I don't affect the cloth, as you know."

"One can't well be anything but friends with the vicar of the place one lives in, Rudolf. But certainly I think he's a good man, and though we've not known him long enough to judge, perhaps, I thought you agreed with me."

"And so I do. I'll go further even, after what he did this afternoon. He ought to have been a soldier, though, instead of a priest."

"How you tantalize us. What's he done?" asked Amy impetuously.

"Oh, you've found your tongue," laughed the Count.

"Isn't he too bad, Blanche? You know I'm ashamed of my French, Rudolf."

"Indeed; then you've got little to be ashamed of. In six months you'll speak like a native. Well, the Abbé is a splendid fellow, and I embraced him on the spot; that's one reason why I am so wet. But so that you may not tax me with teasing you, I'll tell you the reason for my admiration. Some children were playing on the river bank near where I was fishing. The Abbé was close to them, and with his breviaire in his hand, stood watching them and smiling at their sports. The ball they were amusing themselves with fell into the river. A plucky little fellow, the noisiest of the group, tried to recover it, slipped and disappeared in the deep water, above the weir, where there is a pretty strong current. Quick as lightning the Abbé was after him. He just put his breviaire on the bank, and the next moment he had dived and had him in his arms. Then he made a gallant struggle, gripping the child firmly. For a few seconds it looked as though he might be carried over the weir, but he breasted the current, gained the bank, and that's the whole story. Now is he not, as I said, a splendid fellow?"

"I should think so," said Blanche enthusiastically. "How I wish I had seen him do it."

"What, you, Amy? Why, you'd have fainted, and I should have been obliged to carry you home. Not that I should have objected to the burden," added the Count gallantly.

"How stupid of you, Rudolf," pouted Amy; "as if I should have been so absurd."

"You couldn't have helped it. There, you must question the Abbé for further details. I must go and change. Oh, I nearly forgot, Blanche; the Abbé expressed doubts about coming to-night. Wouldn't it be well to send a servant to inquire, and beg him to turn up, if possible? I can't help liking him for his pluck." Having delivered himself of which remark, the Count walked away, followed by his dogs.

There was a silence of some moments, which Amy at length broke by saying:

"How brave of the Abbé; I quite long to meet him."

Blanche did not appear to hear her at first. Then she said suddenly and bitterly:

"Yes, men *can* act like that, as I know, and yet can destroy one's love for them inch by inch."

The words had left her lips almost before she was aware. The startled expression on Amy's face recalled her to a sense of what she had done, of how indiscreet she had been.

"Destroy one's love for them inch by inch," repeated Amy slowly. "Whatever do you mean, Blanche?"

"Nothing."

"I don't believe that. You couldn't speak so and mean nothing."

"Yes, I forgot myself; I was carried away. There, promise me you won't bother your little head any further about a stupid remark without any rhyme or reason in it, and which escaped me only because I was a little out of sorts at the moment."

"Yes," answered Amy vehemently, "but your true

feelings came to the surface then. You may think me a little fool, but I understand you. Trust me, Blanche, won't you? We ought to be everything to each other."

"And so we will be, darling Kiss me, and then go and dress. It is time now. I'll come to you in a few minutes, but I must just go and see whether Rudolf has got all he wants."

Amy went away to her room, but the excitement of her journey and arrival, the pleasure of again meeting Blanche, the pleasant sensation of novelty occasioned by the newness of her surroundings, were dismissed unconsciously, and in a moment, as it were, she became full of her sister.

The apartment which had been prepared for her reception, and received its finishing touches from Blanche's own hands, had, a few hours previously awakened an almost childish delight, now she unpacked her pretty feminine trifles and treasures, arranged them, and set about her toilette almost mechanically. The room itself seemed in every respect suited to its occupant; a fitting receptacle for virginal slumbers and the bright awakening of youth and innocence. The furniture was of some light wood, polished or veneered, adorned with groups and sprays of blue forget-me-nots; the hangings were a charming combination of pale blue silk and white muslin, upon which was a pattern of the same delicate and sentimental little flower.

When Amy, by a few dexterous touches, and the arrangement of her little trifles, had imparted an air of homeliness, the room looked indescribably cheerful and cosy. Meanwhile the Count, occupied in divesting himself of his wet garments, received Blanche's attentions as a matter of course. Clean linen was ready for him, but he never troubled himself to think that his wife's soft hands had put it in order, for this was a task which, from the first, Blanche had taken upon herself, as a delicate attention, rather than as a duty. He answered her gentle inquiries and remarks as briefly as it seemed words would enable him, and having completed his toilette to his entire satisfaction, went off to scan a packet of papers that had just arrived from Paris, to smoke cigarettes, and think of Lisette.

The Baron de Courcelles and Louis arrived at the château almost simultaneously, and when everyone was assembled and Louis congratulated upon having recovered from his exertions sufficiently to come, the Count took the opportunity to dilate upon the part he had played.

"This is the hero of the hour, De Courcelles," he said, placing his hand on Louis' shoulder.

"Indeed, then what better fortune could have befallen me than to meet him?" replied the Baron courteously.

"You over-rate my efforts, Monsieur le Comte. I hope if I am in danger of drowning, that someone will have the goodness to save me," said Louis, shrinking aside and trying to draw Blanche and Amy into conversation.

"Why," began the Count, taking the Baron by the arm and relating all that had occurred, "it was splendid. I never did anything half so brave myself," he added, in a louder voice, at the end of his recital.

"Nor I," echoed the Baron enthusiastically, "that is a fact, though when you allude to yourself I must take exception to your remark, and tell you plainly I doubt you. You see you are known to be brave."

This was true, for before his marriage the Count had, on several occasions, proved himself to be a man of undoubted courage. Cowardice was not one of his failings.

"Do you know, dear, that these water-lilies smell exactly like cheese?" he suddenly remarked to Blanche, abruptly and rather oddly changing the conversation, and plunging his nose, as he spoke, into an old-fashioned china bowl, in which the flowers floated; "why do you have them when others are so much prettier?"

"I like them," answered Blanche simply.

"Am I not right?" he persisted, appealing to Louis, and plucking him by the sleeve.

"I confess I fail to detect the resemblance, Monsieur le Comte," said Louis, smelling the lilies.

"Can't you? Ah, perhaps I'm mistaken. The flowers are all right," he added quickly, with a smile, "but make a friend of the Baron if you can, his influence would get you a bishopric." Then turning away without noticing an expression of surprise on Louis' face, he said jestingly to the Baron, "Yes, the Abbé will have taken the hearts of the peasant women of La Jonquières by storm. The spectacle of a priest risking his life to save a child is not of everyday occurrence."

The Baron said something in an undertone, and the two laughed.

"Madame la Comtesse, dinner is served," announced a domestic, flinging wide the doors of the salon.

During dinner the conversation was animated and general, and was further enlivened by some amusing anecdotes which the Baron told in a quiet, dry manner, peculiarly his own.

After the meal everyone made for the terrace, where Blanche had ordered the coffee to be served.

"Can we not prevail upon you to give us more of

your society, Monsieur le Baron?" inquired Blanche, handing him a cup.

"Nothing would give me greater pleasure, madame."

"Then why don't you come?"

"There are some few reasons against my being much in these parts, madame; still, I fancy, if Monsieur Brunot does not hunt me out of the country, I shall be here oftener than of late."

"Why, what's he been doing?" inquired the Count, with an amused air.

"Trying to buy this estate."

"Buy the Château de Courcelles? Impudence! Why doesn't the fellow make a bid for one's wife at once?"

"My dear fellow, pity him, he has so much money that his simple bourgeois tastes will not permit him to spend it properly."

"Ah, *diable!* I can't see your point, I confess. Not very simple of him to covet the château."

"He may covet as much as he pleases. He won't get it," said the Baron, and he began to talk to Amy, Louis devoting himself to Blanche, while the Count descended the steps which led into the garden.

"What are you thinking of, monsieur?" said Blanche, addressing Louis who had stood at her side some moments without speaking, with his eyes fixed upon the pale, yellow sky.

"May I say what I think, madame?" he asked, in a low voice.

"Of course; why do you ask?"

"Because I have not known you long, madame, and I fear—"

"But you have always been welcome, and although the duration of our intimacy, if counted by weeks, might seem short, we have seen much of you. I shall be tempted to think it an impossibility to break through the shell into which it seems your nature to retire, monsieur, if you don't say just what you think. You see, I am not a Frenchwoman, monsieur."

"True, madame; I understand. We are considered retiring and ceremonious. Of that I am no judge. Perhaps, when we know, we know well."

"I feel sure it is so."

"And you will not consider me egotistical, madame?"

"Try."

"Well, then, to you who are so kind to me I'll frankly admit what otherwise I should bury within myself. To-night I feel prouder than I have ever done, madame."

"Had I been the means of saving a life, I should experience the sentiments you describe, monsieur."

"Madame, you have guessed why I feel as though my life had not been altogether useless. Hitherto, with me it has been all thinking, studying, mere book work; but to have saved this little one speaks to me of action, of having done something; and yet," added Louis pensively, "if that boy's youth is to be as unhappy, as lonely as mine has been, I could almost think him better off were he lying hushed in the death sleep by the murmur of the water, and the waving of the weeds above him."

The tears stood in Louis' eyes as he spoke.

"Monsieur, you must not talk like that. You really must not. In any case, you have left that youth you allude to behind."

"Yet the seeds sown during it will not die. Ah, forgive me, madame, this afternoon's exertion has been too much for me, and I, who ought to cheer others, talk of myself with the selfishness of a child. It is one's duty to lose oneself in others, and then only can one feel happy."

"Then I fail signally. I suppose I am very selfish."

"Ah, you undervalue yourself, madame."

"No, my whole life seems to be spent in attending to household matters."

"Duties, nevertheless."

"But insignificant ones. Mere trifles which leave no mark. The spaces between such work are filled up with recollections of the past, regrets that the present is not different in some way, add to that, hope for the future, a vain effort to peer into the invisible, the hidden, and one's day is gone."

"Yet in between, there is time found to console those who are poor, friendless, and in pain, madame," said Louis, with sly humour.

Blanche coloured.

"Such things, too, are trifles; selfishness the mainspring; to forget oneself, the object."

"What are you two talking about?" interrupted the Count; "anything very interesting?"

"Come and be the judge, Monsieur le Comte."

The Count paid no attention to the remark.

"I told the Abbé that he should cultivate De Courcelles," he observed to Blanche; "explain to him how influential he is."

"But why should I do as you suggest, Monsieur le Comte?" asked Louis simply.

The Count laughed. Louis amused him.

"Because, my dear fellow, nothing is done without influence."

"In the Church, Monsieur le Comte?"

"Even in the Church. You want to get on. The De Courcelles are a powerful family. Why, it's a well-known fact—forgive me for saying so—that men of your calling who are ambitious, are content to haunt the Ministere des Cultes, in Paris, for years, simply to gain their ends. You were ignorant of this? How droll! Really, I must try to instil worldliness into you."

A moment later, when the Count had left them to chat to the Baron and Amy, who had seated themselves at the end of the terrace, Louis asked:

"Is it as Monsieur le Comte has said, madame?"

"I am afraid so."

"Then I shall be the vicar of La Jonquières always, Madame la Comtesse," he said simply.

And when the stars were twinkling, he passed under them, going homewards, tired, but wondering how men could sacrifice their inheritance of manly pride, to become sycophants, paltry toadies, owing their success to others, and content to owe.

CHAPTER VII.

WHILE the Count was amusing himself with Lisette, growing more fond of her, too, than he knew, and Lisette was gradually abandoning herself to the novelty and pleasure of the stolen meetings, though in her turn burning her fingers, André Moriseau was wont to issue forth from the old thatched farm on the hill, to toil through the heat of the day, and then, when the work was done, to make himself smart, and stride off through the lengthening shadows to meet Lisette. His heart had been full of her through all those long, hot hours, and he had sighed for release, and a sight of her. How the blood rushed to his sunburnt cheek, and how his pulse quickened, as she came to him, cool, fresh, full of health, seductive, apparently true. To be with her was like a glimpse of heaven through a mighty rift in the cloud curtain. In his passion, and had he known, he could have sung with his whole heart—

> "There's a bliss beyond all that the minstrel has told,
>   When two that are link'd in one heavenly tie,
> With hearts never changing and brow never cold,
>   Love on through all ills, and love on till they die!
> One hour of a passion so sacred is worth
>   Whole ages of heartless and wandering bliss,
> And oh, if there *be* an elysium on earth,
>   It is this—it is this."

He could have sung this, for thus, in his rustic way, he felt, Lisette having, with admirable feminine tact, cured his doubts, and attached him to herself more firmly than ever. Yet Lisette was not wholly bad. No one is. She was a born coquette; but in Mère Chotard's opinion she was without fault, and that belief had come because Lisette was devoted to her, the best of daughters, loving her with all her heart; and such love covers a multitude of sins.

Within the château events were not motionless. Blanche was restless, wondering at the change—a change she could perceive in the Count's manner and actions. The cause she could not divine; she only knew he was different, and had not gone of late to Paris, where, previously, he had been constantly in the habit of betaking himself.

To have Amy with her was a relief, a great pleasure in fact; but her presence did not prevent her from thinking. Within this cycle of events, Louis went his way, saying his masses, reciting his vespers, doing all the good he could about him, and listening to not a few confessions which could scarcely fail to enlighten him much as to La Jonquières, its web-work, its ways. When the day closed in, and he felt he had done his best, he would seek the château, where to go was his one relaxation, perhaps his greatest pleasure. During all this, he was himself perfectly conscious that his mind was undergoing a change. By fits and starts, as one becomes alive to the passage of time, the advance of age, he became aware that a mental revolution was in progress. It could scarcely have been otherwise. To quit the restrictions, the supervision of the seminary, for intercourse with at least a village world; women kind and charming, and men like the Count; could not fail to produce an effect. Louis prayed that it might be for good, fought against what he thought wrong, but none the less was disturbed. These mutations were only of a sort calculated to enter a thinking, sensitive mind such as his. He felt this. It occurred to him that many had gone before him holding the same position, and would come after him, to suffer as he did. And yet, these sentiments of his were only beginning to assert their existence, only struggling towards cohesion and light.

"Madame," he observed to Blanche one evening, at the end of a sweet and passionate song of Gounod's, which she had played for him, and he had sung in a rich tenor voice only requiring culture, "it is the feeling of loneliness which appals one. You will be surprised at my suddenly saying this, but it flashed upon me as you struck the last chord. I went for a long walk this morning, making visits on the way. Coming back the sun scorched me, I became intolerably thirsty and tired. In that condition I entered a cottage in search of a crust of bread and some milk, if I could get it. The walls of the place were bare, whitewashed, the floor stone, the furniture of wood, without a sign of paint or varnish. Yes, but madame, upon those hard comfortless chairs, round that rough, unpolished table, was grouped a country picture—children and their parents, brown and rosy with health. They had finished their humble meal. The remains of an enormous loaf such as they bake hereabouts, some cheese and a great jug of milk, were thrust to one end of the board. A greasy pack of cards were being dealt round. I begged them to go on with their game. As I refreshed myself, they talked and laughed and seemed so happy—*so very happy*—that when I left, I was tempted to ask the woman—the mother—if it were so."

"'Monsieur l'Abbé,' she said, 'God is good to Jean and me. We have our cares; but yes, we are very happy, for together we can bear them.'"

"Madame la Comtesse, would you believe it? I left her, thinking to myself, Louis Bernard, you yourself stand in greater need of counsel, of human consolation, than that woman."

It was the remark of a very young man, and in the eyes of some people it might have appeared an admission of too much weakness, but its very frankness pleased Blanche. She had, from the first, judged Louis' temperament to be one to which the balm of human intercourse, nay, even affection, was an imperative necessity.

Courtesy had dictated that polite overtures should be offered to Louis' parents. These had been made, but the intimacy went no further, and the impression she had formed, was that Louis was as much alone as though he had no father or mother. This belief had the effect—irrespective of her own opinion—of making her kinder to him, and, in consequence, of causing him to feel that the château was as much open to him as his own home. Hearing him speak as he did, her first ideas prompted a suggestion that he ought not to experience the sentiments he had betrayed so markedly. He was not alone in the world. Why should he speak so? The next moment, she reflected that Madame and Monsieur Bernard were about the last people she could conceive as being likely to afford him the consolation he had a right to expect from such a source. To that belief she added the opinions she had formed of his character, and the conclusion she drew as to his position, struck her as being so painful, that she preferred turning the point of her remarks away from him.

"Yes, monsieur," she said, "you have drawn a very strong picture of the benefits to be derived from companionship, from mutual love, but how often do you get it?"

"Oftener than not, I should think, madame," he replied promptly.

"I don't agree with you. I maintain that the reverse of that outline of rustic bliss, so pathetically described by you, rises before one most often in one's journey through life. Suppose the peasant woman, her husband and the children, to have their hands turned against each other in the majority of cases, and you will have approached nearer the truth."

"I can't credit it, madame."

"Then it is because of the life you have led."

"In that case, what becomes of the beneficence of the Almighty?"

"I cannot explain."

"Does He bring people together that they may disagree, and make each other's lives unbearable, madame?"

"Perhaps you can answer that question. I cannot."

"Alas, Madame la Comtesse, it is beyond me."

"Why should the sins of the fathers be visited upon the children? That the children when they become parents may have the threat before them, and for the sake of their offspring, control themselves, you will say?"

"It is a very deep question, presenting many sides, madame," said Louis gravely.

"To my poor mind, life and its concerns is as a maze, into which the farther one plunges, the more hopelessly one becomes lost."

"Nevertheless, the Divine Hand guides surely, madame."

"Undoubtedly; but if one wishes to comprehend and trace that guidance through its many intricacies, reason fails one wholly."

Louis evaded the remark; perhaps he feared to enter upon a lengthy argument, because of the annoyance it might occasion the Count or the Baron and Amy, who were in the room amusing themselves after their several inclinations.

"It *is* wonderful," he contented himself with remarking, "this spectacle of life, madame; but if to know more of it is only to conjure shadows, to darken the pure golden of the sunlight which kindly streaks existence, by plunging one beyond one's depth, I prefer my ignorance. I know enough already, to call to mind the wedding-party meeting the funeral cortège, to remember the grotesqueness of the laughter and play of village boys beneath the window of the bed-ridden and dying, to conceive the sound of the minute bell from some old church steeple, pealing forth the solemn note, in the midst of feasting, dancing, and merriment."

Scarcely had Blanche grasped the full meaning of Louis' realistic remarks in all their vigour and truth, than Amy prevented an answer by putting her arms round her neck and whispering:

"The Baron wants us to see the Château de Courcelles, and lunch there. Do consent."

Blanche returned the caress with affection, and signified her willingness. Amy slipped aside and began to talk to the Count, while the Baron, no longer engaged in conversation, joined Blanche and Louis.

"Madame," he said, "will you honour me by inspecting the château, and giving me the benefit of your opinion and taste concerning some alterations I contemplate? You see," he added gaily, "Monsieur Brunot is not going to get the De Courcelles' estate."

"But, Monsieur le Baron, I am wholly ignorant of French architecture."

"Oh, I want to make what I think will be an improvement to the interior, and of all things I should like you to give me your advice. I have been suggesting to Monsieur le Comte that we should all lunch there. We had thought of shooting in the neighbourhood some day this week, and if you would consent to drive over with your sister, it would give me the greatest pleasure. Let me entreat you to come, dear madame."

"Nothing would delight me more. But take care, Baron, lest I become envious, for I have heard that to see the Château de Courcelles is to covet it, and I may be like Monsieur Brunot."

"In which case, it is yours, madame," answered the Baron gallantly. "Then all is arranged save the day, which must be for your selection. Monsieur l'Abbé, you will come, too, will you not?"

"Alas, I must remain here, Monsieur le Baron. I have my duties to attend to."

"And you cannot lay them aside even for one day? Come, let me beg of you. I am sure that Madame la Comtesse will agree with me, when I say that without you our party will be incomplete."

"Nevertheless I am forced to excuse myself. To accept would give me much pleasure, but I have no substitute."

Reluctantly the Baron dismissed the subject, for he liked Louis. He knew him to be brave, and his views upon paying court to anyone for the sake of a benefice, had reached his (the Baron's) ears, though in an altered form.

The evening wore on, and at the close of it Blanche stood at her open bedroom window. The gardens, the shady alleys and distant thickets of the park, lay before her. Every star was reflected upon the broad bosom of the river, which was without a ripple, and silvered by the moon, whose rays were foiled by a slowly-gliding network of dappled clouds. The silence was profound, and only disputed by the splash of a hungry fish and the round rich notes of answering nightingales, almost unearthly in their echoing clearness.

"To live in such a spot, loving and beloved, would be too much like heaven," said Blanche, aloud to herself, having locked the door, and left the Count downstairs smoking. "Too much like heaven, and therefore too much to expect. Yet the scene might pass; I would barter it in exchange for a wilderness, shared with some kind being who cared to understand and love me. Why am I so unhappy?"

She ceased speaking, tears preventing further utterance. In the midst of her grief, two soft arms were laid upon her shoulders. Believing herself alone, and therefore greatly startled, she almost screamed.

"Hush, it is only me," said a low sweet voice.

"You, Amy?"

"Yes."

"What a fright you gave me."

"I'm so sorry, darling, but I could not help it."

"How did you come here? The door is locked."

"Why, I was hidden behind the curtains and saw you enter the room. You may have thought I've forgotten the words you said, but I haven't. I didn't like to ask you to confide in me again, dear, but I've watched you, and so certain was I to-night that you felt wretched, although you laughed and talked so gaily, that I risked making you angry and came, confident that, if you would let me, I could be of some use."

Blanche could not speak, she only hugged Amy tightly.

"Did you hear anything I said?" she asked, when her feelings were more under control.

Amy nodded.

"Then you know all. I didn't want to trouble

you. What good could it do? It was naughty of you to come here in this way," she added playfully.

"Isn't Rudolf kind to you, Blanche?"

"It doesn't seem right of me to speak. Why did you come here? I should never have told you."

"But, Blanche, whatever you tell me shall go with me to the grave."

"Don't speak like that. And yet," she added more calmly, "that's what must come of the brightest eyes, the kindest heart. For myself I'm not afraid, but—"

"The grave need have no place in your thoughts, dear. It was stupid of me to use such an expression. But say, isn't Rudolf all he might be to you?"

"No, and never can be now," said Blanche firmly.

"Blanche, you horrify me. Rudolf not love you! There is some mistake, some misunderstanding. It is impossible that any man could see you, live with you, and not love you. You so beautiful. Were I a man I should worship the ground you walk on. I tell you there's some mistake."

Blanche let Amy put her hands upon her shoulders and peer into her face with frank girlish sweetness, but before that steady gaze, and the love and concern it expressed, she felt her eyes grow dim. Her lips trembled. She strove to control herself, and with a supreme effort did so.

"No, dear," she said firmly, "I am not mistaken It is not in Rudolf's nature to care very deeply for anyone. For the first year he overwhelmed me with affection, was never happy away from me, and we went everywhere together. At the end of that time came a change. He began to pay attentions to others, to leave me more and more to myself, and this though I was devoted to him, and for no reason."

"But I should never have stood it," said Amy, becoming scarlet in the face.

"No; and what would you have done?"

"Why, have told him what a brute he was, and that I would not put up with his conduct."

"Which would have made him laugh, given him a pretext for taunting me with being jealous, and in the end, done no good whatever."

"I can't believe that. Rudolf's not bad-hearted."

"No, but he's as changeable as the wind. Any pretty face takes his fancy, no matter who or what the owner is."

"Oh, Blanche, I can't think that."

"No, it may seem difficult, and only by slow degrees have I come to know it. I have at length, and had to bear the pain of the discovery in silence. But I don't feel that I am right in making these disclosures to you. In all probability you won't agree with me, and if you do there is no good gained."

"Now, that's unkind, and not a bit like you, Blanche. Why, I've been so troubled ever since I came."

"I feared it, and that has made me even more unhappy. I've never forgiven myself for making that stupid remark, but I was excited at the time. Why, for whole weeks I have been alone here."

"Alone! where was Rudolf?"

"In Paris, or somewhere. He used to write occasionally, and his letters always bore the Paris postmark; but, for aught I know, he may have been in Vienna."

"How hateful of him. I can't understand any living being treating another in that cruel way. But why didn't you go after him and make him own himself in the wrong? Oh, I should have had a tremendous quarrel, and—and then, if he had promised faithfully never to behave so brutally again, I should have made it up."

Blanche smiled. Suddenly it flashed across her mind that Amy was indeed very unlike her.

"I could never follow a man in that way," she said wearily. "I could never run after him and ask him to love me, as it were. It is not in me. Why, if one were successful, one would own an allegiance not worth having, and if one failed, one's pride would be shattered. It is pride," she added, her eyes flashing, "that has made me bear what I have, as I have."

"But I don't understand you."

"Pride has enabled me to wait and hope that of his own free will he would return to me, perhaps owning himself wrong, but, at any rate, showing by his actions that he knew himself to be so. That waiting was agony. My manner towards him never changed until I felt that the hope was gone, and in losing it, I am afraid I lost a good deal of the power to care. I have quarrelled with him, but not because I sought to bring him back to me by asking. Having married him, I'd rather die than ask."

Her last words were said with tightly-clenched hands and heaving bosom, and with the final one she stamped her foot upon the floor.

"Now, let us talk about something else for a few minutes, and then you must leave me," she added, subsiding into a chair.

"But, Blanche, can't it all be put right?" said Amy softly, and taking her sister's hand. "It seems so dreadful to quarrel in that way. Let me go to Rudolf; I'm sure he'd listen—"

"No, let us change the subject, dear; only, now you know what I meant when I spoke of men killing the love in one, inch by inch, and thought of it first when Rudolf came to tell us that Monsieur l'Abbé Bernard had saved that boy's life. The Count would have acted similarly. As for you, you can do nothing except close your eyes. Be careful that your manner towards him does not change, and—and don't fall in love with the Baron," she added playfully.

Amy grew rather red in the face.

"How absurd! As if he would care for me."

"Well, he seems rather fond of the château of late, and I'm sure I'm not the attraction."

"Kiss me, and let me go to bed," said Amy demurely. "It must be getting very late, and sleep will do you more good than talking."

Then she slipped away.

CHAPTER VIII.

THE court-yard of the Château de la Jonquières presented an aspect of unusual animation. The morning of the day fixed for the shooting and luncheon at the Château de Courcelles had arrived. Some grooms were saddling a couple of horses. A carriage, intended for Blanche's use, was being washed, and in the shade of the walnut trees stood the Count, smoking and leisurely regarding the work that was in progress. Over-night the weather had been stormy, and though the Château de Courcelles was only some few miles distant, the Baron had been prevailed upon to remain at La Jonquières, the understanding being that the Count would ride over with him in the morning as early as a start could be effected. With this object, these two enthusiastic sportsmen mounted their horses, and at an hour when Blanche was thinking about dressing, were actually proceeding at a walk along the roughly-paved street of La Jonquières.

"We shall have a glorious day, if I'm not mistaken," remarked the Baron, settling himself in the saddle, and looking just what Blanche had briefly described him to Amy, " slight, thin, but well-built, fair-skinned, fair-haired, and with nice grey eyes."

His features were good, his manner pleasant. He was rich, entirely his own master, and, springing from an old and powerful family, it seemed as though Fortune, joining hands with Fate, had smilingly produced in Leo, Baron de Courcelles, a man much to be envied.

"I feel a trifle tired. We sat up too late last night," said the Count, stifling a yawn.

"How droll! Fancy a man like you, who has the reputation of being made of steel, talking about going to bed too late."

"Better say iron, steel is supposed to be brittle," said the Count, straightening his small compact figure, twirling his moustache, and looking pleased.

When nearly opposite Pierre Chotard's cottage, he fell back a few paces. The clatter of hoofs brought Lisette to the door.

"Now, there's a picture pretty enough to make you rub your eyes and forget all about sleep."

"Where?" asked the Count, in the most innocent voice, though he had signalled to Lisette, and prepared to smile his best and look his handsomest. "Where?" he repeated, gazing in the opposite direction.

"My dear fellow, on your left, in the doorway."

"Pretty? I don't admire your taste."

"Well, you must admit she's a perfect little figure," contended the Baron innocently.

"Too thick in the waist, clumsy, and a brunette. Give me golden hair any day," said the Count imperturbably.

"Ah, perhaps you're right."

"Of course I am. Come along, we mustn't dawdle or we shall never do any shooting to-day."

"Yes, I think I prefer hair somewhat lighter," said the Baron dreamily, thinking of Amy as he spoke.

"Plentiful, and with a tinge of red in it—auburn,

Only Flesh and Blood. 83

say—eh?" returned the Count banteringly, divining his thoughts.

Scarcely expecting such a home-thrust, the Baron was only too glad to touch his horse with the spur. Turning round to see whether the Count was following him, he was surprised and amazed to detect him in the act of waving his hand, Lisette replying to the gesture by a similar one. Unconscious of having been seen, and no further reason existing for remaining behind, the Count, delighted with himself, trotted gaily after his companion.

"Seems to me that you rather affect brunettes," remarked De Courcelles, as soon as the Count had joined him.

"Eh? What's that, my dear fellow?"

"And have no such rooted antipathy to what you were pleased to call a thick waist," continued the Baron, with a comical expression, and knowing well that the Count had heard his first remark.

Seeing that he had been outwitted, the Count put the best face he could upon the matter, which, after all, was of little consequence, he considered. De Courcelles was still looking at him, so he met his glance, and, with a forced laugh, said:

"Ah, your eyes are too sharp. You can't blame me for trying to throw a little dust in them. An *affaire du cœur* is best kept to oneself, when good-looking fellows like you are so thick upon the ground."

"An *affaire du cœur*! But you wouldn't look twice upon a woman of her class?"

"Who do you mean?"

"You know well, the girl at the door."

"Ah, *diable!* A pretty face is a pretty face all the world over. Women like me, and I have an eye for them. I admire, but, *parbleu!* you are in danger of taking one's remarks too seriously. Come along, we have no time to waste."

The Baron was blinded. He had never exchanged confidences with the Count, and, though very good friends, knew absolutely nothing of his character. For himself, he was of the type of man likely to make an idol of a woman, never thinking ill of the sex, and not knowing them well, for the simple reason that he habitually felt nervous and uncomfortable in their society. But his ideas upon duty were very rigid, and accordingly he had been well laughed at for broaching them.

A prey to a sense of annoyance, the Count persisted in maintaining silence, and under these conditions the two continued their ride.

At an hour when Louis was immersed in those duties which, as he had explained to De Courcelles, debarred him from partaking of his hospitality, Blanche, accompanied by Amy, set forth to join the sportsmen. She herself was arrayed in a charming costume of some light material, pale blue in colour, and trimmed elegantly with white lace. Her golden hair and fair complexion were further enhanced by a becoming straw hat, which suited her to perfection, and with its broad brim protected her from the effects of the sun. Amy looked cool and engaging in a simple white muslin, and needed no richer colouring than her own healthy cheeks.

"Come, let us forget our troubles. Talk to me, will you?" said Blanche, trying to draw Amy into conversation.

"How fortunate I am to be able to say that nothing causes me a moment's uneasiness, except—"

"What?" inquired Blanche.

"You."

"Are all my entreaties to prove ineffectual? Let us consider this subject of myself tabooed. You know, dear, I've refused repeatedly to discuss it."

"Yes, but I can't help thinking."

"Not one yard of this drive, not one minute of this day, must be spoilt by a single melancholy thought. If it is, you will only add to my unhappiness. Now, promise me."

"Of course I will. That is, I'll do my best, but when I think of it, you must feel dreadfully—"

Blanche laid her finger upon Amy's lips, and said, with a smile which lit up her whole face:

"Hush! That is not keeping your promise. You must be radiant. I shall be so, and you are to follow my example. The Baron must be captivated with—"

"If you say another word about the Baron I shall hate him," interrupted Amy petulantly. "I believe I do already."

"Very well, dear, let us talk about something else," replied Blanche good-naturedly. "The scenery between here and the Château de Courcelles is lovely, and interesting, too, from an historical point of view. Now, I'm going to amuse you, and you must not be cross with me. I meant no harm."

Amy's hand slid into Blanche's, and peace was restored.

As the basis of Blanche's regard for the Count, and when marrying him, she had been under the impression that she was receiving as pure and honest an affection as she gave. This, of course, was in a measure due to the long years she had spent at the convent. She remained ignorant of the world. From its walls she had emerged, having acquired all the accomplishments the good sisters could teach her. But she had emerged, too, with a simple and romantic belief in mankind, which, as a young girl of a thoughtful and sensitive disposition, it was but natural she should develop. It never occurred to her to consider the Count, as a man who had roamed the world over, possessed of money, and with the *entrée* to any society caprice might tempt him to select. She had evolved her girlish idol. The Count's knowledge of her sex had enabled him to form a pretty correct estimate of the shape that idol was likely to take, the attributes it would probably possess. Skilfully he clothed himself, so that to her he had soon seemed all she had fondly imagined. To do him justice, in winning her love he had meant well. But he did not know himself. He had been under the impression that the possession of so beautiful a specimen of youth and innocence would work a complete revolution in his existence, would turn him from the pursuit of pleasures which in his better moments he detested himself for seeking. The birth of this idea was due to her. She was so fresh and sinless, he so blackened and *blasé*. Could she not reform him? He thought so.

Approaching her in the disguise he had assumed, she had proved willing to consign herself to his keeping. Charmed, deep in the best love he could give, for about a year, as she had said, his baser nature remained suppressed. At the end of that period it had begun to assert its existence, and finally, in spite of her love and beauty, it had come forth boldly. Had religion supported him, this relapse would have been less possible. But the Count was a *persifleur*, an admirer and feeble disciple of Voltaire.

He had too much sense to attempt any interference with his wife's views. In his inmost heart he did not admire his own, was not sure enough of their merits, or indeed of what they were, to press them home closely. The result, his conduct, proved their looseness and failure to restrain. It was in striving to please and comprehend the manner of man with whom the remainder of her life was to be spent, that Blanche had, particle by particle, dismantled the model, which seclusion, innocence, and youth had combined to construct, until at length nothing but the framework, the mere skeleton, remained to her in the person of the Count. The pain she had endured in the process had been excruciating, and had she herself attempted a description of the anguish she had endured, words would have failed her. Her pride had inflamed, rather than otherwise, because it condemned her to silence. Obeying its promptings, she had never once admitted her weakness and suffering. Resolutely she had scrutinized and torn the veil aside. As the devotee inflicts punishment upon himself, so had her lacerated feelings been scourged by her determination to plumb the nature of the man she had married, *coûte que coûte*, but not to be his dupe.

The Count himself was in blissful ignorance of the scrutiny to which he had been subjected. They had quarrelled, but quarrels, it seemed, were only the natural outcome of the married state. He knew that he had injured her in a thousand ways. But that was of no consequence, provided she were ignorant. He was not troubled. And had he summed up all he knew of her, and given his opinion, he would have vowed he had a wife shaped to his hand.

Woman-like, Blanche was not wholly embittered by the discoveries she had made. Supremely unhappy in the depths of her heart, she still retained the belief that there were beings—men— who, had her lot been cast with them, would have fulfilled, and nobly, all the requirements of her first and fondly-formed conception. Had she been choosing again, she would have paid *less* attention to a handsome face, *more* to threading and comprehending the intricacies of the mind; but she was too young, too hopeful, to be entirely sceptical.

Arrived at the château, De Courcelles and the Count were there to meet them.

"Welcome to the château, Madame la Comtesse," said De Courcelles, aiding Blanche to alight; "and you too, mademoiselle. The master, the house, and all within it are at your disposal," he added, with courtly grace.

"You are too kind, Monsieur le Baron," said Blanche, accepting the Baron's proffered arm. "But what of the shooting? Has it been good?"

"The sport, madame, we have found indifferent. I have been too much away to expect my keepers to remember my existence, and the birds have suffered. But that evil can be repaired," he added, with a swift glance at Amy.

"You will remain here, Baron?"

"As much as possible, madame."

"That will be delightful, for you and the Count are such great friends."

"You would not have said so had you been with us all day," replied De Courcelles, with an expression of amusement and a glance to see if his remark could be overheard.

"Indeed; and why was that, may I ask, monsieur?"

"An argument upon the merits of blondes and brunettes, madame," replied De Courcelles thoughtlessly, and smiling as he spoke.

"Who began the discussion?"

"I really forget, madame."

"But what suggested the topic?" persisted Blanche, with womanly instinct divining that some unusual occurrence had occasioned the dispute.

"Oh, the sight of a most charming face, on our way here," replied the Baron, now fairly drawn into a conversation which had no particular attraction for him.

"Really, you interest me, Baron. And where may this lovely specimen of beauty be found?"

"At La Jonquières. In the village. You probably know her well by sight, madame?"

"Not to my knowledge. At La Jonquières, you say. Then she is a peasant girl?"

"A rustic beauty. A woodland nymph, madame," said the Baron rather awkwardly, for it suddenly occurred to him, that since the Count had been sufficiently interested to wave his hand, he might not be disposed to thank him for making the disclosures he had.

He was consoled, however, by reflecting that if he had been guilty, it was an unintentional error. Besides, if the Count were as good as he ought to be, no harm could be done. But in future he determined to be more reticent, mischief-making in his eyes being a detestable vice.

"After such praise from your lips, Monsieur le Baron, I confess my curiosity is aroused. I should like to see this village Venus."

"Oh, I daresay I am wrong, and you would be woefully disappointed. Since I only caught a glimpse of her, I would not attach much importance to an impression so hastily formed, madame," said the Baron, with an effort to extricate himself, and beginning to wish that Blanche would drop the subject.

"And which type of beauty did the Count prefer, monsieur?" inquired Blanche, more for the sake of something to say than with an object.

"Ah, how can you ask me, madame?" rejoined De Courcelles, evasively but gallantly.

The compliment was too palpable to miss, and Blanche blushed prettily.

"What, have you, too, learned the art of flattery, and are you, too, of opinion that we women set such store by it?"

"The question is an awkward one, madame, but of

course the popular idea is that it has weight with your sex," returned De Courcelles.

"But what is your own opinion, monsieur?"

"It is valueless, madame. But may I inquire whether Mademoiselle Amy, your sister, is to remain with you long?"

"How dexterously you extricate yourself from making too frank an avowal. You would have been a shining light in the diplomatic service, had you entered it, Monsieur le Baron. Really, I shall begin to think that."

"Well, since you leave me no loop-hole for escape, I should say that flattery may be converted into a very potent weapon in dealing with your sex. In a less degree, but yet effectively, with my own."

"I like you all the better for coming to the point. We English are so brusque. But about my sister. She will be with us indefinitely. Our house will be her home. You see I am the only relative she has, except papa, who is in India."

In tendering this piece of information, Blanche adhered strictly to the substance of a conversation she had held with the Count, who when appealed to, was clever enough to remember that the effect of Amy's presence would probably be good, since she would be a source of distraction to Blanche, and likely to draw her attention away from himself.

"Her presence will be a consolation to you then, madame," pursued De Courcelles.

"Yes, indeed, monsieur."

"Well, your husband's annoyance was complete when, do what we would, there was scarcely a bird to be found. Where they've all got to I can't think," he added, fairly laughing. "But my fellows are so fat, and I have my suspicions that they've lived royally, counting upon my usually protracted disappearances. It was so funny, madame. I, who had spoken of a treat in store for us both, in no very modest terms, to be driven to admit that I was no longer the owner of anything worth shooting. Very provoking, too," he added; "but I am afraid that the most profuse apologies I could make, were not as substantial, in Monsieur le Comte's opinion, as the birds would have been. However, I have done my best, and failed signally."

"I shall hear another story when I question Rudolf, monsieur. He will have enjoyed himself immensely, I am sure. But you must feel dull, even in this beautiful place, alone. Are you not?"

"Well, I must own I am, madame. It is given over to lazy servants, closed shutters, and cobwebs. When I set out, I only meant to stay here for a few days."

"And, in a measure, we are responsible for your changed intentions, my dear Baron. Is it not so?"

"To be honest, yes, madame," replied De Courcelles, with trifling hesitation, a slight colour mounting to his cheeks.

"Come and stay with us then. I insist upon it, and shall take no refusal. We can place any number of rooms at your disposal, so it will be hard to invent an excuse. You must return with us to-night. Rudolf will be delighted, I know."

De Courcelles had vague doubts on that score. But the temptation was too great to resist.

"Madame, I shall be only too pleased," he said, with undisguised pleasure.

"Then it is settled. You will drive back with us, monsieur."

The Baron assented, and soon after, contrived to attach himself to Amy, who was as pleased as a school-girl with all she saw. Certainly, it would have been odd had the appearance of the Château de Courcelles failed to delight her.

It was a stately building in Louis XIII. style, the magnificence of which was further enhanced by a terrace, said to be the longest and broadest in Champagne. A handsome balustrade was broken at intervals by spacious flights of stone steps, which descended into gardens designed by Lenotre. The panelling of the grand drawing-room was adorned by groups of flowers painted by Lebrun, and from the windows a view could be obtained which might fairly be said to be unequalled, so exquisitely was water and woodland blended and lost in soft blue distances.

Such was one of the homes almost perpetually neglected by the young and fortunate Baron de Courcelles. He seemed proud of it though, on that autumn afternoon, and it would have been difficult to imagine a kinder and more courteous host. On the first suitable occasion which presented itself, Blanche took the opportunity to tell the Count of the invitation she had given.

"De Courcelles has consented to return with us, Rudolf," she said innocently.

"To return with us! What do you mean?" asked the Count, in no very honeyed tones, for his equilibrium really had been upset at the commencement of the day.

"Why, he is bored here. I invited him to stay with us, and he is coming. I thought you would like it."

"You *thought*, madame. What right have you to *think*? Why don't you consult me before you venture to issue invitations broadcast?" replied the Count passionately. With the Baron at La Jonquières his time would be taxed. He saw that instantly. Hence his rage.

"But we have seen so much of him of late. You have been such fast friends—"

"Friends, *mon Dieu*—"

"He and Amy get on so well, too," pleaded Blanche, still gently. "I am sorry if—"

"He and Amy get on, do they? What have I to do with that? Is not my house my own?" fumed the Count. Then a jealous thought shot through him, and in his rage he did not hesitate to give it utterance. "You are in love with the fellow yourself, madame," he said brutally.

Blanche bit her lip. Her small hands closed convulsively. With an effort she controlled herself sufficiently to falter:

"Rudolf, you are wrong—"

"In love with him yourself," he repeated, "you ought to be ashamed—"

Blanche drew herself up proudly. The moment before, her blue eyes had been dimmed with emotion. They now flashed with scorn and righteous anger. The words which leapt to her lips cut short his abuse.

"Ashamed! You forget. I have never done anything to be ashamed of, in the sense you mean. You *have*, and you know it. You have insulted me also, and that, too, should make you ashamed."

"*Mille tonnerres*—" began the Count.

Blanche swept aside into another path of the garden. De Courcelles was in sight, but at some distance. He was gathering some flowers for Amy, and the two were talking and laughing happily. The Count was left standing alone. His eyes followed Blanche's figure. His rage diminished. Reflection already told the truth contained in her passionate charge.

"A little fury," he muttered; "but what she says is true enough, though that admission is only for myself. Ah, why can't one woman content a fellow always? I must overtake her or it will look odd."

The Count carried out his intention, so that a few moments later, when with Blanche at his side, he joined the Baron, there was no trace of dissension noticeable.

Armed with bouquets of beautiful flowers, which De Courcelles presented with the most winning smiles, Blanche and Amy reseated themselves in the carriage, and the quartette set off homewards, Blanche having delighted De Courcelles by the artistic suggestions she had made concerning the improvements he meditated.

When within a short distance of La Jonquières, and about to cross the river, Blanche proposed that they should alight, saunter along the banks by a path which was wooded and pretty, and so gain the château by taking advantage of Pierre Chotard's ferry. Amy and the Baron enthusiastically supported the suggestion, the Count lit a cigar and was quiescent, so the carriage was dismissed.

Through stubble, grass-land, and an occasional thicket of trees the party proceeded, keeping well together, and pausing whenever the scenery evoked unusual admiration. This was constantly the case, for La Jonquières is justly famous for the romantic beauty of its surroundings, the Meuse seeming to delight in winding amidst rugged cliffs, woods, and fruitful fields and orchards. When nearly opposite La Jonquières, the path plunged into a nut copse, thick enough to exclude the sunshine. On the far edge of it was a stile exposed to the full glare of light, and over it, as though waiting for someone, leant a young girl. She was singing softly to herself, and was oblivious of the approach of anyone. Blanche heard the sounds first and stopped.

"Listen," she said, "what a sweet voice."

Everyone was instantly attentive. The Count knew the singer at a glance. He was still ruffled, as a certain ring in his ejaculatory remarks betrayed.

"Enthrilling, stirring. Holds one spellbound. But the thought occurs to me that you women, like peacocks, are never more pleased, never more brilliant, than when displaying your finery in the sunlight."

Amy and Blanche were both silent. De Courcelles thought the remark unpleasant in its best sense, and was in no mood to recognise its truth, if truth it contained. The Count chuckled as though his satire was incontrovertible. De Courcelles became triflingly malicious. He, too, recognised the singer, for the position in which she stood rendered her conspicuous. It occurred to him that it would be amusing to drop a bomb at the Count's feet; but he was doubtful how to do it. Blanche came to his assistance. The singer's voice died away.

"Have we by any chance discovered your village beauty, Monsieur le Baron?" she asked.

De Courcelles hesitated, glanced at the Count, and was rewarded by a lightning-like gleam from his brown eyes.

"Come, I see it in your face. Have you allowed yourself to be so captivated, monsieur, that you are afraid lest anyone else should admire your Hebe?"

This was too much for De Courcelles to bear. Amy was listening and looking at him. The consequences must be the Count's concern.

"Not I, madame," he answered, shrugging his shoulders.

"Ah, monsieur, it is difficult to deceive a woman." Blanche glanced swiftly at the Count as she spoke. "But beauty," she added, "has no more enthusiastic votary than myself. I am about to have my curiosity set at rest. I want to see your idea of a pretty girl. I wonder whether her looks and words are as pleasant as her voice. Come along, Rudolph."

An oath exploded under the Count's pointed moustache. At that moment he could have kicked De Courcelles. But, divining what had happened, he accepted the position assigned to him by the disclosures De Courcelles had evidently made. The present was no time for sarcasm, behind which it had at first occurred to him to entrench himself. Clearly this was a moment for resolution and *sang froid*, and the Count was equal to the occasion. He offered his arm to Blanche, to enable her to pass some overgrown, brambles.

"Yes, let's have a look at her," he said. "De Courcelles and I both thought her pretty; but then we had but a hasty glance."

In this manner they approached Lisette, for Lisette it was. Waiting, too, on this, the further side of the river, because she judged it to be quieter, her object being to meet André Moriseau.

"Why, is she not Pierre Chotard the ferryman's daughter?" queried Blanche.

"Eh, yes, perhaps so. It's so difficult to remember faces. Don't you find it so, De Courcelles?"

"Sometimes," returned De Courcelles ironically.

"But how changed. She has grown so much," pursued Blanche. "Now I think of it, did she not go to Paris to be with a brother about a year ago?"

"Really I don't know, my dear. You may be right," said the Count, with imperturbable coolness.

"I remember something of it. My good girl," continued Blanche, standing in front of Lisette, "are you not Pierre Chotard's daughter?"

Lisette courtesied.

"Yes, Madame la Comtesse," she said simply.

"Ah, I thought I knew you. I seldom forget a face. But you have grown and altered immensely."

"Yes, Madame la Comtesse," assented Lisette, for under Blanche's beautiful eyes, and influenced by her kind words, a sense of guilt and regret took possession of her.

"What, you think so yourself?" said Blanche, with amusement.

"Everyone tells me so, Madame la Comtesse."

"And did you learn to sing so sweetly in Paris?"

"No one has ever taught me, Madame la Comtesse."

"Dear me, then your voice ought to be cultivated. Don't you think so, monsieur?" she asked, appealing to De Courcelles.

"I do, indeed, madame," answered the Baron abstractedly, for the question interrupted him in the midst of some opinions he was uneasily forming of the Count.

"Get her to come and sing to us," whispered Amy, who was interested and full of admiration for Lisette's beauty.

Blanche took the hint intended for her. But at that moment the Count yawned, and otherwise evinced signs of impatience. He had good reason for desiring a speedy termination to the interview; but he was also a prey to a spirit of jealousy and annoyance, for, to his way of thinking, Lisette's presence, where she was, meant an assignation. She was there to meet some man—therefore a lover. All the same, the compliment Blanche had paid to Lisette in speaking to her, had occasioned him satisfaction. It was at once an acknowledgment of, and a tribute to, her beauty. True, he had experienced some slight twinges of shame at sight of the two talking together—his wife with such innocence and

G

kind intent. But such faint traces of right feeling were quickly put to flight, by the coarser reflection that Lisette might become his toy when he chose. So far, though she was mistress of herself, in thinking of her, he would scarcely admit it. It pleased him to consider her, more or less, as his. This sense of possession and the pleasure it occasioned him, was, however, evanescent, and disappeared before the growing irritation he experienced as he thought of Lisette, perfidious, and permitting attentions from another. The Count's palpable ill-humour was not without its effect upon Blanche, and this became apparent in her words, which, by their brevity, partook of the nature of a command, though of this she was unconscious.

"You must come to the château. I will send to you. You shall sing to me, and I will see what can be done. Who knows, your voice may be of value."

"Yes, Madame la Comtesse," assented Lisette placidly, yet with the words quivering upon her lips, an injurious spirit of false pride entered her bosom. Her ignorance fostered this sentiment. She did not comprehend the nature of Blanche's intentions. Was she to be ordered to attend at the château to sing, just as a ballet girl might be to dance? It was true her father, Pierre Chotard, was a simple ferryman, as his forefathers had been before him. But the ferry brought bread, honestly earned, sufficient, and for the rest, Lisette wanted nothing from those who considered themselves so much above her. The position she stood in towards the Count swelled her resentment. Madame la Comtesse might be in a situation to patronize her. That was so. But could she, with all her beauty and breeding, keep her husband to herself? Here Lisette knew Blanche's imbecility to be complete, and with the reflection that this noble gentleman, this gallant Count, was only too ready to do homage to her beauty, she experienced a sensation of supreme exultation, which instantly choked all struggling traces of good in her.

"You will come, then?" said Blanche sweetly, and in blissful ignorance of the evil she had aroused.

"Thank you, Madame la Comtesse—why, yes;" and then, as she spoke, and fearing lest she should lose the opportunity, Lisette allowed her spirit of malevolence to find vent in a lightning-like glance at the Count, full of meaning, and at once seductive. His answer was as swift. But by mere chance Blanche, on the point of continuing the walk, suddenly became aware of the mute play in progress. When the Count, uneasily, and fearing detection, glanced at his wife, he found, to his dismay that her eyes were fixed upon him, full. of an expression, moreover, which had but one meaning. Surprise, fast developing into suspicion and haughty indignation, was what he read in those blue, fearless depths. Before she had regained her composure, and while some traces of confusion were yet apparent upon the Count's face, some dry, dead branches crackled under a heavy footfall, and André Moriseau, heated and breathless from running, burst upon the scene.

Fear of keeping Lisette waiting was the cause of his haste. But though red and perspiring, nervous to the very soles of his boots, his wits were on edge, and his sharp eyes not idle.

André Moriseau was in love, desperately so, and to throw dust in the eyes of a man in such a condition, when once his suspicions are aroused, is not easy. With enemies of Lisette's like the Widow Lemaitre at his elbow, more came to his ears concerning her doings, or, rather, failings, so far as he was concerned, than gave him peace to listen to. So he was on the alert. Blanche had scarcely begun to realize that a blow had been dealt her, at once the most galling to pride and destructive to peace of mind that a woman can receive, when André found himself in the very midst of innumerable suspicions, which the sight of the Count's symmetrical figure in sober retreat in no way dispersed.

Experience had taught André that remonstrance—words of any kind, were useless. He was powerless to cope with Lisette. His weakness lay in his love for her. So in his heart he shook his fist at the Count, cursed, and resolved to watch and wait. As for the Baron and Amy, they were sufficiently interested in each other. De Courcelles was conscious that the Count had fallen in his estimation. But why should he trouble himself about that? Amy laughed, talked, felt tolerably happy, and fortunately for herself was ignorant of the shaping of this domestic drama, upon the scene of which she had so innocently come.

CHAPTER IX.

ONCE within the walls of the château, Blanche hastened to be alone. Recognising to the full the weakness and error in judgment of wearing her feelings upon her face, she had put upon herself the strain of dissembling. But to do this the effort had been great. The reaction was proportionate.

The violence of this mental struggle may be gauged by the admission that the instant her chamber door closed upon her, and she had secured it against intrusion, she paced the apartment in extreme agitation. No tears came. Her lips were parched, her cheeks, burned, and her eyes flashed with anger. The expression of her beautiful face was the incarnation of wrath. Her *amour propre* had received a crushing blow. Her youth and beauty, nay, her very liberty, she had forfeited in her girlish ignorance, innocence, and blind trust. Ever since, she had been slowly awakening to the consciousness that but trifling value was set upon the priceless treasures she had surrendered. The matchlessly beautiful scales of implicit faith, to which innocence and love had given birth, had been thoughtlessly, harshly, torn from her eyes. Many a woman is scarcely conscious of the metamorphosis her husband's affection is undergoing, or if conscious, her temperament, or poor opinion of men in general, enables her to view it with apathy.

But apathy had no place in Blanche's composition. She was as full of passion, and the power to love, as she was lovable. But her pride was immense, and that pride which had elected that she should endure in silence, had likewise dictated that her bearing towards the Count should undergo no change, which, in the smallest degree, infringed upon duty.

The Count could never have said, with any truth, that he possessed a recalcitrant or callous wife. His position was unique, inasmuch as he believed himself to occupy pretty nearly the same place in her affection as he had secured for himself from the first. She only had suffered, and had she not suffered enough?

As in her excitement her supple limbs carried her to and fro, it seemed to her that what she had endured, would only prove to be a series of preliminary attacks upon her position.

It had come to this, that from the Count's own manner, she had conceived, that a mere village girl, a peasant, might share her place with him. That peasant, moreover, to be actually living within a few hundred yards, upon her very soil. The thought was maddening — and as it came upon her in all its bitterness and force, Blanche glanced about her with a look that suggested despair. Suddenly the repose and luxury with which she was surrounded, and was supposed to enjoy, presented itself in grotesque contrast to the real and pitiable condition of her mind. The very room she stood in was replete with every comfort that money could buy, or the ingenuity of man devise. She had entered it for the first time with the brightest prospects before her. How had they been realized? Looking back over the past, she could remember some, at least, of the thoughts in which she had once indulged when retiring to rest in that very chamber.

" I might have known that I was installed here as

a mere puppet," she moaned, and then, recollections pouring upon her, she could no longer control herself, and her tears flowed fast.

From that paroxysm of weeping, which was, in reality, the greatest relief, Blanche roused herself, and with the calmness she had acquired, began to examine the position in which she believed herself to be placed. First of all, had she misjudged the Count, had she wronged him? Were her suspicions without foundation? Had they sprung from the sense of mistrust which had gradually taken possession of her? Crushing this idea almost as soon as it occurred, came the recollection of the looks which she had so unexpectedly seen, and so swiftly read. Could she, a woman, be mistaken in the meaning of those glances? The answer was short and decisive. No. Then the deduction was that the understanding between the Count and Lisette was complete? Again she had no hesitation in replying to herself in the affirmative. Admitting this state of things then, what was likely to be the upshot? She trembled to think. There could be no possibility of gauging what Lisette's beauty might effect, if a man of the Count's inflammable disposition felt disposed to lay himself open to its influence. The extent of her power over him, at least for a time, depended mainly upon her own conduct, upon her handling of herself.

But Blanche shrank from examining this aspect of the affair. There seemed to be no necessity to anticipate, and was it wise of her to seek to probe too deeply? To probe at all, indeed, was the next idea that presented itself. Where was the wisdom of it? Would it not be tantamount to rubbing salt into an open sore? To occasion herself pain was childish. Clearly she had much better close her eyes. Feign blindness for the present, and the very substance of what she dreaded might dissolve. Her position would remain unchanged. Friction with the Count, which, sooner or later, would be certain to ensue, if she pryed too deeply, would thus be saved her. Policy of a cold kind, there could be no doubt, dictated that she should remain immovable.

On the other hand, was she to be a wife in name and act, and at the same time, to close her eyes to the insults which daily and hourly would be offered to her — she conscious of their existence, but refusing to see them? Pride, and a sense of her own injured innocence, aided her in her decision. She had never once faltered in her allegiance to her husband, though she had been sorely tried. Was she to become his dupe? Was that to be the nature of her recompense? Not if she knew it. If she had her duty to perform, the Count had his, and if he failed completely, and to her knowledge, what tie any longer existed between them? What was to be the nature of the bond which was to continue to hold them together? Slowly, and by a roundabout way, she had arrived at a crucial point. It was this. If she discovered beyond all doubt that the Count was absolutely false to her, what steps was she prepared to take? She was about to solve a problem: should her suspicions, which dictated that attempt at solution, be realized, what must be her line of action? How far was she disposed to go? and in what direction? But philosophy stepped in here, and whispered: "It will be time enough to decide that, when a decision becomes necessary. For the moment it is sufficient for you to stand upon the dignity which is rightfully yours. Your conduct has been exemplary; see, so far as in you lies, that you receive the same genuine dealing."

This reasoning approved of and embraced, the next step was to decide upon her immediate actions, upon the course her own conduct was unswervingly to take.

Had she been in a city like Paris, she would have been tempted to avail herself of the services of those secret agents, who were, she had heard, so dexterous, so silent. Placed as she was, in a tiny village such as La Jonquières, such aid was not only out of her reach, but unnecessary. All she desired to know, she could learn by exercising patience and subjecting the Count to a cautious system of personal surveillance. Her manner towards him should undergo no change; she would simply watch and wait. It would be intensely repugnant to her to do this; but clearly she had the best right to exercise such conduct, and unless she wanted to sit down and play the part of poor patient victim, to know what was going on was her only chance of ever holding weapons which would avail in self-defence.

If the Count had learned her feelings from the expression of her eyes, when he had encountered them, the momentary impression he was likely to have formed would be dissipated by her unaltered conduct towards him. He would become incautious, and then— Triumphantly, though bitterly, she evolved these ideas, until nothing remained to be considered. She clenched her hands angrily, when she reflected that his visits to Paris had not been abandoned without a reason. He had been busy nearer home. Finally deciding to confide in no one, not even in Amy, and with the further resolution on no account to be the means of bringing Lisette to the château, this mentally tempest-tossed woman proceeded upon her rôle of hostess and wife.

CHAPTER X.

"MADAME LA COMTESSE appears to be in unusually good spirits to-night," observed De Courcelles to the Count, when Blanche and Amy had left them, and they were smoking an after-dinner cigarette.

"Ah, do you think so?" replied the Count moodily.

"My dear fellow, how could I think otherwise? She is always charming, but to-night she surpasses herself. I have never before met a woman who displayed so much feeling—mind I am generalizing—and whose tact was so consummate."

"Hem, do you think so?" again replied the Count, in accents which plainly denoted that he was not to be drawn into discussing his wife.

To tell the truth, she had puzzled him. He would have given a great deal to know what thoughts were overlaid and concealed by her apparently bubbling flow of conversation, to which he had sat and listened uneasily and wonderingly.

Blanche had undoubtedly shone, surprising herself, considering her harassed frame of mind. The Count had accordingly drawn in his horns, the better to watch her closely. The expression he had read in her blue eyes, when in Lisette's presence, had alarmed him; but an undefinable *something*, in her manner since, had alarmed him still more. He had flattered himself that he knew his wife; but at the end of a protracted examination of her, lasting throughout the whole of dinner, and during which she had done all the talking, a still small voice had whispered to him: "You never know a woman. You may think you do, but you deceive yourself, and unless you are careful, you may know too much of this one."

The Count wanted to think just then. De Courcelles seemed determined that he should not. After all, time and place were out of keeping.

"My dear fellow, shall I treat you to some more of my ideas?" persisted De Courcelles, knocking the ash off his cigarette, and swallowing a little mouthful of wine.

"Yes, if they are not dull ones," replied the Count lazily, blinking and hooking his thumbs in his white waistcoat.

He was intensely annoyed at De Courcelles. He had not got over his vexation at having him billeted at the château. In addition, and this was his crowning grievance, he considered that the Baron had acted like a duffer in speaking of Lisette to Blanche. He was half disposed, indeed, to set the unpleasant contretemps of the afternoon wholly at his door.

"Well, you seem deucedly silent to begin with," blurted the Baron.

"There is nothing more pleasant than the sensation that one may be, without giving offence. Certainly, one is never quite at one's ease with a person until silence on either side passes unquestioned. But I'll admit I'm a dull host to-night. You must forgive me."

"Please don't apologize or I shall feel uncomfortable. I was only trying to draw you, and did not mean my remark seriously. Your day has been spoilt, and it's all my fault, or rather the fault of those rascals of mine who have been fattening upon the birds I thought we should have the pleasure of shooting."

The Count considered that this last remark was a sufficiently direct allusion to the events of the day, to enable him, under cover of it, to put a question he was itching to ask.

"Ah, that reminds me," he said, in an unconcerned tone, "what induced you to discuss our little brunette with Madame la Comtesse?"

"The chances of conversation, a careless remark, is all I can plead. But I have not offended you, eh?"

"Offended *me*, my dear fellow?" The Count's amazement was deliciously natural. His eyebrows were elevated, his expression perfect. "How could that be? Just think, if you turned the little brunette inside out—er—er—verbally, I mean—what could it possibly matter to me? My allusion to the circumstance is due to the reflection that madame probably spoke to her, thanks to your remarks."

"Lucky for her, I should think."

"On the contrary, you do not know these sort of people as well as I do. Madame la Comtesse's condescension will be a nice fillip to her ridiculous pride. Did you not see how vain the little hussy was?"

"My dear fellow, she has a looking-glass, and has doubtless studied herself in it, eh?"

"Ah, well, that cannot be helped, since a few centimes will buy one; but Madame la Comtesse is naturally so kind-hearted, that she is perpetually forgetting that the lower orders must be kept in their place."

De Courcelles thought this was brazening it out with a vengeance. The recollection of the Count turning round in his saddle and waving his hand, nearly made him laugh.

"As for me," continued the Count, partly divining what was passing in his mind, "I confess my admiration for a pretty face; but what one does oneself, and what one's women do, are two very different things."

De Courcelles made no immediate reply, and soon afterwards Louis Bernard dropped in, as was his custom. He had grown to delight in singing to Blanche's sympathetic accompaniments, and was glad to avail himself of the complete relaxation he obtained by visiting at the château. It was his one great pleasure, thus to steep himself in an atmosphere of refinement and culture. From it, he even believed he gathered strength. His presence enabled the Count to slip away, for with De Courcelles he was an especial favourite, and seeing them quickly launched in an animated discussion, in which Blanche and Amy joined at will, with a sigh of relief the Count sought his own sanctum, where, with the aid of a cigarette, he proceeded to give the rein to his thoughts. To what extent Blanche suspected him, he was, of course, profoundly ignorant, but he preferred to think that she was sufficiently on the *qui vive* to necessitate the use of extreme caution in his future dealings with Lisette. That his intentions towards her were unchanged, his resolution to see her, and that very night, was a sufficient proof. Upon that step he decided, for two reasons. First, the very boldness of it insured success. Blanche would be quiescent, in the full belief that he was on his guard; and, in the second place, he could inform Lisette of the exact state of things, and, having done so, await events more patiently.

The Count was too clever and worldly a man to omit to put the question to himself, "Am I or am I not, a fool, to permit myself to become entangled in a liaison, such as this will probably develop into?" and the reply he made himself was an unequivocal "Yes."

"But if you do not, you will lose her," was the answer. True enough, and he was not prepared for that just then. He thrust his hands in his pockets and emitted a cloud of smoke, saying to himself as it curled upwards, "No, no, my charming little Lisette, you shall not escape me. Such an idea is not to be entertained for one moment. The La Jonquières weakness is my weakness. Supposing there was a rock as high as heaven, and the woman I happened to fancy was at the top, I should try to scale it, forgetting the dangers of the way in the anticipation of the pleasures a-head. There is something so romantic in the pursuit of a fresh and delightful little rustic, something so new and invigorating in stealing forth, when everyone else is abed, to be encountered by a faultless little woman, aglow with health and brimful of affection; something deliciously intoxicating in the pursuit of forbidden fruit. It's the devil's sauce, I should be told. Doubtless, but for me it has a pungent relish."

Having got so far, the Count disposed himself in a comfortable chair, nursed his right leg, and tapped his amplitude of shirt front, while he allowed the smoke from his cigarette to curl slowly from under his moustache.

He now took into consideration another aspect of the affair. Supposing this attractive little peccadillo (for as such he chose to consider it) was really discovered by madame? What would she think—more important still, what would she do? In all probability there would be a squabble of rather larger proportions—a fierce contention, in fact. Well, and what then? Why, madame would settle down to the inevitable. Just that. He, in his turn, would probably tire of the game. His attitude, having done so, would be of a nature to bring about a complete reconciliation, which she would be sure to attribute to her influence over him. He, knowing better, would laugh in his sleeve, and all would be well. But supposing madame developed a fancy for being stubbornly uncompromising, what weapon could he lay his hands upon to reduce her to a more tractable frame of mind? Could no defect be found in *her* armour? To discover a weak spot in her would be to strengthen himself. He would have something to urge in his own defence. Nothing of the kind existed in reality, he knew, but in a war of words, strategy, finesse, the art of discovering and seizing an advantage however trifling might, as in greater matters, serve to turn the whole tide of battle. The idea was worth consideration, and he should not lose sight of it. But after all, his chief strength lay in his personal influence over madame. This he believed to be complete, and, if fully exerted, overwhelming. Was it possible that so handsome a fellow as himself, would be unable to dictate terms? Of course not. He might make his mind easy on that score. So he applied himself to another glass of liqueur, surveyed himself with no small satisfaction in a mirror, and with his brow, which under the pressure of thought had contracted into an ominous frown, once more smooth and smiling, he rejoined Blanche and his guests.

The evening sped its course, but the day having been a fatiguing one, as though by unanimous consent the small party broke up early.

Louis took his leave. De Courcelles and the Count appeared to be inclined to court the influence of Morpheus, rather than a discussion and cognac.

Having exchanged a few affectionate words with Amy, and said good-night, Blanche found herself alone, for the Count having kissed her, and recrossed a small drawing-room which separated their apartments, she no longer feared intrusion.

Physically, she was tired and in need of rest; mentally, beset with jarring thoughts. To undress and lie down seemed best. Whatever she felt, she would have to endure, and to endure she needed repose.

But though she was comfortable, and the apartment steeped in a silence which should have induced languor and sleep, results the very reverse ensued. Ideas swarmed She travelled back over the whole span of her life, as it were, in a second. Her imagination, excited by the events of the day, would not be coerced into restfulness. In vain she closed her eyes, her mind, inflamed and feverish, evolved scene after scene with startling clearness.

At length, dead silence, the semi-darkness, the confined atmosphere, appeared to unite in an effort to stifle her. She rose, examined her watch, and found that she had only been lying down an hour at most. It seemed to her like an eternity. The brilliancy of the moon attracted her; she pushed the blind aside. Then, enraptured with the beauty of the scene, she opened the window softly, and leant forth. In unsullied purity, the pallid lamp of night soared through space, painting the changing features of the rich landscape with a breadth and power, a wondrous softness and delicacy, that, with all its arrogance and vaunting pride, poor human nature can only dimly copy. The gardens, the fields, the lighted aisles of the park, the broad bosom of the river, reposed in a bath of limpid silver, which plunged into bold relief the solid blackness of the woods. The excessive agitation to which she was a prey, struck her as presenting a powerful contrast to the placid beauty, to the perfect repose of Nature.

"Ah," she sighed, and her lips quivered painfully. "All things about one slumber, clad in smiles and peace; but we poor human beings beat our wings against the walls of life, and fret to see beyond. Yes, and dissatisfaction, the restless longing to be understood and loved, are amongst the great causes of this fretting."

A slight sound cut short her reflections. It was that of a footstep on the terrace beneath her. She leant forward and recognised the figure of the Count. His presence there at such an hour would, under ordinary circumstances, have possessed no significance for her. Ever since she had known him, his habits had been controlled by the vagaries of the moment. If it pleased him to smoke when others slept, he did so. But a prey as she was to suspicions, her feminine mind instantly set down this nocturnal ramble as being in some way concerned with Lisette.

"I'll follow him. I *will* know what it all means," she said, and breathlessly she slid her feet into her slippers, enveloped herself in a cloak, and with quick, nervous steps, traversed in succession the spacious staircase and the grand drawing-room itself.

To gain the terrace through the medium of one of the French windows was simple. Panting from excitement and rapidity of movement, her heart beating furiously, she glanced about her. The Count had disappeared. Without hesitating an instant, she descended the stone steps which connected the terrace with the garden, passed swiftly between the *parterre* of gay flowers, and heedless of the heavy dew which penetrated her satin shoes and chilled her naked feet, she bounded over the smooth lawn in pursuit of the man whom she felt confident was wronging her. Until the low boundary wall was gained—which at this point fenced off the château grounds from the high road and the river beyond—Blanche never paused.

Cautiously she peered over the barrier. On her left lay the route to Mezieres; to the right, and only some fifty yards distant, the cottages of La Jonquières. As she had anticipated, the Count had traversed the grounds, passed out through the gate she had guessed he would use, and was in the road on her left. Owing to her knowledge of the locality she had intercepted him, having arrived at the nearest point to the village, and immediately opposite the little copse of willows and alders which grew into the river.

With quick strides he passed under her very nose. She could have touched him with Pierre Chotard's punt pole, and the fumes from his cigarette swept over her face. A few moments more, and he stood beneath Lisette's window. His right arm moved in the action of flinging something against the glass. Breathlessly Blanche watched. Soon the casement opened; a woman thrust her head and shoulders forth, and she could see from the Count's attitude that he was speaking to her. Then the window closed, a light shone in it, and the Count, evidently satisfied, retraced his steps, until when opposite her, he sought the shadow of the trees. A pause ensued, a period of inaction, and during it Blanche could hear her own heart beat, could catch the sound of snapping twigs as the Count crushed them under foot, could see the occasional glow of his cigarette, and when he moved into a favourable position, could discern his form in perfect silhouette, backed as it was by the river.

Suddenly that lull, that period of patient waiting, was abruptly terminated by the Count. Starting forward, he advanced, as though the person he expected was coming to him from the direction of the gardens extending in the rear of the cottages. This was in fact the case. In another moment, the firm, compact figure of Lisette, was exposed to the full glare of the moonlight. The Count embraced her ardently, their lips met. Blanche could even see the expression of her upturned face. Then the shadows hid them, and sick with humiliation, her worst passions roused by the knowledge that another—and that other an illiterate peasant girl—was preferred to her, this proud woman, moving as though her strength failed her, retraced her steps through the dew and the flowers.

Later, when by some slight noises she knew that the Count had returned, she had not closed her eyes. She listened to those evidences of his near presence and shuddered. Even the light of the new day discovered her lying amidst the tossed bed-clothes, still awake, her hair dishevelled, her eyes full of weariness, and bloodshot from tears and want of sleep.

CHAPTER XI.

No one would have dreamt, though, that madame suffered, that a blow had been struck at the very foundation of her home life, and that she was aware of it, had they seen her sitting within the open windows of the grand drawing-room.

With ease, and a grace peculiarly her own, she was laughing and talking vivaciously with Louis Bernard, teasing Amy and the Baron in turn, and receiving some compliments from the Count, who was on the terrace, though well within earshot. Every now and then her white teeth would close upon her under-lip, the heavily-fringed lids would veil the blue eyes, moist with meaning; but those signs of agitation were so well controlled, that as she sat there, her graceful figure disposed easily, and her little feet resting on a carved pearwood footstool, she seemed as perfectly happy as one could wish.

"I never knew such people," remarked the Count abruptly, changing the whole current of the conversation. "I have tried my best, but there is no inducing you to drive or do anything."

"But why should we move when we are perfectly contented?"

"Perfectly contented, Monsieur le Baron? Can you say that?" asked Louis.

"I can indeed."

"What an enviable frame of mind you must be in, monsieur," interposed Amy mischievously.

"Eh, mademoiselle, and you—are you not contented?"

"Ah, that's another matter," laughed Amy. "*You* ought to be, Rudolf."

"Do you hear that?" asked De Courcelles, raising his voice slightly.

"No; what did you say?" inquired the Count lazily.

"Mademoiselle Amy says that of all men you ought to be contented; and, *ma foi*, with the sunlight and a cigarette, you should be."

"Ah, do you think so? Your ideas of what should be conducive to contentment are not bad, but they are not exalted. The sun happens to scorch me, and the cigarette has gone out."

"Sit in the shadow, then; and if you want a light I can give you one."

"Too lazy to move, my dear fellow. As for the light, give it me. Thanks. Tell us something amusing, my dear Abbé. A little scandal even would be refreshing, otherwise I shall go to sleep."

"A distinct compliment to us," interposed Amy pertly.

"Don't stir him up, for goodness' sake, mademoiselle, or else he will drag you out into that sunshine *en revanche*."

"I maintain you are hard on me, De Courcelles. I should do no such, thing; but on a day like this, I think it positively sinful to neglect one's health by remaining cooped up in the house."

"Fancy a man who is made of iron, talking about his health," retorted the Baron; "besides," he added, "we have already been out half the day, and in an hour's time, when it is cooler, mademoiselle is going to teach me how to catch carp."

"Only upon the understanding that you bait the hook, Baron."

"And kill the fish, you said, mademoiselle."

"And kill the fish, monsieur," replied Amy, with mock solemnity.

"A piece of feminine cowardice and cruelty combined," said the Count ironically. "You are willing to teach the art of destroying; but you decline to soil your white fingers. Fie, mademoiselle."

"Don't be so absurd, Rudolf; fish were meant to be caught."

"And so were women, *ma chère*."

"*Peste!* but they catch us," said De Courcelles, with a ludicrous grimace.

"I don't pity you, if you *will* singe your wings," remarked Blanche, laughing outright at the comical expression of the Baron's face.

"Ah, madame had you there," interposed the Count, waking up, as it were, blinking, and puffing forth a mouthful of smoke, which slowly formed circles. "She is right, too, my dear fellow. Yet women are our light; we are content to be destroyed by such warmth, and what we are pleased to consider beauty."

Blanche's lips curled, and her bosom heaved with momentary agitation; the blood mantled to her cheeks, and a slight frown contracted her forehead. At that instant, a deluge of scornful words rose to her lips. She was enduring a species of torture, which, owing to her relationship with the Count, might at any moment become unbearable. His last remark maddened her for the moment. She repeated it to herself, "and what we are pleased to consider beauty." To think that such a man was to determine, to deceive, and yet to ensnare. With the knowledge she possessed, such a sentiment sounded like an insult. But by a strong effort she curbed herself. The frown vanished, the tell-tale blood retreated, her perfectly-developed figure, outlined to advantage by the pale upholstery of the *bergère* in which she half-reclined, was no longer agitated. She trifled with her rings, and then said in the silence :

"Really, Rudolf, our material value might be our only one."

"I did not say so. The idea is yours, not mine."

"You hinted as much. Will your conception of what is beautiful—women, I mean—change?"

"Ah, now I have no words to answer you with."

"Because, if so, some of us will be poor unfortunates. What do you think, Monsieur l'Abbé?"

Louis' grey eyes, luminous with feeling, were turned full upon Blanche.

"A good heart, madame, must always command its value," he said slowly; "for the rest, small-pox may at any moment supervene."

"What a horrible idea," exclaimed Amy, clasping her hands expressively.

"A true one, nevertheless, mademoiselle."

"But appalling. Are we, indeed, so frail?"

"The answer is *within* you, mademoiselle."

"Oh, I prefer not to think, then," replied Amy, jumping up from her chair, and pulling Fidele the spaniel's tail until he growled.

Louis smiled. He had so many thoughts. Strange they might be, but they were his hidden friends. He had no one to tell them to, and already he sighed despairingly in his weak moments for someone in whom he could confide.

"And now, Madame la Comtesse," he said, rising from his chair, "I must be going. There is someone ill at the Moriseau farm."

"Wait one moment, Monsieur l'Abbé," interrupted

the Count, the remark not lost upon him all the same, "wait one moment. There is someone coming, I hear carriage wheels. Let us see who it is, and then I will walk a few yards with you."

"Does Madame la Comtesse receive?" inquired a servant, approaching respectfully.

Blanche signified assent. She welcomed the prospect of a momentary distraction.

"I have an idea it is Monsieur Brunot, by the glimpse I caught of the carriage," decided the Count. "That fellow has a skin like a rhinoceros. Don't see him, my dear."

"Oh, we had better not make enemies. It is so easy to be civil."

"Is it? I don't agree with you. Brunot is unbearable. Don't you think so, De Courcelles?"

"Hush, my dear fellow, here they are, whoever it is."

"Monsieur Brunot," announced a servant, flinging wide the great folding doors.

M. Brunot advanced into the room. Tall, angular, and some fifty years of age, his features suggested sharpness accentuated. His eyes were small and piercing. His jaws were square, massive, and adorned with a grizzly stubble. He was over-dressed, and despite his efforts at easy assurance, he belonged indubitably to the bourgeois class.

Blanche rose and received him politely. An unavoidable introduction or two ensued, and then, in the midst of a rather awkward silence, M. Brunot began:

"The pleasure of calling upon you, Madame la Comtesse, overcame me. I was within a few miles, when the turrets of your delightful château caught my eye. I instantly turned my horses' heads; the recollection of—of—and, madame, I assure you—"

Words suddenly failed M. Brunot. The poor man's

embarrassment was almost painful to behold. Perhaps the self-consciousness that he was not adhering strictly to the truth, was not without its effect. In reality he had planned the visit with a view to gloat over a recent success, to talk of himself in that stately drawing-room, and to let the Count know that he had done without the influence for which he had sued. Yes, pure spite was at the bottom of his appearance at La Jonquières. But there, confronting him, was the compact military figure of the Count, whose keen glances seemed to read his very thoughts, the slight and elegant De Courcelles, whose soft and affable face wore a placidly amused expression. There, too, were the ladies, Madame la Comtesse and someone else, whose name he had not caught, and behind them again, a tall, quiet, and dignified curé. Set in the sober harmony of the tapestry, surrounded by the dull glitter and splendour of the magnificent furniture and porcelain, the actual presence of these people, upon whom he knew he had impudently encroached, took away his breath. Completely out of his element, he made a tremendous effort to recover his self-possession, and, luckily for him, Blanche, who divined his feelings, came to his aid. Really, she felt a little pity for the man, and determined to reassure him.

"You have timed your visit to perfection, monsieur. It has only one fault, you have delayed it too long. I, for one, was languishing for someone to amuse me. Now, come and tell me something new and entertaining."

With admirable tact Blanche drew him aside, thus monopolizing him, from pure kindness. But, though a shrewd business man, M. Brunot failed to grasp the situation. Upon each word of Blanche's he placed his own construction. Here was this beautiful lady, so exquisitely dressed, so altogether charming, telling him, M. Brunot, that her own men-kind were as good as boring her. His self-assurance received an immense impetus, his coarse bourgeois blood became inflamed. He really believed himself to be in especial favour, and some absurd notions instantly possessed him. Besides, he held, he considered, an important card, and was eager to play it. He sank back in his chair, applied his handkerchief to his forehead with inexpressible satisfaction, and said:

"Something new and entertaining, Madame la Comtesse? Well, let me see. But I fear I am at a discount. I have so little time I can call my own. Scarcely sufficient to study the daily papers as I should like. Work, work, work, is, and has been, my motto. True, I scan the political horizon with acute interest. And now—now I have the power to speak of those reforms which I have long planned and cherished. Is it possible that you do not understand me, madame?"

"Indeed I do not. I must plead ignorance," said Blanche, feeling very much like laughing, in spite of her own troubles. "You must remember, monsieur, we live terribly quiet lives here, buried as we are in the country."

"True. Ah, but, madame, how charming the country is. I love it," and M. Brunot flourished his hand with an airy gesture; "but, let me tell you, I have worked, and my work has not been fruitless. I am now a Deputy."

M. Brunot elevated his voice as he made this announcement, glancing about him with unbridled satisfaction.

"Indeed, monsieur, and it was your wish?"

"Since I became rich it has been my loftiest ambition, Madame la Comtesse."

"Then I congratulate you upon having attained it, monsieur."

M. Brunot inclined his head in acknowledgment. "You are too kind, Madame la Comtesse."

He was bursting to add, "And I have done this myself. Monsieur le Comte and Monsieur le Baron de Courcelles have done nothing for me. A fig for them." But since he triumphed, he could afford to rest content. Besides, madame was a superb woman; it was delightful to be near her. Her presence made him forget his spleen. He was confident that she liked him, moreover.

"It is a favourite saying of mine," he continued, still borne along on the tide of egotism, "that nothing is impossible. I have felt the truth of it here," he pointed to his forehead with a dramatic gesture. "I have indeed *proved* it. I wanted to become rich. A few millions of francs are nothing to me. I chose to become a Deputy. I am one."

"Indeed, you are a man to be admired and imitated, monsieur," replied Blanche, already sensible that she was being punished for her good-nature.

M. Brunot failed entirely to detect the sarcasm. He rejoiced in himself.

"I desire only two things now, Madame la Comtesse," he continued, impelled by the sentiment.

"Indeed, monsieur; then you will doubtless secure them. You cannot fail to."

"But you do not inquire what they are, Madame la Comtesse."

"Let me atone for my omission, monsieur. I am curious."

"I covet a delightful old place, such as this. The very atmosphere of it enchants me. I love nature. I worship refinement and art. In addition to this desire, I want to discover someone who can comprehend me, and thoroughly sympathize with my aspirations. Someone who would be willing to become

Madame Brunot. She need not have a franc for her *dot*, but her title to position must be indisputable."

M. Brunot paused, apparently for lack of words to express his varied feelings. Blanche, disturbed, her heart wrung with her own troubles, felt bored to death, and wished with all her might that he would go. It was so grotesque, to be obliged to talk to such a man, feeling as she did. But she contrived, to endure, being too kind-hearted and courteous, to permit her tormentor to discern that his society was fast becoming obnoxious. So well did she conceal her weariness and annoyance, that, when M. Brunot at length took his leave, he was satisfied that he had made a distinctly favourable impression, and was delighted with the reception accorded him.

"What an odious pig of a man," exclaimed Amy, the moment the door had closed upon him.

"An energetic and plain-spoken opinion, if inelegantly expressed," observed the Count, laughing at Amy's vehemence.

"I like to say what I think," she retorted. "Why should one mince matters? I hate people who pick and choose their words, and never say what they feel. But seriously, Rudolf, how did you ever get to know such a person?"

"I met him in public somewhere. At a dinner I think, and ever since, on some pretext or other, he has made occasional descents upon us. But, tell the truth. He is enormously rich. Would you not marry him?"

"How detestable of you to suggest anything so revolting. If he were the only man in the world, I should pray that seas and continents might separate us. Weren't you terribly bored, Blanche?"

"I began by being sorry for him. Poor man, he

was so palpably awkward, but I ended by longing to be released from such an incubus. His vulgarity and egotism are without parallel, still, had I been in the best of spirits, I might have been amused."

"Aren't you in good spirits, then?" asked the Count quickly.

Blanche regretted her remark. She had said more than she intended.

"I feel a little tired, thanks," she said quietly.

"And what has that to do with your spirits? How odd you women are. You never will give a direct answer."

"Not unless we happen to like to be catechised," answered Blanche placidly.

The Count was baffled. He hated to be, and he shot a glance out of the corner of his eye, which said as much.

Amy had sauntered out of the room. She was leaning over the balustrade of the terrace, looking down upon the gardens, half dreaming, and in a decidedly enviable frame of mind. De Courcelles approached her. But as he did so, he thought how fresh and virginal she looked. Little better than a child, too, but a well-grown and very pretty one, in her simple white frock, with her auburn hair reaching far below her waist, and a suspicion of pale blue ribbon adorning it. De Courcelles would have given a good deal for that ribbon just then. To him, Amy seemed so artless, so unconventional and honest. She refreshed him, not because he was the least bit *blasé*. His ignorance of women was against that; but it pleased him to forget the existence of powder, to think of the country, not the town.

"Well, shall we go and catch the carp, mademoiselle," he asked insinuatingly. A nod and a smile on a tantalizingly dimpled cheek was his answer, and the two, who evidently understood each other admirably, were soon busy with rods and lines, on the edge of the pond, in the great court-yard, within the shadows of the walnut trees, and the sound of the deep-toned stable clock.

CHAPTER XII.

So, while the sweet wood smoke, blue as the sky itself, rose over La Jonquières, while the jackdaws chattered and built their nests in the ruined home of the long dead Counts, while the fish leapt in the river, and the river pursued its course, while the little village itself seemed sleeping amidst its apple orchards and its woods, russet, crimson, and yellow with ripened leaves — sleeping there amidst the stillness — men's minds were busy.

Louis' for instance. Mentally and physically, a great change was at work in him. His face no longer wore the hue — as Lisette had said — of the little ivory Christ in the *petit sanctuaire*. The straight, delicate, and clearly-cut features were the same, it is true; but the suns which had painted the trees and ripened the corn, had bronzed his cheeks, and his long walks amongst the golden grain, the woods, and the quaint French farms, had strengthened him wonderfully. His tall, straight figure was erect, and the traces of confinement and close study were no longer discernible.

Mentally, the alteration was as marked. Subject no longer to galling restrictions, and the observance of a daily routine of rigorously imposed and onerous duties, his naturally vigorous intellect began to expand with astonishing rapidity. Questions of a nature which perplexed and alarmed him flitted like phantoms across his mind. These, presenting themselves constantly, becoming clearer imperceptibly, and establishing themselves ever more securely, were only compelled to retreat before the activity with which he set about his daily work. At present, vague, shadowy, and perpetually changing in aspect and outline, he found he could thus rid himself of them. And, in accordance with the principles he had been taught, he did so. Yet the moment he permitted himself to think, his strong common-sense recalled them. Afraid, in sore perplexity, again he would be driven to silence the inward clamour by employing himself in some way at once.

His greatest consolation at this period was derived from the repose, the calm which stole over him, as he reflected that, at least, his life was not useless, since it was in his power to do good. He was in a position to help others, if he could not help himself. The hold he had gained over the minds of the simple and ignorant villagers had only one flaw. This was his intimacy at the château. Blanche was beloved. The Count feared.

Louis' kindness and gentleness had won the hearts of the women, his bravery, the admiration and goodwill of the men. To crown his influence and place it upon a solid basis, it was only necessary that the rustic minds should be *able* to think of him as *their own*—their curé; a prominent feature in their social system who must belong to them, just as did their cattle and their money. He was called to the sick beds of their wives and daughters. He was the recipient of all their confidences, of whatever nature.

Yes, but Monsieur le Comte and Madame la Comtesse were of different flesh and blood to them. Birth stepped in. Pride of race and the possession of wealth, with its concomitant—no need to work—presented a separating barrier. Intimacy at the château, of a marked character, was equivalent to seeking the enemy's camp, and was a species of counterpoise to the good opinions which, it was felt, Monsieur L'Abbé Bernard undoubtedly merited.

Before his varied musings Louis' parents had retreated into the shade. His temperament, his education, his past life, had completely unfitted him to think with them. His culture and natural capacity had, as it were, placed him in another world. They wanted for nothing, which, as a good son, he could offer them. His filial duties, which had become almost mechanical, he never forgot. Beyond that, he barely remembered their existence. This was unintentional on his part; in fact, he was unconscious of it. He only knew that he felt intensely lonely at times, and was at rare moments dimly aware that a great longing for something, as yet undefinable, was springing up in his solitary heart.

Meantime, the Count, vain, fickle, and restless—not unlike many men—had taken an idea into his head, and was not to be put off it.

Lisette, ambitious—desirous of being something that she was not born to be—she could not well have said what, but clearly something a cut above André and her humble station—was in no mood to relinquish the influence she had acquired over Monsieur le Comte.

Blanche, mistress of the château, yet feeling no mistress, wife, yet feeling no wife—growing to detest the name as it stood to her even—was driven to reason with and console herself. To have taken Amy into her confidence would have been, in her opinion, distinctly selfish, of no avail, and, moreover, hurtful to her pride in the highest degree.

There was something brave, something that had a

tendency to soothe her wounded spirit, in wrestling with and bearing her sufferings alone. Ever since the night on which she had gone through the moonlight and the dew, she had striven to repress the anger which was so injurious to her reasoning powers—striven to determine what was best and wisest, to map out some plan of action which she could pursue with the belief that good sense and right guided her. She took her moral stand upon the platform of her own conduct. She knew that her married life had been *sans reproche.*

If she had begun by loving the Count blindly, in consequence of her extreme youthfulness, had then, gaining reason, proceeded to weigh him in the scales, and, alas! had found him hopelessly wanting, *she* had been the sufferer, not *he*. An ordinary woman, loving an erring husband, would have besought him with tears and supplications to remain with her, to be faithful to her. She had not done this. She could not supplicate. A strong will, supplemented by pride, forbade it. In the earlier stages of the Count's disaffection, she had contented herself with redoubling her attentions. Leaving nothing undone to induce him to spend his time with her, ministering to his comforts in every conceivable way, she never once twitted him with his faults. If these proofs of her regard for him could not win him, could not fill the widening rent, she decided that no action on her part would.

Finding her attempts futile, she had simply set duty before her, and had endured. The result had been the steady decay, the perpetual falling to pieces, and, finally, the annihilation of the love her innocence and girlish fancy had conceived. Had she given the Count occasion against her, had she been disloyal, it would have been impossible for her to have judged him as critically. If she gave little, she must expect the same. Good herself, she looked for as much.

She imagined that she should have felt less bitterly, had the object of the Count's attentions chanced to be a lady of cultivated tastes and acknowledged good looks. At all events, she would not have despised him so much, possibly would not have shrunk from his touch with such acute loathing. There was nothing pure, nothing romantic, in this passion for a peasant girl. It could only emanate from base desires. For the Count, setting aside his principles, was an educated man, and his sensitive ear could only be offended by the accents to which he must listen. Sooner or later this would be so. True, there was no accounting for the eccentricities of human nature. The very pages of history proved how men of birth and intellect had stooped to women of obscure origin. However, one resolution Blanche had formed. Since the Count loved Lisette, to Lisette, and those who might chance to please him, he must henceforth confine his affections. She had exchanged her name for that of La Jonquières; it might be well, for the sake of all concerned, to bear the burden she had taken upon herself.

Thus, completely dejected, sore to the heart's core, her existence fenced with unhappiness, at that instant she was in a condition most pitiable, most dangerous to herself. She would have given the world for sympathy, for the love she yet believed in as possible. She had, instead, the bitterness of considering herself defrauded of this consolation which she yearned for with all the strength of her nature. This sensation, this longing, was no new one. She had been stirred to the depths by the discovery she had made, and thus her feelings had reached an acute stage—that was all.

In this condition of mind she had retired for the

night, having had a chat with Amy, and left her to dream of De Courcelles. He and the Count were sitting up playing cards and smoking, so on crossing the little drawing-room, Blanche had merely lowered the light which burnt in a quaint Flemish lamp, and had then shut herself up in her own room.

In accordance with her resolution to hold aloof from the Count, and to receive him as a husband no longer, she had had recourse to delicate feminine subterfuge. This could not avail her much longer, she knew, and she was therefore conscious that she stood on the verge of an explanation, the consequences of which she could not foresee. She had determined to avoid a public scandal if possible. But the Count, having become repulsive to her, she had decided to extricate herself from the degrading position in which she found herself.

The means by which she might attain her ends depended upon the Count's attitude. She was anxious to give him his freedom, but at all costs she would maintain her own. The compact she desired was that they should agree to deceive the world. Would the Count consent? In any case, strong in her right, she awaited the issue unflinchingly and with confidence. The outlook beyond alone appalled her; the future with its dreariness, its humiliations, its utter loneliness, seemed to freeze the very life-blood within her, to quench even the desire to exist. But anything would be better than a continuance of the mockery of affection she had so long and so silently endured.

Pursuing her reflections, and in no mood for sleep, Blanche stirred the fire and sat down before it, for with the falling leaves the night had become chilly. The lamp had burned low, and the light from the half-consumed embers only added to the gloomy severity of the apartment. The ceiling was lofty and profusely decorated, the bed massive, colonnaded, and canopied with russet-hued Genoa velvet. A cabinet of ebony and brass of exquisite workmanship and of Louis XIII. style was fitted with a sliding writing convenience, and on a dressing-table of carved pearwood—upon which two Cupids stood supporting a mirror, and grasping in their chubby fingers brass sconces—were strewn those trifles which women affect. A pastel by Latour hung over the wide stone mantelpiece, and beneath it, gazing into the fire, sat the real, the living picture—Blanche, the young wife, solitary, painfully sad.

A tap at the door made her start and rise to her feet. She recognised that the eventful moment had come. This explanation which she had evaded could no longer be postponed.

The Count entered.

"What! not asleep, not even undressed. Doing your best to destroy your health, and so forfeit your good looks," he said, approaching her.

The words, the tone in which they were spoken, and the sense of ownership they implied, irritated but decided Blanche. There should be no vacillation on her part, but plain speaking without delay.

"Well, I am tired now, and am going to sleep," she said, counting on her reply having a distinctly irritating effect.

"Tired, and going to sleep, eh? Well, that's cool! Decidedly so, when it happens that I've forsaken De Courcelles and a game of cards, packed him off to bed, in fact, on purpose to talk with you."

"Delightful of you, very, but droll, too, since we could only talk, according to you, at the expense of my health and good looks."

"What is the matter with you?" he asked, regarding her attentively from the position he occupied on the chair she had vacated.

"Nothing."

"A woman's invariable reply."

"I was thinking."

"Of what?"

"Of many things; amongst others, of you."

"Ah, now we arrive at the point. But the compliment would have been less doubtful, had you not classed me with the items, the 'many things.'"

"But I have no desire to pay you any compliments."

"And why not, pray?"

"Because you have done nothing to deserve them."

"How disagreeable of you."

"The truth often is."

"Bah! this sparring becomes wearisome. Come and make love to me."

"Thanks, I have no desire to."

The Count was piqued, but not sufficiently so to show it. His passions were partially roused. His vanity fed by the reflection that this woman, at all events, was his.

"Ah," he said, with some amusement, twirling his moustache, "and so you have no desire. But, do you know, I have a great one. Come now, after all these years—what is it? three or so—the pleasure of embracing you is as great as ever."

"Don't touch me!" she exclaimed, starting aside, for he had followed up his words with the action they implied.

"Don't touch you; and why not? Blanche, are you mad?"

She made no answer, but stood before him with palpitating pulse and flashing eyes, her cheeks crimson and her hands clenched.

"What is all this about?" he continued; "what does this absurd conduct mean? Are you rehearsing some imaginary drama? because, if so, I shall be glad when you have ended the part you have allotted yourself. Now I think of it, though, there has been a certain strangeness; a coldness, in your manner for days past."

"If you have discovered that, it is as well. But there is nothing imaginary in the relationship, in the situation existing between you and me.

The Count's face was very white, his calmness forced, for he could no longer deceive himself. Blanche had evidently made a discovery. Yet he had no conception of the depth of the chasm which already yawned between himself and his young wife, and the weakness of his position lay in his ignorance. Once more he made an effort to avert the impending rupture.

"I have never heard you talk like this before, and I don't understand you; but if you've no objection I'll light a cigarette. Smoking soothes one. Come, give me a kiss, and let us say nothing that we may regret."

"I have not the least intention of saying anything that I am likely to regret, anything that I shall ever wish to retract."

"Recollect that."

"I intend to. Just now, you alluded to our three years or so of married life. Shall I tell you what you have succeeded in doing during them?"

"I am listening."

"You have crushed, obliterated, the love I gave you at the beginning of them."

"Ah, and how have I done this, may I ask?" inquired the Count placidly, though with the sensation that he was approaching the crucial question—what had madame discovered?

"To attempt to reply to you fully, would be as wearisome as it would be useless. When you are alone you can interrogate yourself. Your own conscience will supply the answer. Meanwhile, it is enough for me to tell you that I have thought, and that my deliberations have taught me that I have ceased to love you."

Blanche kept her eyes fixed upon him, and the words dropped from her lips like shots from a revolver.

"Really, now, how intensely dramatic. What's the right thing for me to do under the circumstances? Prostrate myself at your feet? Go down on my knees and implore you to retract such a cruel announcement? Tell you with tears and trembling, that banishment from your heart would be worse than death to me? I would do all this if I happened to be acting; but since I am not, I will merely thank you in sober earnest for the touchingly delicate way in which you have tendered the information. For that information itself, most; and then I would remind you, madame, that hearts are as plentiful as chestnuts in autumn time."

The Count's coolness was exasperating. The effect of it instantaneous, and precisely what he desired. Blanche, irritated to a degree, no longer restrained herself.

"Oh, indeed! Well, then, the kisses you spoke of, you may keep for peasant lips and midnight assignations; I have no further need of them," she said, her voice vibrating with scorn.

The Count was startled. He had not expected such a withering volley, yet he maintained his composure admirably. He recognised that there was nothing to be gained by flying in a rage; the reverse, in fact.

"Ah, so you have been playing the spy, and this display of temper is the result. I do not envy you, madame, I assure you. Peasant lips—how sarcastic!

Well, at least, they are fresh and moist. Really, though, I credited you with more sense. To make all this vulgar fuss about a passing whim, a trifling fancy. A mixture of admiration and gallantry provoked by a pretty face. If one is going to be subjected to a system of *espionage*, the situation at once becomes embarrassing. Shall I give you a piece of advice?" he asked, lolling back in his chair as though he considered himself master of the situation.

Blanche made no answer. She had expected a violent display of passion, but the Count's cynicism perplexed and alarmed her. She was doubtful how to manœuvre.

"You have no reply to make," he continued, "so you are not anxious to receive advice from me. Well, I will stretch a point, and tell it you in any case. This is it. Love me as much as you like. It is only natural, and you can't help it; but at the same time, learn to close your eyes a little. Practice this, and you will save yourself enormous trouble, I assure you."

Goaded by his absurd assurance, Blanche became infuriated.

"Love you as much as I like—*love you! You* who have not scrupled to destroy the happiness of my existence, who have striven to shatter all that was good in me; and, to crown your infamous conduct, have bestowed your attentions upon a low-born village girl. *Love you*, I—"

"Take care, madame, moderate your violence, or believe me, apoplexy will assuredly supervene," interrupted the Count, with an irritating little laugh, as though quietly enjoying Blanche's unrestrained vehemence. "What is the use of flying in a rage, pray? Why can't we discuss matters quietly? I am not a volcano, if you are; at least, perhaps, I should say, I don't happen to be just now."

By this last sally, the Count had unintentionally overshot the mark. He wished to enrage Blanche, to keep cool himself. But he had said too much. She instantly divined his intention, and recognised her own imprudence.

"Yes, you are quite right," she said slowly, restraining her anger and the harsh words which rushed to her lips; "to be passionate, when one's passions are not enlisted, is, as you suggest, a mistake. Mine are not, so let me remember the lesson you teach."

"It would be well if you would. But why you are incensed by the discovery of a mere peccadillo, which you cannot even magnify into a flirtation, amazes me."

"I prefer not to discuss it. To you it may seem a trifle—and I have no doubt it is—to tap at windows at the dead of night, to embrace women tenderly, as though they belonged to you; to me, if I cared, it would seem much."

"Why, I do declare you are jealous. I detest jealous people; they annoy one with their insane suspicions. So this is why you have never extended your patronage to Lisette, as you proposed. Well, she will survive it."

"*Probably*, thanks to your fostering care. I wonder how you dare mention her name," she added suddenly, her blue eyes ablaze with indignation. "Do I look like the kind of woman to tamely endure such impertinence?"

"You look amazingly handsome—and—but for Lisette— "

"Don't insult me by speaking of me in the same breath with such a creature. Rudolf," she added passionately, some of the old memories, the old love she had once felt for him, sweeping away her resolution to be calm, "Rudolf, you would make a good woman into a bad one, a saint into a fiend."

"The deuce! Are you the good woman—the saint? How touching! What an ingenious comparison! Really, I shall end by laughing outright, and I have no wish to hurt your feelings. Spare me, I entreat you."

"All I claim for myself is that I have been faithful. It is more than you can say. Such acts as you seem to glory in will not bring you happiness. There will come moments with you, as with me, when sadness will steal upon you, when the life disfigured will seem better ended. When that time comes, you will not be able to forget that you have had one woman's existence in your keeping, and that you have tarnished and embittered it. You can never undo what you have done; you can never give me a light heart, such as I had when the convent doors closed behind me and I came to you; you can never make me love you again as I once did, but you *can* let me feel that although your wife by law, I am free in the sense that my own rooms are sacred to me. To prevent scandal, let us live as friends; but to be anything nearer, I refuse. *This* you can do, and the world need be none the wiser."

For a moment the Count's better nature almost gained the mastery. Blanche's pathetic voice, and Blanche's blue eyes dimmed with tears, nearly had the effect of making him admit himself wrong, of causing him to lay aside what he chose to deem his prerogative as a husband and a man—to swear he was right at all hazards, and without scruple. But no, his authority must be maintained, and his position happened to be such, that a brazen face and sarcasm could alone defend it. Besides, this woman belonged to him. She loved him, too, he felt sure.

"Madame," he said harshly, "you are a superb

actress, and would have made a fortune on the stage. You are a charming woman besides. What a pity you are lost to what the English choose to call the profession. But I am in no mood for mummery just now; the opprobrium you have heaped upon me I choose to take very much in earnest, I assure you. I have only to say, I have no desire to trespass upon the boundary you have fixed. Good-night."

With his small figure erect and perfectly rigid, as though fully impressed with the belief that his honour and dignity had been falsely impugned, the Count walked out of the room.

His disappearance was the signal for Blanche to spring to the door, lock it, and then, woman-like, to dissolve into tears.

CHAPTER XIII.

So Blanche, the young wife, had in reality reached the most dangerous condition of mind at which a married woman can arrive. In succession, she had steadily traversed the various phases which lie between a young and pure love, given, and for a time appreciated, and the ashes, the dead sea fruit of admitted indifference.

She had loved, jealously she had striven to keep the affection she craved in return; finding the power to do this slipping from her, she had sought for reasons why this should be, and in the search her eyes had gradually opened. The defects of this god whom she had set up, and been so disposed to worship perpetually, were no longer hidden from her. The veil of sentiment had parted in twain, and she saw him—this gallant gentleman—as he was. Overwhelmed, she had sought the consolation of prayer, for it had seemed to her that the Divinity alone could support her lacerated spirit. Her natural goodness of heart, and perhaps the answer to her petitions, had enabled her to remain long in a semi-benumbed and suffering condition.

From this partially comatose state, she had been violently awakened by the discovery of the further and more apparent wrong done her—Count Rudolf's amour with Lisette. Thereon had followed her anger, silently endured at first, then, in obedience to events, finding outlet. Attendant upon that had ensued a reaction, a depression of spirit which reduced her to the verge of despair.

Partially recovering from this dejection again, she had become alive to faint glimmerings of a desire for consolation. Was she, not yet in the full vigour of her womanhood, to resign herself to the encouragment of a set belief that life and love were to be forever abandoned; for if she renounced the idea of love, how should she wrestle with, how could she possibly endure the inane monotony, the unutterable ennui which would surely overtake her? The mere contemplation of a perpetual routine of wifely duties, glossed and made palatable by no real interests, was sufficient to appal, nay, almost to paralyze her.

After having permitted herself to dwell upon these thoughts, she invariably rose to her feet with an angry gesture, pushing the hair from her forehead in sheer weariness; but with a spirit of rebellion rife and ever growing, she would tell herself that anything on earth would be preferable, and that she should go mad if she were constrained to live such a life always.

But then, what would change it? Death! To whom would it come, and when? Apparently it was far distant. Then this sympathy, this consolation for which she yearned, whence was it to appear, how was it to be obtained, and at what price? It was this desire, this eminently dangerous, yet most natural craving, that Blanche now confronted. Whatever the Count thought, there had been no attempt on his part at a further explanation or reconciliation. Blanche had sought none, for to what could it lead. She could only hope that the substance of the understanding, already arrived at, might be maintained. For it she had fought, and beyond it she had little that was tangible to expect.

"Mademoiselle Amy, there is something amiss with madame, your sister. I am sure of it," said the Baron, who, in spite of Blanche's clever dissimulation and the impenetrable *sang froid* maintained by the Count, was not to be completely hoodwinked.

"Oh, but is there? I think you must be mistaken," replied Amy nervously, and considering it her duty to mislead, even at the cost of descending to prevarication, the ground upon which the Baron trod, being, she knew, very delicate.

"No, I think not," retorted De Courcelles tenaciously. "I think she looks pale, and I am sure she is out of spirits. Is she coming with us?"

"For a ride, do you mean, monsieur?"

"Why, yes, mademoiselle."

"I don't think so. Blanche, the Baron is particularly anxious that you should come with us. He will insist upon it that you are out of sorts, and that a gallop would be the perfection of a tonic."

"Thanks, my dear Baron, but I don't feel sufficiently energetic. I shall read, and a quiet time will do me no harm."

"Ah, but indeed I think you are wrong, madame. I have it from experience that too much quiet is the very deuce. That reminds me I shall have to get back to Paris soon."

"Madame won't ride," interposed the Count snappishly, "just because there happen to be horses, eating their heads off, entirely at her disposal."

"You don't do me justice, Rudolf," replied Blanche, accepting the accusation, and attempting to smile it down. "You know I am not so unreasonable."

"You say so; very well. But, as a matter of fact, I *don't* know. If there were no horses, I'm pretty confident you would discover that, without your ride, you couldn't exist. There are times when you women are really too provoking. What did you say about Paris, De Courcelles?" he added bluntly, turning his attention to the Baron.

"Only that I'm due there shortly. What are your plans for the winter, by-the-bye, *mon cher* Rudolf?"

"But half formed."

"Well, but have the cold, the rain, and the falling leaves no effect upon you? You should deliberate, and decide without delay. I am not half a Parisian in a sense, but I fancy I shall relish a peep at a good play, and a turn on the Boulevards."

"Oh, it's all very well in its way, and one is in duty bound to turn up there, I suppose. I'm not sure, though. I've half a mind to try a winter here for a change. Fact is, one gets sick of conventionality and perpetually doing what one ought to do. But come along, we had better get ready."

"Let me stay with you, dear," whispered Amy, putting her arm round Blanche's neck affectionately, the Count and De Courcelles having left the room.

"On no account; I should be wretched if I thought I was the means of spoiling your pleasure."

"But I would far rather be with you. We could have some tea, and a nice quiet talk without fear of interruption. We never seem to have a moment together now."

"There, dear, go like a good girl. We can have the talk whenever you like. But give up your ride— no, you won't induce me to hear of such a piece of self-denial. Stay, though, one moment; I have a question to ask you, and mind, it's a very serious one. Do you really like the Baron, because he is evidently very much in earnest, and it would be unkind to trifle with him?"

Amy blushed furiously at the point-blank question, but recognising the necessity for speaking her mind, she said simply:

"Yes, Blanche, I do. He's a darling, and I love him ever so."

Then, as though she had said too much, and was already ashamed of her weakness, she hurried away to put on her habit, her cheeks as crimson as a peony.

"Love and happiness everywhere but within my heart," muttered Blanche the moment she was alone; "and yet, why do I complain, why am I envious? How bad of me, how bad I am becoming. But regrets—regrets bitter and plentiful—will come in spite of all I do to stifle them. This inward emptiness, this pitiful ache, this ashen-grey of cold, harsh weariness, *will* make its presence felt, and there are moments when I become half-maddened. Oh, if I could only escape from myself!"

Mechanically bidding good-bye to Amy, and graciously complimenting the Baron upon the perfection of his horsemanship, Blanche stood and watched them ride away, and then from the windows saw them emerge from the park, and disappear round the curve of the river, on the Meziere road. Still gazing in that direction, she observed a barouche and pair approaching at a rapid trot. M. Brunot and the possibility of a visit from him occurred to her. She summoned a servant.

"I am not at home to anyone," she said.

Then shortly after, changing her intention of remaining within doors, she ran upstairs, slipped on a hat and jacket, and, as the silvery chimes of the Boule clock in the grand drawing-room struck four, she quitted the château, turning into a side path just in time to see M. Brunot whisk round the gravel sweep to the main entrance.

"Thank goodness I've contrived to escape that odious man, at all events," was her reflection, as she buried herself among the trees. "Come, I ought to be unfeignedly thankful that I am not married to that creature. It would be too horrible. If I could only contrive to forget myself and my own grievances, I might succeed in establishing a sort of prosaic contentment. If I had a child, now, upon whom I could dote, and in whose existence I could sink my own. Ah! *if* I had. What is the use of repeating that consummately tantalizing little word? *If* I had another husband, I should be another woman."

Threading her way through the gloomy aisles of the park—for at this hour the shadows were dense, the woods of La Jonquières being justly famous for their superb timber—Blanche hurried on, apparently with an object, in reality with none. Purposely she chose the darkest and least frequented paths, for the profound silence and deep shade seemed to harmonize best with her mental condition. At length, and unconsciously, she emerged from the dense covert, and struck into a foot road which skirted a plantation of young larches. It was a mere grass track, though a public right-of-way to some of the upland farms existed over this portion of the La Jonquières estate.

Following it for some short distance, Blanche's attention became arrested by the sight of a simple stone cross. It rose from a solid pedestal embedded amongst the moss and the hyacinth roots, and carved upon it were the words:

"Ste MARIE PRIEZ POUR NOUS,"

while above them was a little square cavity containing an image of the Virgin bearing an infant Christ. In front of these figures were two half-burned candles, one on either side, and between the bars of the iron grille, which protected them from the vulgar touch, were a few fresh wild flowers. Someone had come and put them there, amidst the silence and the sweet scent of the woods, and someone's simple prayers had ascended into the blue welkin.

"Ste Marie priez pour nous," murmured Blanche, repeating the words. "Ah, I sadly need help," and with the sense of her own imbecility and extreme need, she sank on her knees, and hid her face in her hands.

Pouring out her whole soul, transported with the hope that an answer—comfort in some shape—would be vouchsafed in reply, so completely engrossed did she become, that she was unconscious of approaching footsteps.

Louis Bernard had done many things latterly. He had worked hard, and, amongst other duties, he had listened to a confession from Lisette. What she had told him was therefore fresh in his memory, very fresh, and it had made an unusually deep impression. He was pondering over it, thinking how hard it was to be a priest, to bear so many burdens, to be a receptacle for the deposit, and burial, as it were, of so many secrets. To know so much, and yet, no matter for what end, never to be able to divulge it.

Dwelling upon this, and similar matters, he swung along with a free stride on his return homewards, choosing the near cut through the park, as a saving of a mile or more. He had been to the Moriseau farm. André's mother was ill, and it comforted her to see him, so he had made a point of going there often latterly. When within a few paces of the *petit sanctuaire*, he recognised Blanche's bowed form. Knowing what he did, the situation was grasped by him in an instant. *Why* she knelt there prostrate, having abandoned herself to the torture she endured, seemed clear to him. An expression of ineffable tenderness stole into his face.

It seemed to rise from his inmost soul, to light up the man, as though a lamp of pity and sympathy were suddenly kindled within him.

His footsteps made no sound on the short, springy turf. Taking advantage of this, and obeying a sudden impulse, he glided behind her, and there stood with his eyes fixed upon her, his head bowed slightly, as though he, too, prayed.

Presently Blanche moved, her hands fell to her sides, she rose, turned, and faced him. A cry of surprise at seeing him died upon her lips. Her gaze became riveted upon his, while the blood came and went in her cheeks. The steady gleam of his deep grey eyes conveyed his thoughts; but she was in that emotional condition of mind when such a look stirred her nature to its depths. Such kindness, and the power to feel, as shone in his glance and beautified his face, awoke innumerable echoes within her, and on the instant her blue eyes filled with a light, which caused Louis to lower his and almost tremble. Neither spoke at once. She was the first to do so, and her voice betrayed that her mind had forced her back upon herself. Just as in that flash of feeling as eye encountered eye, the workings of the heart were revealed, so came the reflex action, which reminded her that she was Blanche de la Jonquières, and that before her stood M. l'Abbé Bernard.

Her voice nearly failed her, and sounded hollow and strained, as with a forced smile she said:

"Who could have believed you were so near? I fancied myself alone, and am disturbed and weak."

The natural, but unnecessary apology, was lost upon Louis.

"Those who have suffered, who are *always suffering*, can best sympathize with sorrow. Thank God for the *power* to feel, madame," he said, with a supreme effort, his pulse beating fast, his composure far from perfect.

Blanche looked at him, a certain strangeness in his manner, and a ring in his low, strong voice, thrilled her unaccountably. She dare not trust herself to speak, and her failure to reply at once grew into a silence, during which they walked back towards the château, scaring the white-tailed rabbits and the deer from amongst the bronze and gold of the faded bracken, exchanging no words, these two, for their hearts were full.

CHAPTER XIV.

DE COURCELLES had taken his departure for Paris. Amy was in consequence disconsolate. The Count, not knowing quite what to do with himself, and already missing the companionship of the pleasant and frank young fellow whose advent he had so resented, had betaken himself to his study, with the intention of whiling away the afternoon with the aid of Molière's wit and a box of choice cigarettes. Scarcely had he made himself comfortable and opened his book than there came a knock at the door.

"Confound it," he muttered grumpily, "the devil must be in it, for I never can be quiet. Come in."

Blanche entered with certain resolutions in her mind.

"I have something I wish to say to you, Rudolf."

"Say away, my dear," replied the Count, stifling a yawn, and disguising the surprise he felt at her intrusion, for they had scarcely spoken latterly, except when the presence of others had demanded the civility. "Say away; only I warn you that I'm in a contentious mood, and won't be responsible for myself. Where will you sit? There; ah, now do you mind making a long arm and passing me those matches?"

The Count puffed at his cigarette and reflected.

"What in the world's in the wind now?" he asked himself. "Well, shall I begin for you?" he added, aloud, since Blanche did not speak.

"I don't think you could, thanks."

"Shall I try? Let me see; you've come to say you're—no, on second thoughts, I won't. You shall speak for yourself."

"I've come to tell you that I want you to give up the idea of remaining here for the winter."

"Oh, is that it? Ah, and for where would you wish to exchange the healthy atmosphere of La Jonquières?"

"For Paris."

"Paris?"

"Yes; does it surprise you?"

"No, not in the least. All the world and his wife are, or will be there soon. No, that you should want to go to Paris does not surprise me, since it has been our custom to be there in the fall."

"What do you mean, then? What does surprise you?"

"Monsieur l'Abbé Bernard—"

"What has Monsieur l'Abbé Bernard to do with the question at issue?"

"Well," said the Count banteringly, "you can't take him there very well, and what will become of the poor fellow?"

Blanche had her back to the light, otherwise the Count would probably have remarked the pallor which overspread her face.

"I have come here to talk sense, not nonsense,' she replied calmly, but firmly.

"Well, of course I'm only joking. Since you no longer love me, though, I wondered whether Monsieur l'Abbé had supplanted me. But you know I'm a confirmed tease. However, let us understand each other. If people want me to do things,

I must know what sort of footing I'm on with them."

"By 'people,' do you mean me?"

"Of course."

"Well, we get on famously, don't we?"

The Count glared wrathfully. This refractory wife of his, who, his vanity taught him, was longing to fall into his arms, still had a mind to trifle. He was not disturbed by her vagaries; he would let her see it. She should smart, silly thing that she was.

"Yes, after all, I think so," he said, with an air of boredom. "Individually we please ourselves. It saves one a vast amount of trouble. I like it."

Blanche was infinitely relieved. She had feared that in payment of her requirements, she would be compelled to give and accept overtures. His indifference paved a way for her escape, and to do so, it suited her to pass his remarks unchallenged.

"I have many reasons for wishing to leave here," she said simply.

"Oh, indeed?"

Having insinuated that he did well without her, he looked for some show of annoyance on her part. There was none. Chagrined, he reflected that women were certainly incomparable actresses.

"Yes," pursued Blanche, "there are the best of reasons why we should not remain here."

"Have you any objection to recount them?"

"Well, to begin with, it would be dreadfully dull for us—for Amy and myself, I mean."

"True! What says Molière—'Paris is a wonderful place; a hundred things happen in it every day, of which we know nothing in the provinces.' Naturally a village without a shop, becomes especially odious when the snow is on the ground and you are sighing for chiffons and bonbons, dying, in fact, to be in the midst of these 'things' which Molière speaks of.

But dullness is not at the bottom of your wish to leave here."

"The Baron has gone. Amy is fond of him. What is the use of separating two people who care for each other, and for a whole winter?"

"The Baron can get into the train, if he does not change his mind. We shall be glad to see him, I suppose. That is not your reason."

"How intensely provoking you are. If anything went wrong, Amy would be inconsolable."

"Would she? I doubt it."

"I know my sister better than you do."

"Very probably; but do you fancy you'll hook De Courcelles by running after him? Nonsense, you are too clever for that, and so is he. No, you have another motive. What is it? Come, a fair question."

Blanche hesitated. He was right. She had another motive—a widely different one—so different, in fact, that were it revealed to him he would have been electrified.

"Shall I tell you what it is?" he said, seeing her reluctance to speak. "Let me see, then. I am not so desperately devoted to *la belle* Lisette, as you imagine, therefore, this very natural little ruse of yours to place a railway journey between us shall succeed. I'm—"

"Ruse of mine—"

"There, don't get angry because I happen to have found you out. It could scarcely be otherwise. I only talked about staying here to see what effect it would have upon you; I had not the least intention of doing so. There, come and give me a kiss, issue any orders you like, and leave me to digest Molière in peace. I appreciate your regard for me, my dear Blanche, I assure you."

Without trusting herself to reply, fearing to destroy

her cause, but utterly ignoring the Count's careless allusion to an embrace, Blanche quitted the room. When the door separated them, she turned, and as though looking at him through it, murmured, "How *can* I do my duty, with such a husband? How can I be what I ought? If *he* knew, if anyone knew, what would they think of me?" And just then, Amy came to her from the garden, her hands full of bright blossoms, and that charmingly sympathetic air of Niedermeyer's, "Le lac," upon her lips.

CHAPTER XV.

THUS empowered by the Count, Blanche's restless energy effected the necessary arrangements, the result being that the château was soon tenanted by only a couple of trusted servants.

The blinds were drawn down, the superb furniture in the grand drawing-room covered up. Even the stables were empty, the horses having been trotted over to Mezieres, thence to be conveyed by rail to Paris, where the Count, Blanche, and Amy, were installed in the Hotel de la Jonquières, the family mansion in that gloomy but magnificent quarter of Paris, the Faubourg St. Germain.

As for Louis Bernard, the same world no longer existed for him. The whole face of it was changed. A conventional explanation for this move to Paris had been offered to him, a conventional farewell said, and with that farewell, it seemed to him that the sunlight had departed from his existence. He confronted himself, as it were, and the microscopical examination which ensued was attended with many pangs. No longer could he close his eyes to his own condition. It had come to this, that he saw clearly, too clearly. The phantoms which had flitted across his brain so persistently, and been so repeatedly banished by determination backed by hard work, were phantoms no longer. They had at length assumed a shape there was no mistaking, a solidity there was no denying. He was a living, breathing, thinking man—a *man* in *every* sense of the word—very weak, very erring, intensely human—flesh and blood.

By a rude shock, the approach of which had not been unannounced by tremors, he had come to understand clearly the nature of the vow he had taken. His thoughts carried him backward. He could recall the entreaties he had made that, before taking it, he should be allowed to become a private tutor for a year, that he might think, that he might see something of the world he was renouncing. He could remember the stern answer with which his superior had refused his petition. He must take the vow, and then he was at liberty to do as he pleased. But although he had had in those days dim foreshadowings of the seriousness, the awfulness, of the step demanded of him, he had not fully understood it. It was impossible that he should.

How *could* he grasp the idea that it was asked of him to go down to the grave, wifeless, childless; no sweet human ties for him, no home, as the word is understood; a life of toil, a death of solitude? And he had done this. He had taken upon himself this burden, had denuded himself of these joys, these consolations.

The meaning of those words of his father's, which he had overheard and interrupted was plain to him now: "Ah, well, you have gained your ends, wife. Louis is a priest: our bread is assured, but—" That meant that no woman could ever come between them, that he should have to keep them only and always, and that thus they felt safe in the immutableness of their position. No woman, no; but a woman had caused the scales to drop from his eyes, had made him see as he had never thought to see; bred as he had been between convent walls, cut off from all human intercourse, except that which, like his own mind in those days, had been warped into passive shapelessness by restrictions.

A woman had stirred the passions natural to him, and had made him know himself as he was—poor, pitiful human being. Worse than that, he thought. He had come to ask himself, rationally, calmly, and in the face of day, whether God Himself had ever intended, ever desired, such a sacrifice as he had been called upon to make, from any of the beings it had pleased Him to create. He had come to lie awake and try, with aching head and feverish pulse, to thread his way amidst the mass of theological lore with which his mind was stored. He had come to fall into a heavy sleep towards morning, with all these doubts clashing together unanswered; but last thing of all, last thought of all, he had sunk into that lethargic slumber, so heated, so unrefreshing, with the image of a woman rising up before him— a woman fair and delicately beautiful, golden-haired and blue-eyed.

How those blue eyes had seemed to burn, as he had encountered them! How symmetrical had seemed her form! How he could recall each gesture, each varying expression! Yet that woman was divided from him by a gulf as wide and deep as religious and social laws could make it. No abyss could be more profound, unless death were added to it. For him to think of her, priest that he was, was the gravest sin, and he groaned with remorse and hated himself; but, nevertheless, her image was punctured upon his heart, and pray as he would, he was impotent to efface it.

So this was the upshot of the *carte blanche* which had been extended to him, to come and go at the château as he pleased. The quiet evenings, the pleasant interchange of ideas, the music, the friendship, had developed into something more for him, and that something, he knew now, meant Blanche, Madame la Comtesse de la Jonquières. When he had admitted this to himself, he reflected further.

Here was he, with life before him, bound to the Church by indissoluble ties, looked upon by all as the *ne plus ultra* of goodness, attached to Blanche, wife of the *seigneur* of the parish of which he was curé. He was ashamed of himself. He had good cause to be, he considered.

Setting aside religion and his position, was she not his neighbour's wife? And what could justify him in daring to raise his eyes to her? Was it not madness, and to what could it lead? The destruction of his peace of mind, and, if the world knew, degradation. Besides, how grotesquely ridiculous was the figure he would present to her even, did she but know. Would she not turn from him with contempt and loathing? Would she not brand him with the name of hypocrite? He, a holy man, there to correct evil, to teach good, and by his own life to be a living example to others, pointing them, helping them heavenward. Would it not be a revolting sight to her, this spectacle of himself, reduced to owning that he was worse than any of those whom he had come to teach? And this by a simple admission of his feelings.

His only refutation of these last interrogations, was the vivid recollection of the long, steadfast, wistful glance, before which his own had fallen. Of the walk through the bracken and amidst the shadows of the trees, which he had afterwards remembered, had been a silent one. Curious that neither of them had spoken. Never in his whole life had he walked so far with anyone without talking. And he had been unconscious of the flight of time—

absolutely unconscious of it—and so happy. But that was before he had confronted and cross-examined himself. Now that he had done so, there was only one course for him to take. His *thoughts* were his own, and he had a right to them. No one must ever know, and then—what matter?

If he chose to hide within him this sentiment, this conception of what seemed to him the perfection of womanliness, to treasure it deep in his heart, what harm should he do to anyone? All he had thought and felt would go with him to the grave, and no one would be the wiser. Religiously he felt himself to be guilty, terribly so. But mankind would not be his judges. And as for God—well—he was prepared to answer to Him. That which had come into his existence should remain with him as long as life itself. He would never part with it, but would keep it locked within his bosom. At times it seemed to him that he was less lonely now that he possessed these sweet thoughts, these dreams of what might have been; at others a wild tumult raged within him. Was it not maddening to think that his whole existence had miscarried, and he a mere boy. He felt as though his life had been stolen from him, and that he was bound hand and foot, but that the fetters were none of his choosing. He had not been fit to choose.

But in any case, he was not sure that the Divine Will was not directly opposed to such an existence as stretched before him. Common sense, and all things in nature, were in deadly opposition to it. Then, at the height of the mental strife, when desperation seized hold upon him, and he felt of all men most miserable, would come a lull, a sense of repose, of peace, mysterious, miraculous, as though the Blessed Saviour stood close by him, invisible, yet quite near. And at such moments, the anger, the rebellion within him, would melt away, and with tears, his lips tremulous with feeling, he would go into his little church, and there, in the silence, lose himself in prayer.

To the simple villagers of La Jonquières, to whom a gossip was more refreshing than a meal, now that their *seigneur* could no longer be discussed and abused, their curé stood first in importance. So upon him their gaze was mainly directed. Besides, they had never forgiven him for dancing attendance at the château as he had. Ambition was at the bottom of it, Mère Chotard declared.

"Ah, he knows which side his bread is buttered," she remarked to Lisette one afternoon when the work was done, "for all he's so young, and one would think so simple."

"What do *you* say, André?" asked Lisette, for, since the Count was out of the way, she had André in constant attendance, flirting with him furiously, and making the honest fellow's heart beat as though it would burst his best blouse, specially donned for the occasion.

"I don't know," said André simply, removing his pipe from his lips sufficiently to say the words.

"No, of course you don't," struck in Mère Chotard; "men are always blind, except to liquor and a woman. Look at Pierre, I've taught him all he knows—"

"How to manage a punt even," suggested André facetiously, and with a merry twinkle in his eyes.

"That's enough from you, *Monsieur l'effronté*. You are just a boy, and should be silent," retorted Mère Chotard snappishly.

"Ah, *bien, oui!* just a boy, is he?" laughed Lisette.

"Yes, I can remember the day he was born as though it were yesterday."

"When will he be a man, *ma mère?*"

"When he has carried you off to the farm yonder, in spite of your airs and antics."

André blushed at the blunt suggestion, and looked sheepish to a degree. Mère Chotard favoured his suit, he knew, and that was half the battle, he thought.

"Then he's likely to remain a boy all his life," retorted Lisette, coquettishly straightening her plump figure, and bestowing a killing little glance of encouragement upon André at the same moment; "but let us talk of Father Bernard. He looks older, I think."

"Well, and so he is, child."

"Oh, but I mean much older."

"He is kind and good. I know that," interrupted André; "but for him, I doubt if mother would be alive."

"And he never smiles as he used, they say," continued Lisette, ignoring André's remark; "he used to look beautiful when he smiled. I have thought I could love him."

"Lisette, do you know what you are saying?" Mère Chotard asked sternly.

"Well, mother, I *have* thought so."

"Ah, there is enough mischief in you for anything, I do believe. Friend André, you must look after her well when you get her."

"*When*," repeated Lisette, with emphasis; "that when will be a long while coming."

"But it will come," whispered André, "it *shall*."

"You are so certain. Then you must be happy," replied Lisette provokingly, but in the same low voice.

"Lisette," he said passionately, "if I don't have you, nobody else shall, mind that."

"What are you two whispering about?" exclaimed Mère Chotard, suddenly turning upon them without rhyme or reason, as old folks will at times.

L

"Only about the good Father," asserted Lisette promptly, and with a bewitching glance at André, as much as to say, "we understand each other, my good fellow, don't we? How you *do* love me, and how I shall make you."

André reddened to the roots of his hair beneath that glance. It went through him like an electric shock. The poor fellow positively trembled.

"If there is any change in him—" said Mère Chotard deliberately, and in ignorance of the little farce so cleverly enacted under her nose.

"Who are you speaking about?" inquired Lisette, interrupting her mischievously.

"Why, of Father Bernard, child, of course. If there be a change in him, as I say, it comes of being up at the château day and night. What business has he to go there, I should like to know? Filling his head with nonsense when he ought to be at his prayers and books."

"*Books;* books make him go to the château, I should think," remarked André sententiously.

"And why, pray, *Monsieur la sagesse?*" asked Mère Chotard, standing before him with folded hands and an expression of annoyance.

"Because *they* understand the stuff in them, and *we* can't."

"Besides, he must have *some* pleasure. Oh, how I should hate to be a priest," said Lisette forcibly, turning up her eyes as though she already felt herself a martyr.

"Of course, he must," chimed in André. "It stands to sense. Otherwise, what is to become of a man. I think he ought to have a wife," he added comically.

"*Voyons!* listen to him; André is all for marrying!" cried Lisette satirically.

André got up, and contrived to slip away, somewhat astonished at his own temerity, for he had a wholesome dread of Mère Chotard's tongue.

"Do you know, mother," said Lisette, after a short silence, "I think André handsomer every time I see him. I believe I shall have him in the end."

Mère Chotard gazed with a mother's fondness at her daughter. In her eyes Lisette was faultless. Then, with a Frenchwoman's impulsiveness, she kissed her on both cheeks, and, while embracing her, said:

"Have him; maybe you will. It might be best. For, when André's past his prime, and ugly perhaps, who knows, the farm on the hill will be as good as ever. Remember that, but," she continued quickly, "the man's not born that's good enough for my girl to marry."

Pierre Chotard entered at this moment. Hot and irritable because he was tired, Mère Chotard's remark struck discordantly upon his ears.

"Marry," he repeated harshly. "What, talking about it again? I hear of nothing else from morn to night from you women. If you'd mind your pots and pans instead of talk, talk, talk, it would be better for all concerned. Come, get me something to eat. I'm hungry, and have a thirst, I tell you that."

Mother and daughter exchanged glances. Nothing was said by either. It was of no use to argue with Pierre when in one of his moods. There was nothing for it but to feed him quickly and well, and to keep silence. Lisette got out of the way. From where she stood at the door, she could see André striding along homewards.

"Ah, well," she said, looking after him, "you may be big and strong and well-doing. Yes, but you wear a cotton blouse. No, I shall not have you, friend André; I like someone better. Why did he go to Paris," she added, with a glance at the empty château. "Ah, I miss him. He is so—well—so sweet. I have a mind to go to Paris."

Then she shut herself up in her room, feigning some work to do, in reality to sigh over her lot, and indulge in ambitious dreams.

Foolish Lisette! Why do you aspire? You were not born to wealth and rank. You are not fitted for it if you had it. Take honest André, who would lay down his life for you, and be satisfied. You would save much heart-burning.

CHAPTER XVI.

BLANCHE had entered into no system of deception with herself. After her strange meeting with Louis, and during the whole of the silent walk back to the château, she had been transported.

Those feelings hitherto dormant, had asserted themselves. They had been called into activity by Louis' sympathetic face, and the light in Louis' grey eyes. And she had admitted her weakness. She had betrayed herself as she had looked at him. Of this she was conscious. While he was with her, she had been content to abandon herself to a delicious sensation of happiness. For, with a woman's intuition, she had divined the state of his mind. She knew as well as though he had told her, the extent of her power over him.

By her side, she acknowledged, was a man whom she could respect and love, because of his purity and uprightness. He represented to her the embodiment of all that was good and noble, and she had studied him. If he had been her husband, what a different aspect life would have worn. But by considering, by thinking of him for an instant in the light of a husband, she tacitly admitted her own frailty. Once alone, to think, she recoiled from this weakness. How could she be so wicked? At one bound she had suddenly become worse than she believed her husband to be.

For, after all, Louis was a priest, and mentally, at least, she had descended to the very depths of dishonour. And she had hated herself for this descent. But what was to be done? How was she to act? What was right, and had she the resolution to do it?

When it came to this question she hesitated, and a voice said: "Be passive, remain where you are. Do not seek to alter the current of events. See him just as often; meet him on precisely the same terms. What harm can come of this? Nothing. The gulf which separates you cannot be spanned. You are aware of this. Drift along placidly. If you have been so foolish as to allow ideas to enter your mind which should have no place there, you must lock them up; they must never come to light. In this way they will wither, and finally die. You know your own powers. You are strong. Have confidence. Do not deny yourself the pleasure of seeing this man. Why should you? Will you gain any thanks or satisfaction? On the contrary. *Only* control yourself. That will be easy, and all that is demanded of you."

From this reasoning, so weak, so palpably faulty, Blanche's strength of mind and innate goodness enabled her to swerve. The temptation was strong, but she resisted it. "This is how you should act," her guardian angel insisted. "Leave this place, do not see him. If you would overcome this guilty passion, which threatens to destroy your better nature, that is what you should do. You are human, and as human, weak. Do not cherish evil, counting upon your strength to resist it when you shall have necessity. It may fail you. Then what will happen? This sin has flung aside disguise. It confronts you openly, boldly. Better flee from it while there is yet time. You know what is right now. Do it. It might be very pleasant were you to see each other constantly. Life would seem less monotonous. You might be able to endure, able to crush slowly, and with less pain to yourself, these thoughts which have taken possession of you—this love, in fact, which has entered into your heart. Yes, but it is good to use the knife at times. Clench your teeth, and though the agony be intense, you will discover it to be short, and you will find the cure more complete, more enduring. If you give way to the weaker and more dangerous method of dealing with your malady, there may be no cure at all. By a glance, a pressure of the hand, words said without intent, you may suddenly plunge deeper than you had meant, and that plunge will be fatal to you. It is dangerous to play with fire; lay the warning to heart."

Convinced, fearful lest this admirable prompting should lose force by delay, dreading herself, Blanche had gone straight to the Count, and then there had been no more halting until within the stately home in the Faubourg St. Germain.

Once there, she set herself to enter into the existence which opened before her with feverish activity, and apparently with the delight and *abandon* of the youngest and most frivolous girl. She would give herself no time for thinking. Old acquaintances were assiduously cultivated, receptions given and attended; with her whole heart, it appeared, she flung herself into the vortex of fashionable amusement. Then, not content, this heroic woman set herself another task. The tacit acknowledgment of her own weakness had taught her a lesson.

Previously she had stood upon the pedestal of her own immaculate virtue, and from this height she had examined and judged the Count. After all, had she not been disposed to be too harsh? Had she even exerted all her powers to please and win him? Had she not been too prone to think ill of him, when perhaps no real cause existed? At all costs, it was her duty to make this man love her. To influence him for good. This responsibility belonged to her clearly; failing to discharge it, the onus would rest upon her. *Was* he so indifferent to her, so unimpressionable, so insincere, so wholly bad? Perhaps not.

Besides, now that she knew herself as she had come to, it seemed to her that she no longer had any right to cavil at him. She had been hypercritical, and even absurd enough to expect an angel for a husband; there was little, it seemed, that was angelic in herself. She would try. She would exert herself to the utmost. If an ignominious defeat awaited her, there would still remain the satisfaction of having endeavoured to do her duty. Her hopes rose as the noble impulse strengthened in her. After all, their married life might not prove an utter failure. She would do more than her share; it should be no fault of hers if the future proved no better than the past, and she would begin at once.

The Count was not long in noticing her altered conduct. Dexterously as she aimed at establishing a better understanding, without attracting his marked attention, the Count, shrewdly observant, was aware of the difference in her demeanour.

"So madame's tactics are revolutionized," he remarked to himself, while criticising his faultless attire in a little mirror of delicate Viennese porcelain, which represented Cupid, flower-bedecked, and playing. "If I don't know a woman, no man living does, and, after all, I ought to. The greatest mistake I ever made was in fancying that I could love one only, and always. I begin to think I am too large-hearted. There's something so interesting in a new face, so attractive in a new style of beauty. Features and figure, etc., all different; above all, something so essentially invigorating in the discovery of distinctly new ideas on all points. Am I becoming intellectual, I wonder? Well, well, *this* woman—Blanche—adores me. I know it. But then so does the little milliner in the Rue St. Honoré; what's her name? Adèle, ah! So does Mademoiselle Susanne, *premiere danseuse de l'opera*. Charming she is, too. So does Madame la Duchesse de Brillé. Lisette, too; but then, Lisette, ah, I must see her. Yes, *mon cher* Rudolf, you are certainly wise in your generation; you get as much as you can out of life, and you mean to, eh?

With which piece of doubtful philosophy, he set off to find Blanche, to bid adieu to her, as he was going to his club, and from thence, wherever caprice suggested.

"Are you going out to-night, then, Rudolf?" asked Blanche, as he entered the grand drawing-room.

"Am I going out? why; yes. What a question. As you know, there is a new play on at the Théâtre Français, and De Brillé is giving one of his exquisite *petits soupers* afterwards. There will be the perfection of women and cooking. Do you know what De Brillé pays his *chef* per month?"

"How should I?" replied Blanche wearily.

"One thousand francs, and he is no fool. He understands how to spend his money, and will look to it that he receives its value. And quite right, too, in these republican days. If the ambitious scoundrels want to put by fortunes, with a view to retire and pose as fine gentlemen, we must see that they work and earn their money fairly, *ma foi*. Then, some fellows I served with in Algeria are making a night of it at the Maison Chevet. It will be a gala affair, I assure you. *Am I going out?* I should think so. All Paris is astir to-night. Oh, I forgot; *la petite* Lola appears at the Alcazar for the first time since her illness. She is charming, dances divinely, and, I hear, has invented some new steps, to witness which is positively ravishing."

"You appear to be enthusiastic," remarked Blanche, not without a suspicion of sarcasm in her voice.

"Of course I am. I can only be in the perfection of health and the prime of life, for a brief period, and I mean to enjoy myself. Do you blame me?"

"Not in the least."

"Ah, now, there is a certain *something* in your manner, which tells me that you are not pleased."

"I thought you would have remained at home to-night."

"And why, may I ask?" replied the Count, elevating his eyebrows; "what put such an idea into your head? I thought you promised to go and have an hour's quiet chat with Madame la Marquise? It would be a charity since she is lonely and ill."

"I have already seen her."

"When?"

"This afternoon."

"Oh, so that was why you disappeared. All the same, I am going out. Will you do something for me; will you fetch me my cigarette case? I left it and the matches, just where you placed them for me when I was reading."

Blanche returned.

"Now, will you light one? Come."

"You know I detest tobacco," she remonstrated.

"And I love it. What a pity we don't agree. If we were not married, you would discover a pleasure in lighting that cigarette, I assure you. Ah, if we were only lovers; if two people could remain lovers always, how charming it would be; what tie could be more delightful? But this custom of shackling two lives together is provocative of restlessness, and an absorbing desire to kick."

"There is the cigarette," she interrupted, seeing that no good could come of drifting further into the topic he had started.

"Thanks. Yes, there is the cigarette, as you say. Ah—well, what is the use of moralizing? After all, satiety is at the bottom of this morbid desire for amusement, for originality, for *anything*, no matter how vulgar or commonplace. Let it be an innovation, possessing some doubtful attraction, and it becomes the rage, until, as of its predecessors, people weary, and its little day is done. I wonder how La Jonquières is looking to-night, and what the folks are doing. Do you ever think of the place?"

Blanche made no answer, but she shifted her position slightly, so that he could not see the expression of her face.

"In another hour's time," he continued, "everyone will be in bed, probably, except l'Abbé Bernard. The trees will be waving solemnly in the night wind, there will be no sound save that of the stream and the rustling boughs. Not a sign of a light, I should say, except from the window of Monsieur l'Abbé's study. How confoundedly dull it must be for him, eh?"

"Yes, intensely so, I should think," assented Blanche, in a strained voice.

"I have a notion I should go mad. Truly, I am indebted to the gods that I am here to-night, instead of in his shoes; not but what I could absolve all the women nicely. But fancy striding along over those hills every day, in spite of Jupiter Pluvius, in spite of everything, because an appetite must be had for dinner, and sheer weariness obliges one to quit the fire. Not a soul to speak to, only books, always books, and no one to make love to by any chance.

Yes, what that man must endure daily—educated, refined, and highly strung as he is—would deprive me of my reason in less than a week. I swear it would."

Although he could not see it, Blanche's face was drawn and white, as though disfigured by a spasmodic contraction of the muscles. Her voice was firm and clear, however, as she said:

"To you, of course, such an existence would be the quintessence of misery, and to endure it a man has to be peculiarly gifted, especially taught—"

"I should think so."

"But religion, duty, the love of right, the wish to do it, may make one happy, surely."

"Hem! I daresay."

"Is there no comfort to be derived from doing right, in spite of everything?"

"Perhaps so, but it must be deuced dry work. My opinion on such subjects is not worth having, though. Why do you ask it?"

"Oh! because ideas enter one's mind, that's all."

"Well, *au revoir, à bientôt!* We shall meet some time to-morrow, I suppose, unless something happens to me. What a confounded gossip I am. Really, I must go. Stay, there is one piece of news I have yet for you; it just came into my head. That brute, Brunot, has turned up. Paris is not big enough for him. You should have seen the creature and the concern he was driving in—gorgeous—the worst possible taste. Now then, *en avant.*"

Humming an operatic air then in vogue, the Count did not wait for a reply, but made his exit. With the remnant of a feeble hope strong upon her, Blanche called to him:

"Do not go. Stay here to-night, Rudolf!"

There was no answer. The massive outer doors closed with a crash, and the rattle of wheels next instant, told that he had gone. Passing her hand before her eyes, as though to disperse pain, acute suffering of some kind, Blanche stood looking in the direction of the door through which he had passed. Then with an expression of despair on her face, she paced the whole length of a corridor, returned, and entering the grand drawing-room, sank, pale and trembling upon the nearest chair.

"Why did he speak of La Jonquières?" she moaned; "why did he speak of—of Louis? All day long, and at night as I lie awake, I am haunted by memories of this man I have decided to forget. In the crowded streets I see a priest's dark cassock, a sister's sad gown; in the columns of the newspapers some word, some allusion; when I would sleep, then the church clock of St. Sulpice tolls. There is something to remind one that he lives even in the very atmosphere. I cannot forget religion, and to remember it is to remember him. The distance, the very gulf which separates us, the sin in thinking of him, all seem to have combined together to create a longing within me to be near him—to be something to him. In my own eyes, I have long since become vile, for how can I sink lower than to covet this man, from whom heaven and earth have united to sever me? *Who* or *what* will save me from myself? Rudolf, with his contempt for the tie which joins us, his light opinion of women, his love of them, his delight in any empty pleasure, his dull appreciation of what two people might be to each other if they would, his vanity, egotism, and utter selfishness ; am I to be saved from myself by Rudolf, and if not, how, and by whom? Yet Rudolf seems my last chance, and already the hope I had in him is half gone. What is the use of having set myself this task? To forget the man who has stolen into my heart and who possesses it ; to be faithful to him whose name I bear, yet who neither loves nor is beloved by me. It is beyond my strength. How can I? I am not superhuman. Already I feel the power, the wish to struggle, failing me. To-night a mixture of superstition and hope had made me cling to the belief that he would stay at home; that together we might have endeavoured to go back some little way up the hill we have come so swiftly down; for on this night, though he has forgotten it, we were married. What shall I do—what *shall* I do?"

A weary, hunted glance around the vast and splendid room, as though fearing the presence of someone, a shudder from head to foot as though her agony of mind was too intense to be endured, and Blanche's head sank upon her hands and she wept. From this display of acute feeling she at length roused herself. With her strength gone, her temples throbbing, and her limbs trembling, she again became aware of her own identity. Her eyes smarted painfully, and she could not even think. In this condition the fire flickered and crackled, the clock ticked, ticked until imagination magnified that really slight sound into a deafening one. For a moment the monotony of it occasioned her positive pain. She felt as though perfect cessation from sound would be delicious, and the greatest relief. At that instant, when thus distracted and most anxious to be alone, a curtain which concealed the presence of a door was thrust unceremoniously aside, and her privacy was invaded by a servant.

"Monsieur le Baron de Courcelles, Madame la Comtesse," announced the man.

The Baron stepped up to her. There was a certain indescribable charm of manner possessed by De Courcelles. It was as though frankness and honesty had taken possession of him, to the utter exclusion of those conventional traits which one would have expected to discover in him whom the world had always caressed.

"I am of all men most fortunate, Countess," he said; "I had but one wish—to find you alone, and behold, here you are. But first of all I must apologize for disturbing you—"

"My dear Baron, you know you are always welcome," interrupted Blanche, compelled by courtesy to ignore the fact that no one was welcome to her at that moment.

"Ah, now I know that I have not seriously transgressed, I breathe again. Really, I felt frightfully nervous when your man said, 'Oh, Monsieur le Baron, Madame will see *you*, I am certain;' I had my doubts whether the privilege he hinted at was strong enough to support my audacity. But now let me tell you what I have come to talk to you about, and why I wanted so much to catch you alone. Understand, Countess, I approach my subject with fear and trembling."

At once Blanche comprehended. Was it not like life? She herself was reeling beneath the grief occasioned by recognising that her own existence was a horrible *fiasco*. At that moment she was to be assailed, importuned for her decision, as to the future of two other people The situation was grotesque, there could be no doubt. Keeping her face in shadow, because of her emotion, she smiled encouragingly at the Baron, and said:

"I shall listen with rapt attention, and you will find me so easy to deal with, that you need have no dread of my woman's tongue. Come, let me reassure you."

"Well now, that's kind, that's sweetly said, Countess. So, then, I shall come to the point at once, and confess to you that it is of your sister, Mademoiselle Amy, I wish to speak; in short, I love her."

"Would you be surprised if I told you that I was already aware of it?" asked Blanche, smiling at De Courcelles' earnestness, and trying to forget herself and the embarrassment his inopportune arrival had occasioned her.

"Ah, that's too bad of you," he exclaimed, struggling between the warmth of his feelings and the momentary belief that he cut a foolish figure. "Well, I may as well own I've been *empressé;* but you women are so quick to divine a fellow's thoughts. After all, though, I must admit that you would have been very dense had you not seen the drift of my intentions. Well, I need scarcely say, they are perfectly honest, and I mean to stand by them. I want Mademoiselle Amy to honour me by becoming my wife, and I'll frankly own I've hinted as much to her."

"As to honour, Monsieur Le Baron, you confer it upon us."

"Ah, but I think differently," exclaimed De Courcelles ingenuously. "If everyone will consent, and this can be brought about, I shall be the happiest fellow in Paris."

"You need fear no opposition from me," said Blanche warmly; "but have you thought over it seriously enough? You know it is easy to plunge into an affair of this kind; but since it is for life, a mistake is so fatal."

"But I have examined myself, I assure you, and for me, no other woman exists. It is a fact. And I think somehow that you credit me with being honest. I love Mademoiselle Amy passionately, devotedly; will you help me to win her?"

"No, I won't do that, Baron. To exert any influence I may have in deciding a question which must determine a whole future, would be a responsibility I should not care to take upon myself; but of all things, I candidly tell you, I should like you to marry her, because I think she loves you—"

"Do you—is that your opinion? and you are sure to know. How delighted I am to hear you say as much," interrupted De Courcelles excitedly, and with a great amount of gesticulation.

"You shall have a fair field and no favour," continued Blanche.

"And with that I shall be content, though it sounds rather severe."

"Yes, but I think people ought to decide these questions for themselves, and no one should attempt to bias them. I ought to tell you this though; Amy's *dot*, contrasted with your own fortune, is insignificant. She is very poor."

"All the better. I have ample for us both, and no one will be able to say I married her for her money."

"Have you ever mentioned the subject to the Count, may I ask, monsieur?"

De Courcelles reddened.

"That I have, dear madame, and, practically, I have his approval."

"Well, and you have my best wishes. I love my sister very dearly, but I am certain you will be good to her. I will write to India at once; though papa, whom you have never seen, can have no objection to offer. Amy ought to be here—she only left me to finish some letters; but we'll wait a moment, and then if she does not come, I'll fetch her, and you can plead your own cause."

The Baron fidgetted, and the conversation flagged now that an important point had been decided, for he was too much preoccupied to discuss trivialities, and Blanche was just as anxious that her face should not betray the feelings to which she had given way before his entrance.

"I think I'll go and fetch her," she said at length, "that is, if you'll excuse me."

But at that very moment in came Amy herself, as though talking of her brought her. Ignorant of De Courcelles' presence, she advanced into the room humming an air from a famous vaudeville, her hands encumbered with trifles, and her merry, girlish face full of innocent happiness. When she saw him she started, then, recovering herself, gave her hand, and Blanche came to her rescue.

"We've been chatting here for the last half-hour, and wondering where you were. Is that the silk I asked you for? Thanks. Now, I must get my work-basket."

"Shall I fetch it for you?" stammered Amy, for her own heart told her how matters stood, and what would happen if left alone with De Courcelles. Apparently Blanche did not hear her, and in another moment she found herself alone with him. Tremulous, her heart palpitating strangely, she sank into a big Henri Deux chair, while Blanche, impressed with the idea that she had effected a clumsy exit, went in search of no work-basket, but with a mind sore and overtaxed, reflected upon the strange coincidences of life, the difficulty and danger of her own position.

This was her wedding-day. The Count had forgotten it purposely or otherwise. Unhesitatingly she wished it had never dawned. Convent walls had better have enclosed her perpetually, rather than that she should suffer as she did. In fact the situation was a hopeless one, dragged as she felt herself to be in opposite directions, neither of which presented the flimsiest chance of happiness.

Yet, lacerated though her feelings were, there was a strange blending of the serio-comic, in the reflection that, under the same roof, along a corridor, and through a partition, a love scene was in progress.

Vows of constancy were being exchanged. She could only clasp her hands together, and pray that better fortune might attend them than she herself had experienced.

And so the Baron had Amy to himself, in that superb grand drawing-room, which the antiquity, wealth, and culture of the La Jonquières family had combined to embellish with gems of art. There was nothing disturbing in the presence of Dutch and Italian master-pieces, Sèvres and Dresden porcelain, Limoges enamels, and caskets of gold, chased by Ghirlandajo. In fact, the contents of that stately apartment harmonized well with refined love.

CHAPTER XVII.

THINKING it about time, Blanche forced an expression of serenity, and obeying the dictates of propriety, rejoined the lovers. Amy was smiling and radiant, De Courcelles evidently delighted. It was easy to see that the young fellow had not been repulsed.

"Countess," he exclaimed enthusiastically as Blanche entered, "she has consented, she is mine"; then gallantly slipping his arm round Amy's waist, he added, "Behold the future Baronne de Courcelles, and instead of only being able to talk about it, as I did to you just now, I am, in fact, the happiest fellow in Paris. We shall all be so jolly together, living within a short distance, as we must. The Château de Courcelles shall be completely renovated, workmen shall be despatched there, and then you two will never be separated. With your incomparable taste, madame, we shall make a palace of the château. Between us, it will be superb. Through the summer we shall all be within a drive of each other, and take my word for it, we shall lead the most delightful existence."

They stood talking for a few minutes, and then the young fellow suddenly exclaimed:

"Ah, I am saying too much. You will both laugh at me; that will be my reward for behaving extravagantly as I have. But I am overjoyed; and being no longer master of myself, I think I had better go. Then you can discuss matters uninterruptedly."

"But not just yet—not so soon surely?" inquired Blanche, with some amusement at his almost boyish frankness, and liking him all the better for his simple behaviour.

"Yes, I'll be off, Countess; I shall only cut a ridiculous figure if I stay, and I have a lot to think of."

"But you'll come again before long?" inquired Amy playfully.

De Courcelles took her hand in his, kissed it passionately, and then, not trusting himself to say more, went off.

"So this was a little plot of yours," said Amy, the moment they were alone; "you two were conspirators? I had my suspicions when you deserted me so abruptly."

"Yes, I plead guilty; but I knew how I should please you best, and, as I have told Rudolf, felt that should anything unforeseen happen to estrange you two, there would be very little happiness for *you*, at least. So you see I did my best to hasten the crisis. Am I to be forgiven?"

"Are you to be forgiven? Do you know, I think I could just squeeze you to death, you dear old thing. But let me look at your face. Blanche, something has troubled you. You can't hide that from me. Oh, I know I've been horribly selfish of late; I've allowed Leo to engross me. But, dear, I love him so; all the same there is no excuse for me. I have been a little brute, for having thought of anyone to such an extent that I forgot you."

"You haven't forgotten me, dear."

"No, but I've been absorbed in my own concerns."

"I find no fault with you."

"No, I blame myself. But of late, I have thought

you so changed—so much happier since we came to Paris; you have entered into everything with such zest. Once or twice I have said to myself, 'The quiet of the country depressed her, since the change to town she is a new being.' Well, as it is, I am going to begin, I shall reform at once. I shall sit at your feet, and you must tell me everything."

With playful force Amy compelled her to sit down, placing herself as she had said, then she drew Blanche's arms about her neck, and reclining against her looked up into her face.

"Come, be good, and begin at once," she continued half-jestingly; "I know you have been worrying yourself, and you are not to do it. It's naughty of you. You must first confide in me, and I shall be able to cheer and comfort you."

With charming naïveté she looked at Blanche, her eyes sparkling, and seeming almost black in the subdued lamplight, she herself a perfect picture of innocent freshness and robust English girlhood; while Blanche, upon whom she thus gazed expectantly, displayed womanliness, refinement, and beauty. Clad in a white dress which revealed the shape and hue of her broad marble-like shoulders and splendid bust, the purity of her complexion was such that nothing could have contrasted more favourably with the dead colourlessness of her dress, which was without ornamentation of any kind. Her golden hair was coiled in a careless knot, placed high and rather at the back of the head, and in it appeared a simple diamond crescent. The sad pensiveness of her expression increased the charm of her face, and with the impulsiveness of a girl, Amy, upon whom her beauty had its effect, exclaimed:

"Do you know, Blanche, you look positively lovely. Oh, if I were half like you, Leo should adore me."

"He does that already. But how ridiculous you are."

"Indeed I'm not, unless speaking the truth has made me so. No, but if I were a quarter as beautiful as you, Leo should be in such a condition that he could never leave me."

"Poor fellow, would you reduce him to such abject slavery?"

"Yes, I should like it of all things."

"Well, you are a dear girl, and in his eyes perfection. Beauty," she added, in a more subdued voice, "may have fallen to my lot, but it has brought me no good."

"Don't talk like that, I hate to hear you," exclaimed Amy impetuously. "I feel in the dumps at once. Don't move your arms, keep them as they are. Now I'm prepared to listen, and as I've said, to comfort you."

But Blanche remained silent. Amy's suggestion only served to increase her distress. Memory carried her back to the night when Amy had stolen into her bedroom and learned her feelings for Rudolf. If she needed comfort then, now she was in a condition when to confide unreservedly, to be permitted to unburden herself of the weight within her, and to receive in exchange, genuine sympathy, perhaps advice— would have been the most effective curative earth could bestow. But how was this to be? Could she have persuaded herself to own her weakness, and even guilt, in harbouring thoughts of Louis Bernard, she still would have been prevented from doing so by her desire to do right and not wrong. Although only a small difference in age existed between them, Amy, a maiden, and brought up under the eyes of a religious spinster aunt, was as innocent as a child. It would be a culpable act on her part, to describe her feelings and sentiments for Louis, to one so simple and artless. The idea of such a step was not to be entertained for an instant, even if she were willing to take it at the sacrifice of pride. The conflict within her was a severe one, but it terminated as might have been expected from a woman of her force of character.

"No," she reflected, "I may be weak enough to love hopelessly and in spite of myself; but though the burden I bear is heavy, it shall be borne in silence. I am mistress of myself yet, at any rate."

"Come, why don't you talk to me, why don't you speak?" asked Amy; "are you vexed with me?"

"Vexed with you dear—no. What have you done to vex me? To be vexed with each other we should have to quarrel. No," she added, deciding to change the conversation, "I am very much interested in all that has happened, and shall think of nothing else for months. You will be in my thoughts, until that which you so much desire has come about. Do you love him with your whole heart, dear?"

"Love him, Blanche; I worship him," was the short and emphatic answer.

Satisfied, Blanche made no reply. She could not help contrasting Amy's remarks with the sentiments she so well remembered a short time back, when she too had felt that she worshipped Rudolf. Now she half-shuddered at the recollection of it, wondered how she could have been so blind, so easily deceived, and yet was disposed to tax herself with lacking depth of character, since anything could produce such a change in her nature. "Ah, but one has to live the life," her heart told her in reply to the accusation; "one has to live the life, to understand what it is to have the affections sapped by the perpetual attacks of a thousand antagonistic and petty details. After all, the myriad grains of sand compose the sea beach."

"Was it not sweet of him to think of living so that we might be near to each other?" exclaimed Amy, scattering reflection to the winds. "I think it was splendid," she added enthusiastically, and without pausing for a reply.

"So it was, dear," assented Blanche, almost absently. "He has a number of estates, of which the Château de Courcelles is the oldest, but it is certainly the smallest of his possessions, and he has been in the habit of going there so little."

"Oh, but it's just like Leo!" continued the delighted girl; "he is so generous, so thoughtful, and so utterly unselfish! He considered me, not himself."

With a woman's intuition Blanche recognised how absolutely Amy's heart had been surrendered to De Courcelles, and impelled by a sudden rush of feeling, she bent over her, saying, while she kissed her:

"I know how much you love him, darling. I can understand. If thinking and praying for you can bring you happiness, it will be yours," and following swiftly upon the words, came the consoling reflection that this engagement and marriage, would furnish a distraction of which she could honestly avail herself. With an effort on her part, she might really become absorbed in Amy's concerns, and in those of this young and amiable fellow whom she had always liked and thoroughly respected. But following fast on this plan, this scheme which was to enable her to lose herself in others, came an idea which threatened its destruction. The Count's allusion to La Jonquières recurred to her, and Louis Bernard's slight and yet vigorous figure arose before her. She could discern his clear-cut features and expressive mouth. Even the grey eyes, luminous and truthful, met her own. He was as near to her at that moment, retained in fancy's grip, as though they once more talked together. What was he doing? Of what was he thinking? She was impressed with the belief, at times, that he was as unhappy as herself, and the idea would present itself that she was not wholly irresponsible for this condition of affairs. She shook herself. These reflections must be dismissed, she decided.

CHAPTER XVIII.

SHORTLY after the night on which Blanche had betrayed her knowledge of his amour with Lisette, the Count had decided upon following a certain line of conduct towards her, and this he had pursued. His inordinate vanity supported him in his belief that Blanche really worshipped him.

Women were so prone to fall at his feet, good-looking fellow that he was; and this one with whom he lived, could not fail to adore him secretly. The best proof of this was the neat way in which she had got him to leave La Jonquières. His feint of remaining there for the winter had been a master-piece.

However, he had resolved that this unruly wife of his should be brought to her senses, compelled, in fact, to retract her words, and to admit that she longed for him; otherwise he would never be anything to her again. He would take good care of that. A reconciliation should not come from his side. She was a deuced fine woman, but fortunately Paris swarmed with fine women, and it just suited him to amuse himself with them. He could reduce this wife of his to submission, without interfering with any of his little amusements. He was going to have no feminine supervisor over him, and he would let her know it. When once she had learnt that, they would get on much better.

He had not forgotten Lisette—not in the least. He had seen no one to compare to her physically. But then, his life was such a round of amusement, and since they were separated, he would be a fool not to console himself with the reflection that with the return of the warm weather, if not before, he should meet her again; she would be radiant with health, and just as ready as ever to put her arms about him.

So he fenced, rode in the Bois, indulged in *petits soupers* after the theatre or the opera, played at anything that was going till the morning light struggled through the venetian blinds of the club, then went to bed, and, after a cold douche, appeared as well as though he had been snoring all night. The men at the Jockey Club grew to discuss his constitution. "They were no chickens, and could make a night of it; but really, Monsieur le Comte was a wonder. There was no tiring him, and, no matter what he did, he was always as fresh as paint when it was time to begin again." Monsieur was rather of their opinion himself. He had told Blanche that he meant to enjoy himself, and he kept his word, going the pace to some purpose, until his name as a *viveur*, blended with no trifling suspicion of the *roué*, was thoroughly established.

Of course, his behaviour towards Blanche was precisely such as completely frustrated her well-intentioned efforts to approach him. The barrier erected between them was apparently insurmountable. Had the Count known what was passing in her mind, and had the good sense to pull up, and try to appreciate the amiable qualities of this woman to whom he had a right, there would have been the best of chances of re-establishing himself in her favour. But he acted as though he were oblivious of her beauty and reckless of her virtue. She had never come to kiss his feet, as it was his intention that she should, and, after all, the freedom he enjoyed was not displeasing to him. But in the face of this, with unwavering steadfastness and admirable perseverance, Blanche continued the policy she had decided upon following. Her kindness and attention was marked and constant. She struggled heroically to overcome the indifference he meted out to her with such persistency. She had a gentle word, a kind look and act always at hand, and witnessed his obdurateness with growing concern.

This man, who was her husband, could alone fortify her against those weaknesses, of the growth of which she was aware; and, in spite of her efforts to prevent it, this man seemed determined to estrange himself from her.

Bent upon her purpose of conquering her fondness for Louis, she indulged in every species of gaiety, and was always to be seen where fashion and wealth met; Amy with her, the young Baron, amiable and admiring, in constant attendance.

In the love of these two young hearts for each other, she foresaw the realization of the affection she had fancied and steadfastly believed in. There *were* people in the world who could love passionately and sincerely, and she refused to think otherwise. She set herself to examine the Baron's character with microscopical care, and the result was that she felt confident he would make a model husband. She was indefatigable in conceiving plans for their enjoyment and closer intimacy, so that thus thrown constantly together, they might know each other thoroughly, before taking the irrevocable step they contemplated. This she considered a part of her duty towards Amy. She placed herself in the position of a mother to her, and the responsibilities thus entailed she discharged with admirable affection and forethought.

By these means, and in a perpetual whirl of festivities, the weeks passed. Already the trees in the Bois were clouded with bursting buds, and in some instances a more decided tinge of fresh bright green was noticeable. People were beginning to talk about summer, and a trip to the seaside. The wealthier ones were tempted to discuss the delights and fascinations, to say nothing of the health, which they would derive from the approaching yachting season, or to plan, as usual, the descent upon some distant, but charmingly situated, château.

Soft, balmy winds, and more protracted gleams of sunshine announced the approach of warmer weather. People lounged and sipped their *liqueurs* outside the cafés. Paris was awakening as from sleep; joyousness prevailed. It was in the atmosphere.

The restraint Blanche had imposed upon herself was not without its results. Fearlessly she had compelled herself to scan the horizon of her life, and had come to think as a woman might, who accepts the belief that she must jog along soberly, and yet not without some enjoyment. Her health was superb. She was an object of admiration.

Without in the least encouraging them, young men flocked around her. Was there not much to be thankful for in this splendid vigour, in this undoubted homage? Possessed of wealth, the respect of the world followed. What had she done to merit these benefits? Absolutely nothing. Instead of being clad in Worth's *chefs d'œuvre*, and attended by liveried servants, solemn, respectful, and ready to obey her slightest behest, why was she not sitting in rags on the steps of the Madeleine, hopeful of receiving a few coins from the numerous lords of creation who flocked thither to be married? What had she done, she asked herself, that this poverty and pain should have been spared her? And how wrong she was ever to rebel, because God had not seen fit to grant her that earthly love for which she yearned. By a kind of self-imposed hypnotism she became soothed.

She coaxed herself into imagining that it was not love, not passion, she experienced for Louis; or, at least, if she had been so far culpable, she had cured herself of such frightful impiety, and was no longer stirred by aught deeper than a sincere friendship for him.

Was it not a proof of what could be done by determination?

In reality, she was in a more dangerous condition than ever. She had put out all her strength to erect a line of defence, which a word or a look would cause to crumble into ruins. The consequences would be terrible when, this fortification so stormed, she would have to acknowledge her utter weakness, and bow to the inevitable.

Her chief dissatisfaction and anxiety, lay in the recognition of the complete failure of her designs upon the Count. Yet even here, impelled by the sense of right which triumphed in her, she did not despair. Some day or other he would be bound to acknowledge her devotion, and then, ashamed of the grief he had caused her, and weary of the empty pleasures he had been wedded to, there would be a reconciliation between them. They would be fast friends. She would have been his guardian angel, and her reward would be the peace which springs from doing right.

As for the Count, during the pauses in his gaiety, he would sometimes half regret his treatment of Blanche. Latterly he had begun to think he did not understand her. What could he gather from her conduct? She was certainly obstinate to a degree, in whatever she undertook. If she really loved him, she curbed her feelings to perfection. Her kindly attentions, her evident desire to live amicably, could not be mistaken for a warmer sentiment. There was a distinct line of demarcation between her actions, as he began to understand them, and love.

An immense contrast presented itself between her conduct latterly, and the affection she had lavished upon him in the early days of their marriage. This was, in reality, the case. No longer loving, Blanche could not pretend, so as to bear the least critical inspection. Her manner was that of a sincere friend, not a lover. And the Count began to have his doubts. After all, did she love him?—he, the spoiled darling, rich, handsome, and well-born. He was no longer absolutely confident. Nettled, he cast suspicious glances around him. Had madame a lover? he asked himself. But, keep his eyes open as he would, not even the shadow of one could he find. Satisfied on that score, he relapsed into a more complete state of mystification. Hating to be foiled, he would occasionally vent his irritation, with a view to induce Blanche to commit herself. It piqued him to think that he, an undoubted lady-killer, should produce nothing more violent than sensations of the most lukewarm character in the breast of his own wife.

" What an odd woman you are," he would assert as a commencement.

" Why? " Blanche would naturally ask.

" Oh, you ought never to have been married."

" Can you tell me of a single duty I neglect? " she would inquire mildly.

" Duty be hanged! Are wives only to amuse themselves and entertain one's friends, I should like to know? "

"Well, certainly, to do that is a great deal."

"A great deal—the deuce! but do you suppose you were married for that?"

"One is possessed of a great many illusions at the outset of life; unfortunately one gradually learns that they are as tantalizingly unsubstantial as the Fata Morgana."

"Oh, a lot you know about it. Who filled your head with such sentiments?"

"Experience—life."

"*Hélas;* all I know is that you are the coldest woman I ever met. It strikes me that when a man marries, he ought to know what he is doing. If the majority of women were like you, my dear, the world would very soon become a desert, and there would be no one left in it to witness the mirage you allude to."

When the conversation reached this stage, Blanche would take refuge in silence. There was nothing else for it. Evidently the Count's appreciation of her resolved itself into a low physical one. And right or wrong, knowing him as she did, she could not stoop to encourage such a sentiment.

One morning when they were breakfasting alone—Amy being confined to her room by some trifling indisposition—the Count rounded off some previous periods, by an assertion which had some effect upon her.

"By Jove, you can say what you like," he observed, munching away energetically, "but if fellows don't sail straight, their wives are at the bottom of it. You women are quick enough to discover the bad side of one's nature, but are you ever on the look-out for the good? I know what I'm talking about, and many a fellow wishes to be a first-rate husband, but is prevented by his wife's attitude towards him."

After all, there might be something in what he said, she reflected. The words had the ring of an entreaty. Could it be that, in contending as he had, he had alluded to himself? Was it his wish to "sail straight?" She had certainly treated him well of late; but had she gone honestly to work, and as a fair beginning, retracted her assertions that she neither loved him nor sought his affection, her entreaty, in fact, that there should be nothing between them? And, after all, in what did her own perfection consist? What right had she to set herself up? Her conduct was none of the best. In her heart she knew that she was not sinless. As she hoped to be forgiven, surely she was constrained to forgive. She was touched, softened.

Her feelings for Louis partially benumbed, it occurred to her that, if the Count would act uprightly, she could strive to forget Lisette, and such similar faults, completely. It would cost her a great effort, but expiation for her secret weaknesses was due from her; could she not make it in this way? With this desire to discover good in him strong within her, and prepared to sacrifice her pride should her reason dictate it, Blanche observed the Count's actions attentively.

CHAPTER XIX.

DINNER was in progress at the Hotel de la Jonquières. The gloomy prospect presented by the Faubourg St. Germain, with the rain falling determinedly amidst gusts of wind, and from a sky without a break in it, was shut out by blinds and closely drawn curtains. Grouped around a table, tastefully decorated with exquisite silver-plate, sparkling crystal, and a profusion of rare and beautiful flowers, sat Blanche and the Count facing each other, with Amy and De Courcelles on either side.

"Well, we shall soon find ourselves at La Jonquières again," the Count was remarking, while glancing suggestively from Amy to the Baron, and again at Amy.

De Courcelles reddened like a turkey cock.

"Yes," he stammered, taking the remark upon his own shoulders; "have you heard anything of Monsieur l'Abbé Bernard?" he added, recovering himself, but sipping his wine with some signs of nervousness.

"No, we haven't," answered Blanche quietly.

"You have never written a line to the poor man have you?" asked the Count.

"No."

"Well, don't you call that rather too bad, De Courcelles, considering the intimacy which existed? Why, Monsieur l'Abbé was perpetually at the château, and was welcome, there. I like him, I must say."

"And so do I. I felt drawn to him from the first moment I saw him," responded De Courcelles, with perfect frankness.

"I should think he'll feel hurt and neglected. I know I should, were I in his place," resumed the Count.

Blanche made no answer. Each remark, with the reflections awakened by it, occasioned her a species of slow torture. She preferred to take refuge in silence.

"We shall be able to organize some first-rate shooting-parties in the De Courcelles preserves, eh, my dear fellow?" observed the Count abruptly, but with evident relish.

"Oh, now I call it mean of you to rake that up against me. Don't you agree with me, Countess?"

Blanche nodded smilingly, but became grave next instant. The whole events of the day spent at the Château de Courcelles were at once vividly recalled by the allusion. Lisette's face and figure were daguerrotyped upon her mind. She seemed to see her as upon that evening, and she fancied she could even hear her voice, which she had so remarked upon and admired.

The Count, who was looking at her, guessed her thoughts. He had no particular wish that Lisette should furnish food for reflection, so he rattled on.

"We shall drive over to the Château de Courcelles occasionally—eh, Amy? You know, as near neighbours, we really owe it to Monsieur le Baron, and should do our best to enliven him in his bachelor quarters."

This time it was Amy's turn to blush.

"Thanks," replied De Courcelles, coming to her rescue, and darting a glance full of meaning and affection at her as he spoke; "but I hope the said quarters will be as lively as I should wish to see them, some day."

The truth was, that the marriage between Amy and the Baron had been arranged to take place early in the year. There were to be only a few friends present, and the ceremony was to be celebrated in the chapel at the Château de Courcelles. The affair, it had been decided, was to be simple and quiet, though after it, a fête was to be given to the tenantry, the park illuminated and thrown open to the public, in honour of the event. This was De Courcelles' idea.

"But you need not joke me about my shooting," he continued, reverting to the Count's previous remark. "I have issued strict orders for the preservation of the game, and, under my eye, things will soon improve."

"All right; but meanwhile, had you not better buy some first-rate farm-yard fowls to stock the covers? They will carry you on until—"

"How provoking you are, Rudolf," interrupted Blanche.

"Am I, dear? I thought I was making a really valuable suggestion," replied the Count, who was not to be repressed. "You will have to wear an old blouse and a straw hat, De Courcelles, and stalk about the woods all day long, or those fellows of yours will assuredly continue their poaching practices. It will be capital exercise for your long legs, my dear fellow."

"Ah, do you think so?"

"Indeed, I do. You must have a hobby, mind. It is essential. Is it to be that, or shall you prefer to turn horticulturist, and peer into melon-frames and hothouses, become great on manures, soil, etc., and wax into an authority upon the growth and treatment of grapes? Now, that would really be very interesting, I should imagine. I can picture you with Amy on your arm, sauntering amongst those old box-edged walks, hoeing up a weed occasionally with a spud fitted to the end of your walking-stick. Yes, my dear fellow, you must certainly have a hobby, and had I not known your love for the fresh air, I should have suggested old china, pictures, or something of that sort; but, then, you would have to be in Paris to do the thing properly. You can't very well have the Rue de la Chaussée d'Antin in the grounds of the Château de Courcelles."

"You can chaff me as much as you like," returned De Courcelles resignedly, "but I don't intend to go mad about anything. We shall have the perfection of jolly times, I am convinced, and if we tire of being quiet, it will be easy enough to pack the place with guests. I know a sprinkling of really nice, good-natured people, and there are always plenty, who, for a bed and good living, are content to spend their life in moving from house to house, and who really make a business of being agreeable."

"I had no idea you were so familiar with the ways of the world," replied the Count satirically.

Determined to give him as good as he gave, the Baron thought a moment. Then he said:

"You see, I am young. Oh, I am proud of it. Wisdom is the only compensation one gets in return for gray hairs. Of course, *you* know very well—"

"The deuce, do you mean that my hair is gray?"

Amy tittered.

"Why, it's certainly grizzled, Rudolf," she exclaimed.

"Grizzled, is it?"

"Why, yes. Don't you know that?"

"Know it—and suppose I do? I should speedily forget it if I consented to descend to the trickery you women think nothing of. What about a suitable dye, judiciously applied—eh, mademoiselle?"

"Oh, you need not talk at me. I don't dye."

"Or rouge?"

"No."

"Or use patches and powder?"

"I have existed without them so far."

"Bravo, but then you are not a fair representative of your sex. You know that. De Courcelles, you will be fortunate in possessing a model wife, who neither paints nor powders, and that's something nowadays. But, as for you, my dear fellow. Your words have produced this attack upon me. I shall have my revenge. So look out. Gray hairs, indeed. I feel younger to-night than I have done any time this last dozen years. Younger than I did when, at the head of a handful of Chasseurs d'Afrique, I charged through and through clouds of Arabs. I can tell you, in less time than it takes to relate it, there was nothing to be seen but the backs of a lot of dirty bernouses scudding off through the dust."

"Eh, they couldn't have fought much, then," laughed De Courcelles provokingly.

"Couldn't have fought much," repeated the Count indignantly; "a fine judge of fighting indeed. Well, anyhow, I maintain I feel younger now than then."

"So you may, and I am glad to hear it; but it is impossible for me to say how you *feel*, I only know how you *look*."

"Eh, all right, all right," growled the Count, with the sensation of being worsted; "your time is coming, my fine fellow. After Amy has taken you in hand for half-a-dozen years, you'll begin to get gray, I promise you."

"Now, that's shameful of you. What a wicked insinuation," asserted Amy, crimsoning.

"All right, we shall see," the Count contented himself with retorting.

The dinner drew to a close. With solemn slowness the sedate footmen flung open the doors leading to the drawing-room, and the two men followed closely upon Amy and Blanche. A little later, the Count, with his hands in his pockets, was beginning to get enthusiastic over the rival merits of two famous stars, who were at that moment taking Paris by storm, when a servant entered and respectfully handed him a telegram.

"May I be permitted," he inquired politely, and then, his face bent over the thin blue paper, he read it attentively. Blanche happened to be looking at him, and as an expression of pleasure swept over his face, she innocently asked :

"Who is it from, Rudolf?"

Thus suddenly appealed to, he started slightly, and the hue of his bronzed cheeks deepened.

"Oh," he said, recovering his composure, "it is from the Baron. You know those two magnificent blacks of Pauloff's, De Courcelles?"

De Courcelles nodded.

"Well, I have entreated him to let me have them. They are the grandest animals I have ever seen ; match so perfectly, too, and—"

"Has that telegram to do with them ?" inquired Blanche, interrupting him quietly.

The Count glanced at her sharply.

"Certainly, my dear. That is, in a way. Pauloff wants to see me. I am to meet him at the club. De Courcelles, I know you'll forgive me for running away, and you, too, Blanche, won't you ? Amy will look after you both. You won't mind my absence, and really this is important."

De Courcelles was glad rather than otherwise. He would be perfectly free to talk to Amy A few moments later the Count left the room, returning almost immediately, having slipped on a silk muffler and an overcoat. His crush-hat was under his arm. He advanced to Blanche, touched her forehead with his lips, smiled at Amy, and nodding to De Courcelles, left them, the clash of the outer doors announcing that he had gone.

In the subdued light, Amy and De Courcelles made love in whispers. Blanche, immersed in her own thoughts, became unconscious of their presence. She had divined that the telegram the Count had received, was certainly not from the Baron.

CHAPTER XX.

THE following morning was a lovely one, and intent on shopping, Amy induced Blanche to set off at an early hour. Having executed their varied commissions satisfactorily, the delicious buoyancy of the atmosphere tempted them to order the coachman to turn into the Bois.

The excitement of the day was over for Amy. She had set her heart on purchasing certain odds and ends, and since they were actually at her side, she felt tranquil and supremely contented. As for Blanche, she had talked herself tired in the shops, and was disposed to enjoy the brilliancy of the scene in silence.

The sky was of the most perfect blue, and the sun shone in uninterrupted splendour. The rainfall over night had cleansed and freshened the roads, and a succession of stately equipages bowled along them, the sun flashing upon the harness, and causing the glossy coats of the horses to shine like satin. The trees were wearing the perfection of green tints, and freed from the occasional sameness of full leaf, delighted the eye, while the birds twittered and evidently revelled in the return of warmth. It was a morning to be remembered, and events had decided that it should not be forgotten. The coachman unchecked, and probably enjoying the drive as much as his mistress, was soon spinning along the road to Boulogne.

"Let us get out and walk, the carriage can follow us," Blanche at length suggested, and giving her instructions, the two paced along, enjoying the exercise. Ahead of them, at the angle of an intersecting avenue, a man was standing, apparently debating in which direction he should proceed, then, seeing them, he no longer hesitated, but approached with a jaunty and confident air. Amy was the first to notice and recognise him.

"Why, here is Monsieur Brunot. How annoying! I can't bear that man," she exclaimed.

"So it is," assented Blanche. "Well, you know I don't like him either; but he is quite harmless. Do be civil, we need only exchange half-a-dozen words, and he may not stop."

But, alas, M. Brunot had no intention of allowing two charming ladies to escape him. Besides, since he had become a Deputy, and so realized his ambitions in that direction, other desires had sprung up, and he did not disguise from himself that his admiration for Blanche was profound. In addition, her unvarying politeness to him had actually awakened a belief that she was partial to him; M. Brunot, like many excessively plain men, being inordinately vain.

"Good morning, Madame la Comtesse, and you, too, mademoiselle," he said, bowing obsequiously, and even in that action betraying the parvenu. "Like myself, you have evidently been inspired by the charms of this superb day. Undoubtedly this is the perfection of weather."

"Yes, we were unable to resist the pleasure of a walk, monsieur."

"And there can be nothing better for one. I seldom come so far as this myself, but I ordered my carriage to meet me at this point, and can discover no trace of it. I was getting very angry, madame, I can assure you, when I was fortunate enough to catch sight of you."

M. Brunot was no longer oppressed with nervousness. The Count's eyes were not upon him. Besides, he had called as often as he dared at the Hotel de la Jonquières, and though received with freezing politeness, was foolish enough to consider himself quite on a friendly footing.

"Well, I hope you will find it," said Blanche consolingly.

"Yes, indeed," echoed Amy.

"Meanwhile we'll continue our walk, monsieur."

Brunot longed for an invitation to accompany them, but seeing no chance, in despair, he proceeded to prolong the interview by affording a piece of information.

"I presume you are in search of the Count, madame?" he inquired.

"The Count, no," replied Blanche, a trifle surprised.

"Oh, forgive me, madame; since you are within so short a distance of each other, I naturally thought you had arranged to meet hereabouts. Monsieur le Comte is in that direction. I don't think he can have gone far, for he was on foot; though, just amongst the trees there, a man was holding a horse I took to be his."

"Thanks very much for telling us, monsieur," said Blanche pleasantly; "we shall doubtless find him." And with a bow she linked her arm in Amy's, and drew her in the direction M. Brunot had indicated. Then, when some distance separated them, she signed to the coachman, and entering the carriage, told him to continue along the avenue.

"I don't see much good in going further," remarked Amy; "for my own part, I'm tired, and we are sure not to find Rudolf. Besides, I'm simply famished. Come, Blanche, take pity on me and let us turn back."

"I should like to go as far as the corner of the road. Then we'll go home. It's just possible we may meet him, from what Monsieur Brunot has said."

"Oh, for that matter, his 'short distance' may mean a mile. Some people are so stupid," retorted Amy, bent on dissuading her.

But Blanche had decided, and nothing short of the point she had indicated would satisfy her, though as she approached it, a certain uneasiness affected her. She hated to think she was suspicious, but the Count had done so much to shake her faith in him, and cause her at this juncture to say to herself:

"What can he be doing here? This is quite an unfrequented part, and had I wanted him— Ah! I have my doubts."

The telegram, and the uncomfortable sensation she had experienced that he was not speaking the truth, recurred to her. Disturbed, she leant forward in the carriage, glancing searchingly amongst the already thick foliage and maze of tree trunks. A grave and troubled expression stole into her face, which the neat, close-fitting hat she wore suited to perfection.

"Why do you look so serious?" inquired Amy, surprising her in the midst of her unpleasant speculations.

Before she could make any reply, they swept round the angle she had indicated, and almost collided with a man who was pacing a horse up and down automatically.

"That's Tunis certainly," exclaimed Amy, recognising the animal as a favourite hack of the Count's, "so Rudolf can't be far off."

The words were still upon her lips when Blanche

caught sight of two figures, a man and woman, amongst the tree stems. A score more revolutions of the wheels, and but a few paces separated her from them. Her heart beat rapidly. She was frightfully agitated, but had just sufficient presence of mind to remember that she did not wish the coachman to see the sight that lay before her. Tremulous and white to the lips, she contrived to call to him sharply:

"You may turn and go home."

The man did as he was told. Experiencing some slight relief she sank back in her place, for the moment overcome. She had surprised the Count in the act of embracing a woman, over whom he was bending. Thinking himself safe from observation, he was so absorbed in his occupation of making love, that he had not heard the sounds made by the approaching carriage, until too late. And Blanche's long sustained glance had told her that this woman whom he was fondling was Lisette.

It was then that she had acted, and her first impulse had been dictated by pride. It seemed detestable that a servant should see how lightly the Count esteemed her, how little the ties that united them were respected by him, so she had given the order which had flung the horses upon their haunches, and sent them flying homewards.

By Amy's silence Blanche understood that she, at any rate, had observed and comprehended the situation. This was sufficiently annoying. But what neither of them had remarked, was the presence of a third party, further away in the deeper shade of the foliage, and sufficiently hidden to escape them.

This person was a man, young, powerful, and of the peasant class. A peaked and high-crowned cloth cap shaded his face, and he was clad in his holiday attire—his best blouse—and, as he watched, his energetic face, was distorted by suppressed fury. This man was André Moriseau. Lisette, having at length fulfilled her intention of going to Paris, and having given out as an excuse a desire to visit her brother, Pierre Chotard, André, whose doubts of her had steadily increased, had left his farm, and with the caution of an outraged lover, had tracked her. Paris had robbed his beautiful Lisette of her simplicity to begin with, he had thought. This time he had a mind to see for himself who her friends were.

During the homeward drive Blanche never spoke. Amy ventured to once.

"I am so sorry, darling," she whispered softly, and her hand stole into Blanche's, and remained there until they alighted at the Hotel de la Jonquières.

Then Blanche went straight to her own room. The necessity for being absolutely alone was imperative. No one must know how she suffered; no one ever could know, in fact. This long-sustained fight, this wearisome wrestle for good, had brought her nothing but humiliation. She had clung to the skirts of hope; but, cling as she would, not even the shreds remained in her grasp. This was her reward for days and nights spent in grappling with her secret faults, for having endured a mental anguish such as seemed, by a retrospective glance, worse even than her idea of death.

It occurred to her to wonder whether Brunot was aware of what was going on, when he told her about the Count. But this, she instantly decided, was not possible. He would not have dared to insult her so cruelly. But was not her position a maddening one? to know that whatever came of it—unless she was content to face a public scandal—her life was indissolubly bound to this man, who dishonoured her in the face of day!

Was it not infamous? And what was to be done? How was she to conduct herself? And to think that she should have harboured all the kindly thoughts she had—heaped nothing but consideration upon him! What a consummate little fool she had been! This time, at least, there should be an end of all such sentiments as she had been stupid enough to indulge in.

At length, she confronted the bitter fact that her home life was ruined beyond the possibility of repair. And the sooner she clenched her teeth, and compelled herself to become accustomed to the idea, the better it would be for her. She had striven and prayed so hard, too, for the appearance of some little ray of light to illumine the gloom which threatened to engulf her. Henceforth she must harden her heart and ignore fine feeling. She must be content to grope in whatever light she could find. Meanwhile she had to assume a placidity and cheerfulness she was far from feeling. People must not suspect. Her face must be wreathed in smiles; she must appear as though her path were one of roses. She was curious to know what line of conduct the Count would pursue. He must have seen her. Would he allude to the affair, and attempt to excuse himself with the aid of as many lies as the occasion demanded, or would he adopt the bolder course—ignore, behave as though nothing had occurred? She was not left long in doubt.

The Count's audacity rose superior to the occasion. He alluded to *nothing*. His cheerfulness and courtesy were admirable. He adapted himself to the rôle he had set himself, with perfect *savoir faire*, and he was not guilty of that commonest of errors, over-acting, because he desired to act well. Being in the wrong, he forgot to open his lips on the subject. That was all. The telegram he had received had been from Lisette. He had at once met her, never going near his club, or the Baron, as he had said; and on parting, they had arranged for a quiet talk in the morning, which quiet talk Blanche had shown the stupidity and bad taste to disturb. That was how *he* coloured the picture.

So far as his future plans were concerned, they were simple, and remained unaltered. There was this marriage between Amy and De Courcelles on the *tapis*. Then he had really been going the pace, and stood in need of rest and change of air, so that everything seemed to point to a move to La Jonquières. True, it was rather early in the season; but, after all, he was becoming tired of Paris, and the life and air of the country would be refreshing, for a time, at least. The upshot was, that one fine morning, the blinds of the hotel in the Faubourg St. Germain were drawn down, and an inquiry elicited the information that Monsieur le Comte and Madame la Comtesse had that very day retired to their château in Champagne.

The prospect of the return of *le grand propriétaire*, the approaching marriage of the Baron, and the probability of the Château de Courcelles being the chosen place of abode, had leaked out, and become known in La Jonquières, forming, for the simple villagers, food for a nine days' wonder. There were to be grand doings, so the speculations and contradictory opinions were varied and amusing.

Louis Bernard, as an intimate friend of the great folks, was constantly appealed to. Evasion was his only resource. But it was terribly irritating to be perpetually reminded that he did not possess knowledge for which he yearned. Through the long winter, he had looked for some news of Blanche with feverish and unwearied expectancy. It was so hard to remain in ignorance of where she was, whether she was ill or well, happy or sad. Though, on this latter point, he had little doubt. She could scarcely be happy, he knew. And this belief increased his suffering.

In his bitterness of spirit, and when fits of despondency seized upon him, he told himself that since his existence was ignored, he was forgotten. She was indifferent. And was it not what he might have expected? In the opinion of this great lady, whose beauty of mind and person had filled him with admiration, he was evidently of no consequence. It was true that at one time she had shown him marked kindness and attention; but that was because he had afforded her some small amount of distraction. Out of her sight, he was evidently out of her mind. What a fool he had been to imagine that it could be otherwise. He was being punished for his audacity, weakness, and sin. What right had he, a poor priest, to think as he had done? Was he not among the most insignificant of God's creatures—a very worm on the face of the earth? Did he not richly deserve the chastisement meted to him? And what excuse had he to offer in defence of his own vile conduct?

His chief delight, when his thoughts completely arrested him, was to merge his present existence in that of the delicious past. During such moments he would recall minutely and lovingly Blanche's appearance, gestures, peculiarities of speech, even some trifling change of dress, which, at the time, he had remarked and admired. By a strong power of will, aided by a singularly lucid memory, he compelled himself to recall almost word for word, long conversations, to which, when they had occurred, he had attached but slight importance. It was delightful to him to remember them. But when forced to rouse himself from these dreams, in which he had dwelt with ecstasy, the reaction which ensued was agonizing. He had imagined that she was in the same room with him. Her lips moved, her eyes met his, and they were talking softly, while the very perfume of her hair was inhaled by him as he leant towards her. He was enraptured, intoxicated. Suddenly someone would move in the house, enter his room, speak, and, with the swiftness of the lightning, the imaginary vision would vanish. In place of it, appeared the bare walls of his little room, his few books, his poverty, above all, *himself*, not as simple erring man—man, *free*—but himself as priest, severed from human beings, human ties, human aspirations, semi-apotheosised, *profoundly solitary*. Sometimes he would cry aloud in the acuteness of his anguish; sometimes he would sink upon his knees, and, closing his eyes with feverish vehemence, strive to lose himself in prayer. But always, when stronger and calmer, he would silently permit Blanche, as he conjured and conceived her, to enter into him and take full possession. He could never be anything to her, she never anything to him, but he would not have parted with her image, as she existed within him, for whole worlds. No threat, no punishment, would have availed to make him give up this woman who was enshrined in his heart.

From the moment he had acknowledged to himself his feelings for her, he had silently decided, that with him, it should be one love, one sin. He was powerless to will it otherwise. If to respect, to worship silently, hopelessly, as he did, and intended to do, was to commit a sin, he was content that it should be laid at his door, and, when the great reckoning should come, content to suffer. What could be sweeter to him than to suffer because of his love for her? Fired with this spirit of devotion and adoration, he would go swiftly, midst the waning light and the shadows, with a few delicate flowers he had grown clasped in his hand, and his footsteps never slackened, never swerved, until he had gained the edge of the larch wood, and the *petit sanctuaire*. Then, he would place the blossoms between the bars of the grille tenderly, lovingly, and, on his knees, in the exact spot where she had knelt, he would pray for her, for forgiveness, for guidance, long, earnestly, his face bathed in tears. Tranquillized, comforted, he would pace back to his little home, thinking as he did so, that, occasionally at least, he must be treading upon the very ground her feet had touched.

Louis Bernard had come to love Blanche in this fashion. Yet, when he heard that she had actually arrived, was within a few hundred yards of him, though he would have given all he possessed to see her, without the delay of a moment, nothing would induce him to go near the château. She had not written. He had never received a line from the family. If they wanted him, they must seek him. He would not go to them. So he shut himself up, kept out of the way, but had to own to himself that the self-imposed restraint was torture.

As for Blanche, so far as the Count was concerned, there had been no scene between them. Like him she had been silent. Words could do no good. There would only be a tremendous quarrel between them. So it was best to spare herself further mortification. Henceforth he must do as he pleased, and in her turn, she should consider herself free to act as she thought proper. For the present, she was absorbed in Amy and her affairs. When that excitement was over, she must seek a fresh one. Much depended upon her choice. In her opinion, to forget herself was the most powerful specific for the condition into which she had sunk. After a few hours had passed, the novelty of the return to her old home had worn off, and a sense of uneasiness began to gain ground. The reception-rooms and the furniture contained in them, reminded her in some shape of Louis. There was no sign of him, however. No one alluded to, or spoke of him, and this silence concerning his presence and well-being grew intolerable. She had no actual proof that he was still at La Jonquières, or even alive. Of course she might assume, that had anything unusual happened, she would have been amongst the first to be apprized. But this amounted merely to conjecture. It was in her power to seek him, but from this step she shrank. Knowing what she did, such conduct would not be right.

From some of the windows she could see into his garden, and with a glass, could distinctly trace the form of the walks, the fruit trees, neatly trained over the espaliers, and, with an effort, fancied that she could distinguish the very beds of early flowers which he loved and cared for. She deprecated the return of her weakness, but she no longer made the same spirited resistance. The old sensations were awakening within her momentarily, but she no longer strove to repress them. Her heart fluttered like that of a young bird. She longed to see and converse with this man, whose dominion over her was so complete. Not made so by words either, but by his simple bodily presence. This spirit of restlessness had laid such violent hold upon her, that she no longer said:

"I am not guilty of loving him. He is merely a friend," but she allowed her heart to throb. She unhesitatingly acknowledged, that to be with him would be a delight. Though nothing could come of it, earth could afford her no greater bliss.

At length her feelings became unbearable, and she summoned the oldest and most trusted of the servants who had been left in charge of the château. Having issued a few orders, she carelessly questioned the man.

"Oh, yes, Monsieur l'Abbé was well," he affirmed, "and though changed—"

"In what way?" demanded Blanche curtly.

"He is thought to be graver and older looking, Madame la Comtesse," replied the servant respectfully. "But he is as good to everyone as ever. He was born to be loved, and he has come to the right place."

Blanche did not care to ask any more questions. Fearful of betraying herself, she dismissed the man, experiencing relief when he was gone. So Louis was well, and loved, though older looking and graver. Reflecting upon these remarks, she instantly strove to set the allusion to his appearance down to mere gossip. One thing was certain, he was offended at the silence she had maintained, and had no intention of coming near her. From her speculations and misgivings, she was at length aroused by the Count entering the château with his arm through Louis'.

"You must prevail upon Monsieur l'Abbé to dine with us," he said to Blanche. "Come, I have caught him, now I leave him with you."

Then he went off on to the terrace, to enjoy the sunlight.

Louis and Blanche thus confronted each other. A curious sensation of awkwardness stole over them on thus being abandoned to a *tête-à-tête* in this somewhat brusque fashion, and after so long a separation. Louis' embarrassment resulted from no change of sentiment. As he had acknowledged to himself, this woman had undoubtedly attached him to her for life. His uneasiness was due to his doubts.

What did she think of him? Had his disguise been so transparent that she had penetrated it, was on reflection disgusted, and showed it by maintaining the silence which had so pained and perplexed him? His heart was torn as he stood before her. Besides, he felt like a criminal, look on which side he would. He *was* one, in fact. For the life of him he had not been able to resist the Count's friendly advances. Dying to enter the château, when asked to, he had acceded. Blanche's image, as she always appeared to him, decided him. But when the Count marked the friendliness of his attitude towards him by taking his arm, and in this manner leading him to his home and his wife, shame completely possessed him. He could only assuage the torture he thus endured, by saying to himself:

"What can this woman ever be to me, though I do love her to distraction? I can never tell her so. Death might release her, but my fetters are indissoluble. Thus, where is the sin in seeing her? It does not matter. The sweetness of worshipping her I reserve to myself. It is my solace, and nothing living shall rob me of it. Were I deprived of life in the twinkling of an eye, her likeness would be found graven upon my heart. I can never efface it. I even glory in it. The sin I commit, the church tells me is heinous, and I am sufficiently unhappy in the acknowledged hopelessness of this passion which absorbs me; yes, but all the same, I have come to glory in it."

With these thoughts in his heart, his mind, alas, suddenly a blank, he stood before Blanche, who, in her turn, with a swift, comprehensive glance, scanned him. Was he indeed changed?

She received a shock, for she was forced to admit that he was. Study, the winter season, his love, had caused the return of that hue to his countenance which had made Lisette compare him at first sight "to the little ivory Christ in the *petit sanctuaire*."

Yes, he was paler and older looking. What had

done it? Was she responsible for alteration in him? Influenced thus—saying to herself that in her desire to do right she had really behaved unkindly, cruelly—she at once decided to make amends. The very sight of this man told her that the position he occupied in her heart was that of master—master, whatever should come of it. And this instantaneous admission occasioned her shyness and nervous reserve. But since he was silent, she obliged herself to take up the thread where the Count had broken it off.

"There you see, Monsieur l'Abbé, you will be subjected to our united entreaties," she said, with affected gaiety, "and you will be unable to resist them. Yes, the dinner to-night would be incomplete without you. You must rescue us from the reaction which is sure to set in, on exchanging Paris for this quiet existence."

"You have been very gay, then, Madame la Comtesse?" he answered, at a loss for words, and with his eyes upon the ground.

"You cannot conceive how gay," she replied, with admirably assumed animation; "we were scarcely ever at home except when we entertained—a perpetual round of amusement. The days were accounted for weeks before they were due."

"And you enjoyed them, madame?" he ventured to ask.

Blanche hesitated momentarily. The vivid recollection of her suffering made her.

"Well, yes," she said at length, "in a measure. Society makes demands, the payment of which cannot be ignored. One recognises the inevitable, accepts it, and from that moment experiences a certain amount of horribly unreal and equivocal pleasure. You see, one is irresistibly carried along by the current."

There was evasion and a ring of dissatisfaction in

this reply, Louis thought. How could she have enjoyed? Knowing what he did, he deemed it impossible. He took heart. The desire to ascertain how he stood with her strengthened. It would be delicious to know that they were allied by a bond of unaltered esteem, such as he imagined had existed in days gone by, when he had regarded the château as a refuge, a home, where he was always welcome. But he was puzzled how to begin. At present he must content himself with groping in darkness.

"Of that current, that stream of fashionable life, I am, and always shall remain in ignorance. Do you think it fortunate that it should be so, madame?" he asked, not without some misgivings.

"For you, for one of your temperament, yes," answered Blanche, unhesitatingly.

Louis experienced a delightful sensation of pleasure. She had evidently studied him, and owned as much, in this opinion so frankly given.

"You think I should have been an object worthier of pity, had my lines fallen in more worldly places, madame?" he inquired, with the diffidence of one who fears to occasion annoyance by talking about himself.

"You would not have been any happier," she said simply.

"But I should have had less time to think," he answered gravely. "Oh, I assure you, madame, when the snow lies a foot deep in the roads, when for relaxation one must depend upon oneself the whole winter through, one begins to question and cavil."

"Have you felt very dull, then?" she demanded suddenly.

"Such a sentiment ought never to have entered my head, I suppose; but, yes, madame, at times, very."

Blanche's heart smote her. She understood him

perfectly. As though he confessed it in plain language, she comprehended that he wished to say to her, "You ask me, have I been dull? and I answer you, I have been wretched. I, who have no right to think of you, have had you in my thoughts day and night without intermission. You know what you have done. You, who conferred upon me the honour of your friendship, who taught me to consider that I was no longer without the consolation of a genuine sympathizer, have abandoned me. You understand. Why did you do this? Have I deserved such treatment at your hands?"

Blanche's pity was instantly appealed to as much as her love. Seeing him, being with him again, had kindled them both. To have given this man—who hung upon her looks, her words, her slightest gesture—six months or more of comparative tranquillity, it had rested with her to take up her pen and indite a few kindly lines from time to time. She need have done no more. And she had failed in this. But it was in her power to atone for the anguish she had caused him. Did she require to have him go upon his knees, and in a torrent of impassioned words declare his admiration for her? Did her intuition deceive her? Not for one instant. Very well, this man loved her, and would continue to love her.

Added to this, she knew how little of her heart she could call her own. Well, as mistress of the situation, she could contrive to bring the colour to his cheeks, and remove the careworn lines which had suddenly advanced his seeming age a good ten years? There need be nothing criminal between them. It rested with her. Certainly, then, they could indulge in a delicious friendship, a delightful and unrestricted interchange of ideas, without a particle of aught that was harmful tincturing this ideal intimacy.

Her own knowledge of the world, and this man's simplicity and total ignorance of it, was a combination which lent itself to the maintenance of her authority and influence over him. Seeing the position into which they had fallen, no more tempting and yet reasonable course could be adopted. They would grow to understand each swiftly changing expression, each altered intonation, each gesture, and in the existence of this bond, never made tangible by admission, they would mutually experience ineffable delight. There no longer existed the stern necessity for tearing herself away from him, and thus plunging them both into misery. That was at an end. With this suddenly-conceived idea, she prepared to become charming. All doubts in his mind must be cleared up, and he must suffer no more.

"I fear you have thought me unkind and forgetful," she said abruptly, acting upon her resolve.

"I, madame?" stammered Louis, overcome by the nature and suddenness of her remark.

"Yes, you. I must have appeared to you in the light of one who, when with you, promised great things, but when separated by a railway journey, no longer remembered the protestations she had made?"

"I, madame?" again exclaimed Louis, his cheeks red, and nervously twisting his hands. "How could I think such things?"

"Oh, but you have, and you had a right. It was thoughtless and inconsiderate of me never to tell you of our doings. I admit it. But come, let us forget everything unpleasant. Forgive me. I assure you I was not silent because I—I—"

Louis had simply raised his eyes, those superb gray eyes, so capable of betraying sentiments as yet but partially aroused. Blanche had encountered the fire, the power that burned in them, and her words had died upon her lips. Again, as at the *petit sanctuaire*, their very souls seemed to mingle. While that glance lasted they were indestructibly one. But at the end of it, there no longer remained a doubt in either heart. Louis' pulses tingled and throbbed with an unspeakable joy. During those lightening seconds his gaze never wavered. He only wished to look, undisturbed, enthralled, united to her thus. Why should it be otherwise? Why should he return again, as it were, to himself, lonely, restless, fighting perpetually? Blanche's glance was the first to waver, to quiver, and then the magnetic link was broken, the charm for the moment destroyed. Louis stirred, and regaining possession of herself again, Blanche faltered:

"—Well, and I had not forgotten that we had seen so much of you."

"How could you condescend to speak of forgiveness? What have I to forgive? You made my gloomy moments bright; you went away, and full of gratitude, unable to forget the pleasant hours spent with you, I remembered. That is all."

"Then you are not hurt, you are not offended?" she asked eagerly, unable to refrain from seeking a complete understanding, while the opportunity presented itself. Carried away by the same desire, she had, while speaking, extended her hand.

"I hardly know how to answer, madame," gasped Louis, with the nervousness of a child, and affected powerfully by the touch of her cool, firm flesh.

Blanche saw the effect she had produced, and, secretly delighted, though recoiling instantly, she said:

"Hush, nonsense, we are very good friends again. I wish it so. You must come and see us just as you have always done."

Before Louis could reply, a shadow darkened the

room. The long French windows stood wide open. It was the Count's figure that, filling one of them, obstructed the light.

"Well, it is decided. Monsieur l'Abbé is going to dine with us. Am I not right?" he inquired affably, while twisting his moustache and supporting himself against the window frame.

Louis started at the sound of his voice. How long had he been there? What had he heard, what did he now suspect? The recollection of the shadow he had noticed so pointedly, in his earlier visit to the château, recurred to him. Then, as now, the darkness was due to the Count's person. He was not superstitious, but was the Count destined to cast a gloom over his life? The reflection, and his momentary silence in consequence, obliged Blanche to speak.

"Yes," she said gaily, "I have prevailed upon him, and moreover, he is going to give us an unabridged account of everything that has happened in La Jonquières since we left."

"Well, let me think," replied Louis, rousing himself, and entering into the spirit of the suggestion, "shall I begin at once, madame?"

"Yes, or you will have so much of importance to chronicle, that you won't have time, unless we sit up talking half the night," interposed the Count ironically.

"Indeed you are right, Monsieur le Comte; such a catalogue of aches, pains, and petty grievances would send you all to sleep, I am confident. You would not be at home, madame, when I next called."

There was a laugh, and then the Count said abruptly:

"I'll tell you what, though; I know two people who really do need your assistance."

"Mine, monsieur?"

"Why, yes; come and look at them. And I assure you they are resolved to have it."

As he spoke, the Count drew Louis to one of the windows.

"Who does he mean, madame?" asked Louis wonderingly; "can you not solve the mystery for me?"

"Yonder is the solution," replied the Count, indicating Amy and the Baron, who, with heads bent close to each other, were pacing to and fro within the shade of the timber which fringed the gardens.

"But, Monsieur le Comte, are you sure that they want my aid?" he asked.

"Certain. Ah, my dear fellow, you have made no effort to ingratiate yourself with the Baron. I'll give you credit for that. But, all the same, you are a great favourite of his. Ah, you churchmen are very subtle. De Courcelles will have you marry him. The bishopric I once talked to you about will follow in due course, and that, without wearing out your patience and shoe leather by haunting the anterooms of the Ministère des Cultes. I am now divided in my opinion as to whether you should have been a soldier or a diplomatist."

"If I have won the Baron's approval, monsieur, I am delighted. It is pleasant to be liked. I am, however, conscious that I have done nothing to gain his good-will. I certainly merit such good fortune in no way," replied Louis modestly, and with some show of nervousness.

"De Courcelles may think differently."

"In any case, I shall be proud to place myself at his service, Monsieur le Comte,"

"That's right, you shall marry him, and I will sing the epithalamium," rejoined the Count gaily.

There was certainly nothing in Count Rudolf's manner to occasion Louis the least uneasiness. He was singularly ingenuous and cordial. Thus impressed, Louis ceased to trouble, surrendering himself completely to the delight he experienced in being once more in Blanche's society.

In reality, the Count had experienced a momentary sensation of surprise, on coming upon Louis and Blanche as he had done. But he had detected nothing unusual in the attitude or expression of either. He had arrived upon the scene late, and with his eyes dazzled by the sunlight. But being of a cynical turn of mind where women, or more especially his wife, was concerned, he had said to himself: "Dear me, dash it! one would scarcely think that those two have not met for months, and that during them, madame chose to treat that poor man quite unkindly. To look at them now, one would say that they could barely exist without each other. But that is madame's doing. Such hypocrisy is positively sickening." And after reflecting thus, he had troubled himself no further. By nature he was intensely suspicious though, and at any moment a trifling incident might suggest the advisability of putting two and two together. In which case awkward complications might arise.

Enjoying the last bright rays of the sun together, Blanche and Louis sauntered midst the trim flower-bordered walks, extending their promenade even to that part of the gardens where choice pears, venerable, yet bearing to perfection, grew side by side, with superb specimens of the peach, apricot, and cherry The substantial and lofty old walls were nearly hidden by the carefully-trained boughs, and the air was laden with the delicate perfume of herbs and the blossoms of old-fashioned flowers half-forgotten.

At length, with the increasing gloom, came dinner, and the pleasures of sustained and animated conversation. More than that, for these two, this night marked the commencement of a new departure—an epoch. They already began to indulge in the delight of a secret, and yet silent, understanding. They began to affect and sway each other by look and word. Their glances met and mingled, their voices became attuned to harmonize and thrill. They were beginning to indulge in the dangerous intoxication of approaching each other, morally, as near as they dare. Blanche had surrendered herself so far, and Blanche pervaded Louis' being.

Finally, having returned home, mechanically, and upon air the whole way, it seemed to him, Louis again found himself enclosed by the bare walls of his little sleeping-room. What a metamorphosis between the Louis who had looked on them last, and the Louis who now sought their shelter. He had been sad, almost devoid of hope, devoured by misgivings and anxiety. Now his cheeks were flushed, his eyes sparkled, and the expression of a conqueror marked his face. Ideas as extravagantly varied as the colours of the kaleidoscope filled his mind. He was transported with joy at the thought that this woman, who had become the very breath of his nostrils, the arbiter of his fate, instead of being indifferent to him, had not hesitated to admit, by many indefinable subtleties, that he was a potent factor in her life.

What admiration her beauty must have awakened, in the breasts of those who had been fortunate enough to enjoy the privilege of her society while in Paris. And yet, now, he was disposed to nourish the enchanting belief that, in the midst of a whirl of beauty, fashion, and wealth, such as he could not even rightly conceive, his image had dwelt with her. He, the poor and simple village priest, had not been forgotten.

More than that, he had good reason to believe

that he possessed the power to quicken her pulse, to force the blood to her cheeks, to compel a languorous light, which thrilled him, to gleam and burn in the shadowy depths of those eyes which no beauty of hue could rival. What had he done that he should be so favoured, that this great lady should condescend to smile upon him? And her heart, he was firmly convinced, was pure, and, like his own, incapable of change. Was he not of all men most fortunate? Never again would he experience the agonizing sensation of loneliness, the dull despair which, previously, it had been his lot to endure. His cup would never again overflow with such bitterness. Surely, too, he need have no dread of God's anger, for if He had not countenanced, would He have permitted this great love to enter into and possess him? After all, circumstances had combined to draw them together —this woman and himself. There was a similarity in the actions which had decided their earthly condition.

When in her childish innocence she had bound herself to the Count, her age had prevented the formation of a sound judgment, and thus her happiness had been destroyed. Had he not, too, plunged into an abyss, the depth and nature of which he had neither fathomed nor understood? In his heart of hearts, the more he reflected, the more he felt disposed to think that the Almighty—in whom he did not doubt existed the perfection of beneficence and love, who indeed was love itself—had never intended, and did not wish, any of His creatures to take such an oath as the Church thought fit to exact. He could not associate it with the teaching of the Blessed Saviour. No, no, there was some mistake, something wrong. Man had invented it, and man had erred. Why should he live in solitude, why should he die, and even on his death-bed, in that last

P

supreme agony, be cheered by no sweet human ties? Again he fell asleep, as he had often done, thinking these things.

Surrendering herself to the greatest happiness she had known, since recognising the failure of her marriage—perhaps the greatest happiness she had ever known, for, after all, was she not a child in those days?—Blanche had retired for the night. Louis was near to her. They understood each other, and a summer during which they could be constantly together lay before them. True, the position in which they stood to each other was a terribly unfortunate one. But why regard the unfortunate side of it? There was a bright one. And, after all, life seemed a misfortune, a constant battle, in fact, so long as the pulse should continue to beat, a perpetual and heart-breaking struggle to stem the tide.

Well, she had fought till she was tired, and in this tired condition, she was disposed to shrink from the contemplation of stern, uncompromising actualities, and to allow herself in spirit to glide midst the flowers and the sunshine, to inhale the sweet odours, and allow the soft, balmy winds to caress her heated cheek, and play midst the tresses of her hair. She and Louis could go thus hand in hand for a little, during which they would be supremely happy, and then— Well, she was tired, and could not penetrate the profound gloom beyond; so, while shrinking from peering into it, she slept like a child.

CHAPTER XXI.

DREAD lest her influence with the Count should suffer, had supplied Lisette's reason for visiting Paris. Absence, and the distractions afforded by the gay capital, might well cause him to forget her. She had returned to La Jonquières cured of such doubts, richer by the value of costly presents, triumphant. Her great physical beauty, she was now assured, was sufficient to enchain the Count.

Intoxicated with her success, ignorant and vain, she indulged in the contemplation of a number of preposterous ideas and schemes for the future. Count Rudolf was wealthy, and so far as she was concerned, weak. This was a very pretty basis upon which to build castles. Anything for her but the prospect of a peasant for her husband, no matter how thrifty and hard-working he might be—a peasant home in which she would have to do the drudgery, and count, with care, the francs—a peasant life ever and always, with its uninteresting, intolerable monotony. No, she would rather die than endure it! And, with her beauty, why should she? She was convinced that no one would become a stately hotel, fine clothes, and dashing equipages, better than herself. And it was in her power to obtain these luxuries if she only played her cards well. Foolish Lisette! Has not the familiar adage much truth in it for you: and such as you, "A silk purse cannot be made out of a sow's ear"? Perhaps you may yet learn wisdom, but, if you do, you will come by it only through much suffering. Meanwhile, for André, and such as André, you have a contemptuous shrug of your plump white shoulders, an insolent pout of your red lips. With degrees of difference there are not a few in the world like you, Lisette.

As for André Moriseau, what he had seen in Paris he had kept to himself. Returning to the farm, each day saw him working early and late midst the wind and the sunlight. When he saw Lisette, his manner towards her was unchanged. He pocketed her scorn, as he did his pipe, when he had done smoking it. Of what use to remonstrate with her? Better maintain a phlegmatic silence, better keep his pride intact. He had a dull, dogged sense which taught him this. He could watch and wait.

Only when alone, sometimes, would his pent-up fury, his hatred of the Count, explode. He had to thank *him*, and no one else, for the misery he endured, for the wreckage of his hopes. Vigorously he spat and cursed him, yet his rage, instead of abating, burned more fiercely.

And Count Rudolf, dressed to perfection, looking the embodiment of health, with his gun over his shoulder, and his dogs at his heels, amused himself with consuming a vast number of cigarettes, with *la chasse*, too, and with Lisette when he could get her.

CHAPTER XXII.

THE stately Château de Courcelles was at length ready for the reception of its new mistress. Lavishly, and yet with the perfection of good taste, the Baron's instructions had been executed. Nothing was wanting but the arrival of the marriage-day. And it approached swiftly, the two young people, lover-like, watching it draw near with rapture and impatience. In spite of her protestations of future amendment, Amy had again become absorbed in the Baron and the coming event, which was to change her whole existence as radically as her name. She had no time to notice Blanche attentively. This was fortunate, for, being a woman, under other circumstances she could scarcely have failed to detect much that would have surprised and puzzled her. Blanche was no longer the same being.

What sober judgment would have declined to permit, love, combined with pity, had effected at one bound. How laboriously, and with what mental anguish, had she succeeded in erecting a rampart, which, she had believed, rendered her proof against Louis. Yet it had been assaulted, and carried with a few soft words, a sight of the man, and at a first interview. Now, with the unreasonableness of love, she failed to see that she had been weak. She regretted nothing that she had done; believed herself strong still, when really defenceless. Content to be blinded by love, she abandoned herself to the blissfulness of the sensation, with a recklessness that love alone could have produced. What would happen, what would be the result, she made no attempt to anticipate. Her romantic temperament was responsible for a new idea which seized upon her after again meeting Louis. "I will worship this man," she said to herself softly. "He shall be to me an earthly Saviour, for through him I shall be saved from myself. He whom I know to be good and pure, is worthy of all the love I can bestow upon him. Fate has cruelly separated us, but my heart shall be none the less his, and I will be true until, perhaps, in some brighter and better world I may belong to him. I can make him happy. Is not that something—some reason why I should feel contented, satisfied?"

But, alas! were human beings ever contented and satisfied? Was it not more probable that passion, sudden and irresistible, would make its demands—would refuse to listen to the voice of reason, and, like the mountain torrent, would sweep away all obstacles? She did not realize this—did not dream that it could be so with her. But then she did not know how much she loved.

"Tell me everything that happened to you during those years when I was at the convent of the Sacred Heart, and you were at the seminary at Rheims," she said to Louis, during one of their conversations, which she now regarded as daily luxuries. "Do you recollect that I once said I should persuade you to tell me about your past life?"

"I remember perfectly," replied Louis gravely.

"It seems strange to think that we two were living during all those years, receiving the impressions that have made us what we are, and yet were totally unconscious of each other's individual existence."

"Strange, indeed."

"Were you happy, as, after all, I believe one is, during one's school-days?"

"I experienced a little pleasure, due, I now know, to the fact that I was so young; and a great deal of misery owing to the restrictions and severity with which I was treated. I know I may confide in you, dear madame."

Blanche winced. She always did whenever Louis, impelled by propriety, let slip the ceremonious appellation. She longed with all her heart to hear him call her Blanche. Would the time ever come when openly he might speak to her so? How could it? The reflection was a heart-breaking one, and overcome by it, she found strength only to nod her head in reply to him.

"Then I was profoundly wretched. The life in the seminaries is little known, little understood. I was sent to *le petit seminaire* at the age of twelve, and remained there until I was about seventeen. During that time, even the letters which were sent to me were always opened before I received them. I was never allowed to stir out without an attendant. The greatest care was taken by the Superior to prevent us from coming into contact with what is termed (*une personne du sexe*) females. We were strictly forbidden to possess any other than school books, and I remember that one boy was nearly expelled for having hidden some amusing secular work. Even during our holidays, we were forbidden to attend any festivities, such as a simple country fair, for instance. But does this really interest you?" he asked suddenly.

"Yes, go on, please. Whatever has so much affected you, must interest me," she said simply.

The blood leapt into his face.

"How can I thank you enough? What can I—"
She held up her hand to silence him.
"By relating everything, as I have asked you."
With an effort Louis recovered himself.

"Well," he said, "let me think. A really good seminarist would never look one of your sex in the face, even if obliged to talk to her. I have known some, who were so zealous that they would studiously regard the toes of their boots. To prove to you how severely treated we were, I will quote as an instance this occurrence. A boy was found to possess a box —some paltry sweetmeat box—upon the lid of which was a coloured picture representing a woman's figure. It was immediately confiscated by the Superior, who, not content with that, made a speech in which he dwelt upon the wickedness of such things. He then tore it up, in the presence of the assembled seminarists. Now, how can such an education as this fit one to be launched upon the world, when but a little older, simply because a vow which has not been understood has been taken? At the end of five years of this kind of surveillance I was sent to *le grand seminaire*, where I first wore the cassock and lived in a separate cell. All the rigours I have related to you were there amplified.

"Once a week only were we permitted to go out for a walk together. We were allowed no amusing books. No kind of recreation, in fact, except on wet days, when we indulged in backgammon, dominoes, or draughts. Fancy, on the finest and brightest of days, our only exercise was to pace backwards and forwards, in groups of three and four, but always facing each other. Oh! it was so tiring, so monotonous, so heart-breaking, shut up in a huge court-yard, when the sun was shining, and one knew that everything was bright and fresh and free, outside those gloomy walls.

"During all this, the principal theory taught us by the Superior, was that salvation stood at the ratio of perhaps five in one hundred. Five souls rescued, ninety-five lost. In some instances, where passion, an unsuitable temperament, dislike for the life, were pleaded as reasons why the vow should not be finally subscribed to, *la discipline*, or self-inflicted flogging, was invariably recommended. The theory of damnation so perpetually and untiringly taught, as I have described, depresses and strikes such terror into a young, sensitive and credulous mind, that the torture endured is indescribable. It sometimes causes madness."

"How terrible."

"But you can easily understand how it occurs; a weakly constitution, combined with an acutely sensitive mind, cannot endure the weight of such a burden. Then, in addition to that, add the fact that from the age of twenty-one we were compelled to fast, having but one meal a day, and always rising at five o'clock in the morning.

"Many men have ruined their constitutions through fasting, and not a few have actually killed themselves. The Marquis de Gonzaga and Jean Berchmans, for instance, did so, and were canonized. If I attempted to tell you how wretched I myself felt, words would fail me. How I envied the birds, how I envied anything that was free. I remember looking out of the window of my cell one morning, and seeing on the sloping roof before me two sparrows playing contentedly with a straw. As I watched them my tears flowed fast, so supremely wretched did I feel, for it seemed to me that those birds were far more fortunate than myself. For them, during their brief life, there was love and happiness, and after life, annihilation; but for me, if I believed what I was taught, what hope was there?

My heart was torn, my mind distracted, my—" Louis' voice failed him, the anguish of those dead years was with him again as he spoke. At length huskily, and after a long and painful pause, he added the next disjointed words. "So now you will understand something of what I went through. Such was my boyhood, my youth, and so I felt when I became a man. Will you think less of me for being so weak and telling you so much?"

The only answer Blanche made was to look at him, and, as she did so, his heart bounded within him, for her lips were quivering and her face was wet with tears. At that instant, a passionate, a maddening desire seized upon him. With his whole soul he longed to fling his arms about her, to kiss the trembling lips, and dry the dear tears which fell for him. But swift as the heart-felt longing, there arose before him a vision of the Count, the recollection of himself as priest.

Were these thoughts honourable? were they manly? were they right? He shuddered, for he knew they were not. Yet had they cost him his life, he could not have prevented himself from thinking them. Already it was almost beyond his strength to control himself. And the man to whom this woman belonged—this woman who had awakened such sentiments in him—he knew to be neglectful of her, incapable of appreciating her nobility of mind and beauty of person. Beyond all that, thrusting it into the shade, dwarfing it completely, as priest he was tortured by the knowledge that this man was untrue to her, wholly unworthy.

Was this not a powerful picture of life, turned to meet his gaze? As he comprehended its grotesque proportions, and remembered the isolation to which he was condemned, the sharpness of the pain he endured became intensified. He averted his face, with clenched teeth, not daring to speak, until he had recovered his tranquillity. At length, as the sun struggles to pierce a mass of wintry clouds, so through his lacerated feelings came a feeble and forced attempt at a smile.

"I am going to show you that sometimes funny things happened to us, too," he said, with a painful effort at light-heartedness, "although it is but another instance of the severity with which, what were deemed the vanities of the world, were concealed from us. I think it will make you laugh. I daresay you may have noticed the little carts upon which itinerant vendors of plaster figures display their wares?"

Blanche nodded.

"Well, one of these men, probably impressed with the imposing appearance of our seminary, which was a huge building of three stories—and believing that where so many people lived, he would be able to drive a brisk trade in statues, crucifixes, and images of saints, directed his donkey to the gate, and rang the bell. The door-keeper, a good brother of mature age, on seeing such an array of saints, experienced much gratification, and, without hesitation, allowed the man to pass into our court-yard. We were at that moment amusing ourselves by pacing up and down the ground, as I have described to you. At the sight of so many pretty things, we abandoned our exercise and surrounded the donkey cart. Amongst other saints, I remember a St. Louis de Gonzaga in an attitude of devotion, clasping a crucifix to his breast, several statues of the Blessed Virgin in the attitude of immaculate conception—hands clasped together, and eyes directed heavenward, as though rapt in contemplation. But in the centre of these small devotional objects, prominently placed, were two busts of women.

"'What saints are those?' inquired one of our number, an innocent lad who knew nothing about feminine evening dress.

"'Those two are not saints,' answered the owner of the donkey cart; 'but they are well known, and I sell a great many of them. This one is our dear Empress Eugénie, and this, Queen Victoria of England.'

"These words were scarcely uttered, than like a bird of prey, his eyes lighted by the fire of indignation, our Superior himself descended upon us. With a gesture of supreme authority, as one accustomed to be obeyed, he seized the donkey by the bridle, and led him out, quick march, to our intense surprise, and to the unfortunate owner's amazement. Poor man, he had not remarked that as soon as he had entered our court-yard, both he and his wares had been the cynosure of the Fathers, who were themselves enjoying their recreation on the first floor of the seminary, and from the windows were watching all the proceedings. I am not sure whether they at once perceived the two *décolletés* busts, but the Superior did, and promptly turned this emissary of Satan out of the place. Not content with this, the Superior, having made inquiries, discovered that the guilty one, the one who had so recklessly imperilled our innocence and peace of mind, was a *brother*. In order to teach him to be prudent and watchful for the future, the Superior sentenced him to be flogged for fifteen minutes during three consecutive days, and to kneel in our private chapel throughout the morning service."

Louis paused and looked at Blanche. He naturally expected some evidence that she had listened to and appreciated his story. He received nothing of the kind. She was perfectly silent, and her usually mobile face was expressive of gravity only. She was thinking. What an existence Louis had sketched, and in a few words. What wearing and ceaseless torture he must have endured! She had no idea that every priest had to go through such a fiery ordeal. And after all those long years, years robbed of lightsomeness and freshness, what followed? The spectacle of Louis, lonely, unhappy, morbidly desirous of human companionship, human ties. If ever a nature was formed to love and be beloved, it was his. And yet for him to think of love, in the carnal sense, was a grave sin. There was something unnatural in such a condition, it seemed to her; and, placed in it, she felt that she should have rebelled. But how rebel? and with what result? Here she came to a stand-still.

The next reflection, following this pause, was the oft-indulged-in and enthralling one, that certainly, Louis had never loved any other woman. She had awakened the sentiment in him, therefore she might the more absolutely believe in its purity and depth. But was she not hideously to blame, then? Of this interrogation she shook herself free. Had she not struggled? And what had been the use? Now, no penalty or threat would have induced her to forego this dear delight, which warmed her heart and made it pulsate as she had never thought to feel it. And everything rested with her. She could do as she pleased with this man, of that she had no doubt. But such knowledge as this was almost too delicious. It made her tremble. Was it not too much power to possess, and might she not well fear, that in some wild, weak moment, reason would be annihilated by passion? The more she realized the depth of the chasm dividing them, human-like, the more vehemently did she long that it might be bridged. When she attempted to measure her affection for this man, who appeared to be so hopelessly lost to her, she shuddered; for already she felt that she was capable of doing and enduring without limit, if by such means she might come to call him her own.

She did not comprehend that she was balancing herself upon the extremity of a precipice, and that though struggling to grow accustomed to the dizzy height, it was questionable whether she would be able to preserve her equilibrium. She was disposed to consider herself strong—the greatest proof of weakness; and in reality, she no longer possessed the power to extricate herself from the dangers which beset her. In her condition of mind, her judgment was so warped that it amounted to no judgment at all, such violent hands had love laid upon her. Its grip, too, was tightening.

She awoke from her reverie—Louis having remained at her side without attempting to speak. And they were seated thus, in the kiosk, at the back of which Louis had so distinctly heard her sobs, and the Count's voice raised in anger.

"I shall not tell you what I was thinking," she said suddenly. "I heard every word you said, and was deeply interested. But just as you finished speaking, ideas crowded into my mind, and I preferred to evolve rather than scatter them."

"I knew it, and took care not to interrupt you," he replied simply.

"Well, in return for your forbearance, you shall have the best cup of tea I can give you; and here it comes." Then, to the servant who entered bearing the precious equipage, she added: "Be good enough to tell Mademoiselle Amy that we are waiting for her."

Seated before the steaming stimulant, doling out the crystal sugar and rich yellow cream, no one could have seemed further removed from aught that could disturb. True, she was engaged in pouring out tea for the man she loved. No wonder, then, that her eyes sparkled, and that her golden hair and fair complexion, further set off by a perfectly fitting and yet simple attire, made an irresistibly dazzling combination.

The interior of the kiosk was bright and even elegant. The cunning art of the Japanese had embroidered the hangings which adorned the walls, with a lightness and brilliancy which was almost startling. Pale blue mountains, calm pellucid lakes, temples, gaudy butterflies and birds soaring beneath blossoming trees and azure skies, were portrayed with a daring but peculiar skill. Thick straw mats deadened the sound of footsteps. The lacquer furniture was profusely enriched with gold, and a subdued light was obtained by means of closely-drawn silken curtains, while from the roof a splendid bronze lantern, with coloured glass panes, hung suspended by a metal chain. And it was to this luxurious retreat that these two now frequently came, in the cool evening time, the hour when, with his day's work done, Louis abandoned himself rapturously to breathing the same air as Blanche, feasting his eyes upon her, listening to the soft, bell-like ripple of her voice.

"But, do you know," remarked Louis thoughtfully, while tapping his cup with his teaspoon, "it seems to me that you don't quite realize how much I suffered, in the days I have spoken of. True, words are inadequate to describe what I endured."

"There may be truth in what you say. It is difficult to place oneself in the exact position of another, impossible in fact, for one thinks with a different mind. But I must have convinced you that I sympathized very sincerely," she replied, in tones of reproof.

"Yes, yes, indeed you have."

"Shall I tell you how to treat anything disagreeable?"

"Consign it to oblivion?" he suggested, hap-hazard.

"That's it, consign it to oblivion. The worst aspect your revelations wear, is when one says to oneself—yes, but these abuses are going on at this very moment. Human beings are enduring, and preparing to endure, what you have felt and are still feeling."

"Yes, that is it; and what I shall continue to feel all my life, unless—"

"Unless what?"

"Ah, I cannot say. At least, not yet. I have thought very deeply, I assure you, all this long winter through. Some day, when my ideas are clearer, I'll come and tell you, though, when I do, you are more than likely to say, this man is a depraved monster."

"That's absurd; but you should not tantalize me by throwing out so many vague suggestions. I am half inclined to try what persuasion will do now."

"I could not tell you, until I am convinced that my judgment is sound."

"Dear me, how seriously you speak."

"It is a serious subject," he answered gravely.

"More enigmas. Well, I will not question you. I shall await the result of your cogitations. For the present, though, let me entreat you to forget the unpleasantness of the past, and you shall have my friendship to enable you to do so. Come, is it a bargain?" she asked sweetly.

"A bargain, the benefits of which are all on my side."

"That can scarcely be said, when it affords me so much pleasure."

The appearance of Amy, looking radiant, put an end to the conversation.

CHAPTER XXIII.

At length the ardently-desired marriage day had stolen its silent march upon the two young people. At La Jonquières, it was evident, during the earliest hours of the morning, that something unusual was in the wind.

There was to be a general holiday for miles round, which was to terminate with a fête in the beautiful old park of the Château de Courcelles. The Baron had persuaded Amy that instead of rushing off to some outlandish place, where they would probably be made excessively uncomfortable, it would be much nicer to spend their honeymoon in the spot so endeared to him by the recollection of his boyhood. Besides, they would be near everyone at La Jonquières, and could see them, should they wish it. And what could be jollier than to celebrate their happy union by giving the peasants, who cared to come, a feast, and freedom from toil for that day at least? The suggestion charmed Amy; so while a stir was taking place at the Château de la Jonquières, De Courcelles, escorted by a relative or two, whose existence it was impossible to ignore, inspected the preparations, giving hints and directions to the workmen, who were employed in erecting what was intended as a ball-room for the country folk. There was to be a pyrotechnical display upon a grand scale.

The lake was to be illuminated. There were to be boats decked with flowers and Chinese lanterns, from which musicians were to fill the air with sweet strains. Merry-go-rounds had been put up for the children, an abundance of good things had been provided, and everyone was expected to eat, drink, and be happy. From the first peep of day, the sky had been anxiously scanned, but when the mist cleared away the sun shone forth with a brilliancy that banished all misgivings on the score of the weather. The party from La Jonquières, consisting of Blanche, Amy, Louis Bernard, and the Count, arrived at the hour arranged. And, at the last moment, M. Brunot, who had got wind of the affair, drove over from Mezieres in his gala barouche, and, as it were, bounced upon the scene, bringing a superb present of sapphires and diamonds.

"Never mind, my dear fellow; the man means well," replied De Courcelles, in response to the Count's growls and objections to his presence; "we can't very well turn him out."

"But fancy the cheek of the fellow; was there ever such a piece of impertinence?" retorted the Count, with unappeased wrath.

Arranging themselves in the chapel—which, if diminutive, was a masterpiece of sculptured marble and costly stained glass, bearing the De Courcelles escutcheon—Louis, in a firm and impressive voice, performed the simple ceremony which bound these two together. The park gates were then thrown open, and the public began to take possession of the place. The open-air orchestra made itself heard, and the sounds of laughter and merriment penetrated even into the château.

Amidst mirth, good wishes, and much health-drinking, darkness stole over the sky. The Baron, who had made a speech which had been cheered to the echo, was on the terrace with Amy and those who had come to do him honour. Louis and Blanche were leaning over the balustrade watching the brilliant scene, preparatory to an early return to La Jonquières, upon which the Count had insisted. The lake was ablaze with dancing lights, beneath which the rippling water, curling before a gentle breeze, shone like silver. Coloured lanterns, of all shapes and hues, had been fixed to the sweeping boughs of the ancient trees, and these, with their flickering light, illuminated the woodland aisles and stretches of smooth turf, upon which soldiers from the garrison at Givet strolled and made love to the pretty village girls. André, who was looked upon as already done for, in consequence of his passion for Lisette, was there; but Lisette, in accordance with the fine ideas she had developed latterly, had preferred to remain at home. This assemblage of peasants was no longer to her taste.

Louis Bernard's heart was full. The events of the day had suggested much. Had he not united the sister of the woman he worshipped to the man she desired? And loving Blanche as he did, was it possible for him to stand at her side, with marriage and the thoughts of marriage borne, as it were, upon the soft night air, without thinking of what might have been had Fate decreed otherwise? Was not his condition one in which the struggle between the fleshly desires of the body, and the purer and loftier aspirations of the soul, was sure to be a desperate one, and on this day more than on others, Amy and the Baron's happiness being so apparent?

To enjoy the intimate companionship of a woman of Blanche's beauty, on such a night, without in his weak moments coveting her madly, was beyond his strength. He felt himself to be a man, not a saint.

Had there been the least chance for him, a hope, however faint, that time might remove the obstacles which separated them, he would have experienced greater contentment. But his position afforded him no hope. Look on which side he would, darkness confronted him. Morally he was convinced that she already belonged to him; materially, that they were lost to each other. Beatitude, ineffable bliss, was his on the one hand; on the other, an abyss, the obscurity of which was profound.

Nothing either could ameliorate his condition. At first it had appeared possible to him to rest content with her friendship, to lay aside all thoughts of a closer bond, to be satisfied to see and speak with her, to enjoy this inestimable boon of social intercourse, and to wish for no more. He had come to recognise that this was not enough, and now, as he leant over the balustrade at her side, more imperatively than ever. If she had been happy, if she had not loved him in return, he would have torn himself away, sought the rigid discipline of some monastery, perhaps, and trusted in that, and time, to effect some sort of cure. But she did love him, and assuredly she was unhappy.

Almost identically the same thoughts had entered Blanche's mind, and intuitively she had guessed what was passing in his. She knew that, like her own, his heart-strings were wrung with conflicting feelings, but with a woman's tender devotion, she forgot herself, in her desire to alleviate his sufferings. Could she not say something that would sooth and cheer him, though to make the attempt was like playing with gunpowder? Obedient to this impulse, she remarked softly at his elbow:

"You are depressed to-night, I think."

He was conscious of a slight shock, for he had been absorbed in his reflections.

"Depressed—what makes you think so?" he asked, recovering himself.

"Because I have watched you through the day."

An expression of mingled delight and triumph played over his features. It was so sweet to him to hear her admit that he was an object of interest to her.

"Oh," he answered, in a low voice. "When looking upon some brilliant scene, by some strange perversity of human nature, I often feel tempted to conjure a gloomy one; to anticipate a metamorphosis. With festivity before me, so much joyousness in the atmosphere, I have, perhaps, been selfish and foolish enough to think of myself, to contrast my own existence and prospects with the lives and probable futures of those about me."

"And is the comparison so unfavourable for you?"

"Sometimes I think so."

"But you would not change places with any of those people about us? With the gardener, for instance, who is busy letting off those rockets, with the peasants, or even the soldiers, who are going to eat and drink till they can eat and drink no more, make love to anything in the shape of a woman, and return to the barracks in a glorious condition of imbecility?"

"I am not prepared to say."

"Would you wish to possess coarse features, a clumsy frame, and blunted susceptibilities, in order that you might enjoy life as they do? You surely prefer learning and refinement to ignorance and vulgarity?"

"But is there any necessity to coin such violent contrasts? Why could not one be simple, honest, and free, without being stupid and vulgar?"

She did not choose to notice the remark.

"Hush, I want to make you recognise how much you have to be thankful for."

"I ought to need no such lesson," he retorted bitterly.

"Please don't be offended with me for speaking my mind."

"You may make me ashamed of myself, but you can never offend me."

"Ah, you don't know how terribly brusque and disagreeable I can be."

"No; experience may teach me much, but it won't teach me that."

Blanche smiled tranquilly, but her heart beat fast. It was so sweet to her to receive these apparently trivial compliments from this man, knowing that he meant so much more than the actual words he used implied.

"But listen," she went on, "just consider what the last twenty-four hours have been. You have had a roof to shelter you, every luxury, and any number of friends."

"All of which—the roof and the luxuries, at least—I would gladly exchange for the constant companionship of someone who loved me," he answered, lowering his voice, yet in tender though vehement accents.

"Oh, nonsense; you imagine all that."

"*You* can say so?" he interrupted, almost threateningly.

She silenced him with a gesture peculiar to her.

"It is an acknowledged fact that human beings are seldom contented with what they possess, or can acquire easily. What they have, they think least of. Those one has lost, one loves best. Come, try to be contented. I implore you to be more, even; be brave, and help me to be so."

He understood her perfectly. Like him, she was devoured by the fire which love had kindled in her. In her calm moments, perhaps, she hated to think herself so weak—so erring. The nobility of her nature rebelled against this partial material triumph. And, rather than succumb, she was disposed to call upon him for aid; to derive strength from an appeal to those good qualities which she credited him with possessing, to urge him to prove that, in a deadly struggle, matter stood no chance against mind. But what a delicious admission of her weakness—what a convincing proof of her confidence in him. And thus, having practically said to him, "Come, let us do what is right, let us adhere to the most rigid lines of honour, let us be true to our better natures—true to ourselves," was she to be subjected to the pain of finding out that he was less of a man than she thought? He it was who should have set this example, and yet, though his life had been spent in studying the sacred writings, in the pursuit of good, here was a woman who could teach him his duty. A sense of shame overcame him, but, despite it, his admiration for her was strengthened. Her face, pale and expressive of fear lest she should have said too much, lest she should have given offence, was turned to him inquiringly. Resolutely he encountered her gaze.

"You are quite right," he said, almost in a whisper; "I deserve reproof. I assure you, I am often disgusted with myself; I, who ought to know what is right, and who should be able to do it, but—"

"No, no, you misunderstand me," she interrupted, while casting an anxious glance over her shoulder, as though dreading observation. As she again turned her head, satisfied that no one was watching them, the Count appeared at one of the windows, almost immediately behind her, through which opening a strong light was flung upon the terrace. Striking a favourite attitude by leaning against the woodwork, the Count appeared to be sufficiently interested to notice them narrowly. In this intention he was further aided by the position in which he stood, and the powerful rays from the magnificent crystal chandelier. He had merely been making a tour of the grand drawing-room, amusing himself by examining some exquisite pastels and certain pieces of china which the Baron set immense store by, but, having completed this inspection, his progress had been arrested by the sight of the two figures before him.

"You misunderstand me," repeated Blanche eagerly.

"Oh, no; indeed I don't. As I have said, you are perfectly right, and certainly, if I contrast my position with that of many a man who has perhaps undergone all, and more than I have, I ought to be unfeignedly thankful. Had there been, for instance, no living soul in this place in whom I could confide, I should have been a thousand times worse off. In that case I might have been justified in indulging in despondency; as it is, I am ungrateful, and don't deserve to be happy."

"Listen to me," said Blanche, in anxious tones.

"But I want you to hear what I have got to say first, or it will be driven out of my head. With you to take an interest in me, to see and be with me, almost every day for at least half the year, instead of grumbling, I should be as joyous and light-hearted as any peasant in the *arrondissement*. That I am not so is my own fault. I am not genuine—not what I seem. If I only had the welfare of others uppermost in my mind, instead of my own, I should be a different being. Come, I will ask you to help me—to enable me to become a better man; and you—*you can* do it."

This speech, which he believed to be as harmless as true, produced anything but the effect he had intended. She became alarmed. He was annoyed, mortified, she felt certain. Once before, on her return from Paris, fear of a coldness, dread of occasioning a breach which might not be filled up, had caused her to fling prudence to the winds. Without a moment's hesitation she did so again.

"I have offended you, and you are sarcastic," she exclaimed. "Well, you have a right to be so. I have said enough to make you angry with me. You whose life has been one long sacrifice, who are beloved by every soul who has ever sought your help, and who would give the very coat you wear to the poor, *you* are to be altered into something better, and I am to do it—I, who have been the one disturbing element in your life. Do you think I don't know that but for me you would have lived here, respected and at peace? It's all my fault. Better a thousand times that you had never seen me. I am the cause of—"

Her words died upon her lips. With his face transfigured, scarcely believing his ears, he gazed upon her, and as he did so the power of speech forsook her. The blood deserted her cheeks. Consumed by her love, she longed to abandon herself, to rest her head upon his shoulder, to cease this strife that was costing her such terrible suffering, and the end of which seemed shrouded in chaotic gloom. Subjugated, trembling, Louis' head swam. The mastery over himself hung as by a hair.

At that critical moment a step sounded behind them, and in his polished accents the Count said:

"Ah, I have found you at last. I had a sort of idea that you were strolling about in the gardens, but was beginning to believe myself doomed to search in vain, until I thought of looking for you here. Really, the illuminations are most effective: under the influence of the magic power of light the place has become a sort of fairyland—eh? Well, we have spent a most delightful day, have we not? However, I am bound to convey the unpleasant information that the carriage is waiting, and, since we have a long drive before us, we must not start too late."

While dropping every word deliberately, as though firing them from a revolver, the Count's eyes were not idle, but darted from Louis to Blanche, who had just sufficient presence of mind to say:

"Then, in that case, we will go. Will you give me your arm, Monsieur l'Abbé?"

Then, with quickened pulse and crimson cheeks, she swept past the Count, directing her steps towards the Baron, who, with Amy clinging to him on one side, was, on the other, more than balanced by the heavy arm of an enormously fat maternal aunt, the old Duchess D'Aiguillon, whom he really wished far enough, but with whom he was laughing good-naturedly, having just returned from a tour of the gardens.

"Countess, we must have a last little chat together," he said to Blanche, as they all met. "I have seen positively nothing of you." Then contriving to elude the vigilance of the stout old lady, he drew Blanche aside, and together they descended the steps into the garden. "I fear," he went on, "that this fête of mine has bored you. No; well I am glad, then. But while I think of it, I want to say a few words, and since the occasion I have chosen is an eventful one, perhaps we shall both remember them better. Now that I am Amy's husband, I don't want to lapse into the orthodox specimen of a legally-made relative of the rather-to-be-avoided type. You may want someone you can depend upon some day; who can tell? If you do, will you come to me, that's all?"

The young fellow slipped his arm through Blanche's as he spoke, as though he would say, "Come, I have a right to you now. From to-night we are relatives in earnest," regarding her at the same time with the ingenuousness which had always so strongly prepossessed her in his favour.

"Indeed, I won't forget. I *will* come to you. You are so kind," she answered, endeavouring to bestow upon him her whole attention, for her brain was still whirling with thoughts of Louis and the Count's interruption.

"Yes; but mind we must be sworn friends," persisted the Baron. "Now that you have entrusted me with a priceless treasure, you must bestow upon me what stands next in value in my eyes—your friendship. You know the worst of me by this time."

"I'm not going to tell you what opinion I have formed of you," replied Blanche, with pretty coquetry; "but I have lived long enough to know how to value disinterested friendship, to remember that blood is thicker than water, and as a proof of the importance I attach to all you have said, see, you may kiss me, and we will be brother and sister."

Presenting her soft cheek, De Courcelles gravely and reverently impressed upon it the caress she had invited.

"Now that our compact is sealed," she continued, "you must take me back, or Rudolf will be angry. Already I must have kept him waiting." Then with a sudden burst of feeling, as she recollected her own loveless hearth to which she was returning, she added, "May you be happy, very happy always, happier ever so much than I am."

No reply was possible, for at that instant M. Brunot joined them, and in his loud, vulgar voice said:

"Ah, Madame la Comtesse, this odour of orange blossoms is intoxicating. The sight of so much beauty disturbs me. Only a moment ago I found myself telling Monsieur l'Abbe Bernard, that I might apply to him sooner than he expected. Ah, I am keeping my eyes open."

"Quite right; that is what you should do, Brunot. You will never be complete until you have ceased to be a bachelor, mind that," interposed De Courcelles cheerily, and drawing Blanche past the noisy and ambitious Deputy, he observed, "We have got rid of that fellow, at all events; but here is Amy with some wraps."

"Are you coming, Blanche?" called the Count, from the terrace. "Come along."

"Rudolf has again been in pursuit of you, dear," remarked Amy affectionately. "He is grumbling at the prospect of a jolt over bad roads in the dark, and declares he wanted to start an hour ago, but that you have eluded him like a phantom. You must come and have some wine before you go, and put this round your throat."

"But I'm not delicate."

"Monsieur, to you I intrust this wrap. Envelop my sister in it," retorted the lively girl, addressing Louis. Then, literally making her swallow the wine, they all trooped to the carriage, near which the obsequious M. Brunot had already stationed himself. With a last vigorous hug from Amy, Blanche was suffered to take her seat.

"Now, mind, we must meet soon," called the Baron, and then the wheels began to crunch over the gravel drive, and midst the sounds of merriment from the revellers in the park, they set off for La Jonquières.

CHAPTER XXIV.

The Count had both seen and heard enough, not only to arouse his suspicions, but to convince him that Louis and Blanche were actually in love with each other. He made no attempt to mince matters, by endeavouring to place some more moderate construction upon what he had witnessed. His fury, then, may be imagined.

During Blanche's brief saunter in the garden with De Courcelles, he had time to consider how he should act. And for the moment he decided to dissemble. They should never suspect anything until he was ready, then the blow he might strike would descend with more crushing effect. In accordance with this determination, he became a model of amiability through the whole of the drive, talking with much *verve*, and concealing his real feelings with such consummate skill, that Louis, and even Blanche, was completely deceived.

Once alone, however, the Count presented a very different spectacle. After a violent explosion, and with features distorted with anger, he began to examine the situation with some semblance of calmness. All the same, he continued to pace the room, puffing at his cigarettes as though he felt himself capable of disposing of those who dared to cross his path, with the same ease and promptitude. So this was madame's lover—the lover for whom he had kept such a sharp look-out. And this lover was a priest. *Mille tonnerres!* Was it not enough to choke him? This woman, who was in the best Parisian society, who had been surrounded by the most distinguished representatives of the foreign colony, who was a power in the Parisian fashionable world—this woman had taken it into her stupid head to fall in love with a poor devil of a priest.

By Jove, no wonder he ground his teeth. Had she not posed as the most immaculate of her sex? And really he had believed her to be proof against all attacks. And she chose to open his eyes thus. He reflected with greater deliberation. Like a detective sifting the information placed at his disposal, he cautiously felt his way backwards, laboriously recalling words, and reckoning up events, until he stopped dead before his interview with Blanche, the result of which had been their return to Paris.

Why had she come to him with that suddenly conceived desire? Why had she urged him with all the eloquence and determination at her command? Fool that he had been! Her reasons were plain enough now. From that day, or near upon it, the serious aspect of this love affair dated. And to escape from it, she had recognised the necessity for quitting La Jonquières. Lisette and his amour with her had nothing to do with it, conceited ass that he had been. As she had told him, she was not in love with him. But in that case, her hasty departure, which, now that he thought upon it, amounted to flight, was the action of a good and noble woman, obeying the prompting of a virtuous and upright heart. Her conduct, too, during those months in Paris. It was perfectly obvious. She had sought to discover in him the protection she felt she stood in need of. Under his wing she had endeavoured to shelter herself, and he had done his best to drive her from him. But why, then, had she not retracted the expressions she had used to him? They had stung him to the quick, raised the pride, the devil in him.

Ever since the night on which she had told him of her desire to be his wife in the world's eyes only, he had kept aloof from her. They had maintained the outward appearances she had asked for; beyond that, they had been dead to each other. For, whatever he was, he had not sunk so low as to force himself upon any woman. She had chosen to continue cursedly obstinate, content that her words should lie and rankle in his heart. Well, that was no fault of his. In addition, it was true, she had occasionally stumbled across some peccadillo or other of his; this had set her by the ears, and here was the result. What was he to infer, then, from the fact that though she had treated this Abbé even rudely while in Paris, on meeting him again—and he like an idiot had brought him to the château—she had received him with open arms? He recalled the slight feeling of surprise he had experienced when, on returning to them, they had appeared to be sworn friends. Did this mean that she had struck her flag, and, in fact, ceased to make further resistance to him? Taken in conjunction with the intimacy which had since continued without intermission, it would seem so. A cold sweat broke out upon his forehead. He had not thought he could feel so keenly about this woman. But she was his wife; she bore his name. And never before had she given him cause to think that she favoured another man.

All at once he became furiously jealous. What he did himself was one thing; what he might do was another. No comparison could be made between them. There never had been such a comparison rationally attempted since the days of Adam. A little looseness on his part might not be quite right—certainly was not right; but then had he happened to live a few centuries earlier, he could have had as many wives as he pleased. But polyandry had practically no place in civilized history. Where he was to blame was in having let her discover his little weaknesses. But how the deuce could he have helped it?

And all this had come about—been brought to a crisis, at all events—in consequence of a stupid *penchant* of his for a peasant girl. Certainly she was pretty, adorably so, and possessed a matchless figure; but, well, what was to be done? What proportions had the affair assumed? Were these two really anything to each other? He could not induce himself to believe that she was false, actually bad. However, in any case, she was to blame. She had made love to the man to begin with, or he would never have so far forgotten himself. Certainly, she was very much in love with this Abbé. He had known *that* the moment he had looked at her. And for the Abbé himself, he was ready to swear that he had never seen such an expression on any human face. Creeping up close to them unobserved, as he had, he had been amazed.

There remained no longer a doubt, then; she did not care for him.

Well, was there not enough to infuriate him in this sensation that he was not beloved? He, Count Rudolf, who had won and trifled away so many hearts, counted for nothing with his own wife—absolutely nothing! And was he the sort of man to submit to this state of things? Hardly. This infernal scoundrel, this Bernard, should rue the day he had dared to raise his eyes to a woman who bore the name of La Jonquières, even if she did forget herself sufficiently to encourage him.

What had a priest to do with love? True, he was a human being. Warm blood coursed through his veins, feeding the fires of affection, tenderness, love of companionship, longing for aught that he might coil about him and cling to; but by the terms of his vow, this blood should have stagnated, this susceptible heart withered. In any case, this man Bernard must leave La Jonquières. His—Count Rudolf's—influence would effect that. It was certainly in his power to ruin him if he pleased. And he might please. This done, madame would come to terms, sue for pardon, do anything to avoid scandal, anything he *told* her to do in future. For the weapon he now grasped could be wielded as he should see fit. And for his method of dealing with this ridiculous pair of lovers, he would strike terror into their hearts when they least expected it.

Were his feelings to be outraged?—his honour tarnished? They should see. In this kind of mood, the Count shut himself up in his room, keeping his anger and jealousy so warm that he forgot something. He had not insisted on returning to La Jonquières so early that evening without a purpose. Lisette was at the bottom of this. But he did not remember her, so full was he of his discovery; and so she cooled her pretty little heels, and stamped them, too, while he slept. Poor Lisette! Honest André would not have treated you so. *He* was not sleeping—could not sleep for thinking of you.

CHAPTER XXV.

So, while the Count slumbered, Lisette fidgeted, fumed, and finally regained her bed with the stealth by which she left it—hugging something tightly though, and this was her newly-conceived wrath.

Beneath the red-tiled roof of the old farm-house amongst the poplars, André Moriseau lay staring at the white-washed walls of his room, and at the ceaseless moving shadows caused by the waving boughs and fluttering leaves of the trees, as the moon soared behind them, and the night wind sped on its way. This waiting, this keeping his own counsel, while love ate him up, was killing him. He was being robbed of his dark-eyed, dark-haired, bewitching little Lisette, by this *grand seigneur*, against whom he could not raise a hand. He was as impotent to contend against him, as the poplar leaves were to cease quivering in the wind. And no good could come to his darling—only dishonour. *Her* dishonour—she whom he worshipped. He pictured the scene. The amorous Lisette, her head turned, yielding, conquered, won. In an agony of mind, this strong man lay thinking, goaded to madness, the sweat rolling down his face.

De Courcelles and his fond girl-bride were alone

with each other, for the fête was over, the château plunged into gloom.

Blanche, blushing for the weakness she had displayed, yet while blushing, rejoicing in the delight she now experienced in living, folded her pretty hands last thing of all, and, borne heavenwards, prayed with the tears in her soft blue eyes, that God would give His angels charge over her.

Louis, afloat upon the high fever of the day's doings, with sparkling eyes, paced between the limits of his four cheerless walls, too excited, too happy to rest for a long while, and finally succumbing to physical exhaustion only to enter into a new life with Blanche. And what bliss, to sink into a delicious slumber and live with her, as he so longed to in reality. During this complete mental transmigration, he joined Blanche where the sky was blue, the sun unclouded. He was her husband. No longer was he fettered. The gulf between them was at last spanned. She was his. He could sit at her dear feet, and listen to her clear, soft voice, pouring out in return all the promptings of his overcharged heart. Those lovely lips he had watched so long, and wanted, were now pressed to his. Her arms encircled him; their hearts beat only for each other. What rapture thus to merge his being in hers, to see no one, to remember nothing, to have no wish but to be always with her. Then, soon, they were not alone. This exquisite woman had developed into a mother. Children played about them—their children. No rough winds shook the blossoming boughs which sheltered these darlings from the dancing sunbeams. The very gravel was smoothed, that the rosy feet of Blanche's dear ones might stray unharmed. His heart was not large enough to hold all the love they inspired. Birds filled the air with their choicest songs, and amidst clear water, the tinkle of fountains, the perfume of flowers and luscious fruits, they rested in harmony, honouring God by the purity of their love—*one*, as He in His goodness had made them. All night long Louis remained steeped in the delights of these vivid conceptions, roused at length from them only by a thundering knock at his door, and his mother's voice, harsh, impatient, bidding him rise.

What a metamorphosis! His little room again, with no Blanche; their dear ones, myths. He, no husband, but Louis Bernard, bound by oath never to become one. He could have wept in his anguish. Everything had been so real, he so rapturously immersed in it. Striving to recover himself, he became willing to accept the dream as a happy omen. "Let me be thankful," he murmured, "I shall see her to-day;" and, like a child anticipating pleasure, he leapt from his bed, flung open his windows, and inhaled the balmy air, in the sweetness of which there was no deception.

Dressing rapidly, full of what the day might have in store for him, he was on the point of hastening downstairs, when something on his black coat sleeve caught his eye. A long, shining thread, like fine-drawn gold, had adhered to the surface of the cloth. It was a single hair of Blanche's. Tenderly he handled it, drawing it through his fingers until he measured its full length. Then, winding it into a little coil, he kissed it tenderly. He would keep it always. Chance had given it to him, and while he breathed he would not part with it. So sacred was this treasure, that, his mother calling to him to tell him that people waited for him in the church, he unhesitatingly placed it between the leaves of his *breviaire*.

Returning from his duty, he ate his breakfast in silence, while the wind blew in through the windows, bulging out the curtains like two balloons, and filling the room with the homely scent of wall-flowers, roses, and mignonette. It was no day for work; he could do nothing conscientiously. So he sauntered off, beneath the cool shade of the trees, through fields waving with ripening grain, scarlet with poppies, and purple with clover, the pleasant rippling of the river in his ears, Blanche in his heart, and God's blue sky above him. The breeze had died away as the heat increased; even the tiny leaves of the silver birch trees were motionless.

In the meadows the cattle no longer browsed, but remained huddled together in the shade, flapping their long ears and whisking their tails in their efforts to rid themselves of the flies. The birds were silent. Only the butterflies and bees stirred freely, fluttering gaily in the warmth, or buzzing with drowsy hum from flower to flower. The blue-bloused workers in the fields paused to wipe their heated brows. The strong scent of the rich land and of the cattle was almost overpowering. This blaze of light deprived Louis of the desire for exercise. He had thought he could enjoy a walk, but his knees felt weak, and, overcome by an irresistible languor, he lay down in the shade with a sigh of intense relief. But though bodily enfeebled by the oppressive condition of the atmosphere, mentally he was restless and imaginative. He endeavoured to recall his vision of the night—to live again in that paradise into which sleep had transported him. And to do this he closed his eyes, shutting out all opposing thoughts and sounds by an effort of will, and striving by these means to pass into the elysium in which he had so delightedly dwelt. Then gradually he forsook the imaginary for the real. Again he was on the terrace at the Château de Courcelles, and Blanche's dulcet tones rang in his ears. She was urging him, appealing to him, and each entreaty was a confession of her weakness, an admission of her love. Almost word for word he repeated all she had said, and surrendering himself to this intoxicating pleasure, it was long ere sober sense asserted itself sufficiently to destroy the flimsy fabric he had indulged in creating.

He had dressed that morning, expectant, hopeful. To what was this due? Had he anything to expect? Literally nothing, unless it was a further development of the alarming malady, which already practically subjugated him. Was he not, then, mad, thus with his eyes open, aware of what he was doing, to merge his being, to surrender himself to the keeping of this woman? By constantly seeing her, her power over him must become more firmly established. Could he be so weak as to court this result? Alas! he could only sigh. He *was* so weak. What had she to offer him, what could he yield to her, that would not be dishonouring to both of them? For this friendship that he had dreamed of was becoming a farce, a mere subterfuge. Did he not well know that it had already been within an ace of overleaping its bounds? Peevishly he turned from the contemplation of this aspect of the affair. Whatever existed could not be altered. He was prepared now and always to close his eyes to everything that suggested severance from Blanche. He owned to himself that the temptations which had already assailed him, had nearly undermined him. Morally, he was at that moment in a tottering condition. And yet he had the audacity to say to himself, "I shall not be so sorely tried again. What am I troubling myself about? When the time comes I shall be sufficiently strong to grapple with all that may present itself." Thus he plainly showed that he had become, as a man, as unmanageable as a rudderless ship. He was completely dominated by the subtle charms of this woman, and whatever came of it, was content to be so.

The shadows were lengthening by the time he had roused himself sufficiently to turn his steps in the direction of home. But while doing so, he became alive to the sensation that some crisis was at hand. The depression which this feeling occasioned him increased, and he found himself unable to stifle the idea.

On arriving at his own door, he was informed that a man was waiting to see him. He went to him at once, and on entering his sitting-room was confronted by André Moriseau.

The sleeplessness and distress of the past night had proved too much for André, and to ease his mind he had come to unburden himself and make his confession.

Louis listened patiently, while, with rustic simplicity, André described his love for Lisette, dwelling upon the happiness they had enjoyed together. Then he drew in the Count, showing how completely he had turned Lisette's head, and transformed her into another woman. Finally, when touching upon the hatred with which he had thus become inspired, his gestures became more threatening. His long pent-up fury obtained the mastery over him, and, with a sweep of his powerful arm, he indicated what he would like to do to this unprincipled aristocrat who had wronged him so atrociously. His brown face became blanched, as the venom hissed and whistled from his lips, and at length, quivering from head to foot, the strong fellow sank at Louis' feet, and in a paroxysm of despair exclaimed—

"I tell you I shall kill him!"

"You will do what?" demanded Louis.

"What I say. I shall kill him."

Horrified, Louis fixed his eyes upon him, as though in that glance he was collecting all the mental power at his command, for the purpose of crushing this terrible desire for vengeance.

"You will not," he at length thundered forth; "you will do no such thing, for God would never forgive such a sin, and I should never absolve you."

At these words, as though willing to defy even the minister of God, André deliberately turned his back upon him and left the room.

"Poor fellow," muttered Louis, in amazement; "to such lengths will love lead one."

Perplexed and troubled beyond measure, Louis felt unfit to go anywhere that day, and it was long ere he could recover himself sufficiently to set off for the château, but he did so, convinced that if goaded to it, André would be capable of any act of violence. And whatever he did, were there not many excuses to be urged in his favour? Was it possible to imagine a situation in which a man might more readily become dangerous? But by what means could he pour oil upon the troubled waters? His hands were to a great extent tied. Still, he should endeavour to warn the Count in some way.

Having pondered deeply, and resolving to do what he could, he entered the château grounds by a wicket-gate, the stable clock chiming five as he crossed the court-yard, his object being to reach the kiosk by this short cut, and there to find Blanche. He was disappointed. The summer-house was empty. In quest of her, he mounted the steps to the terrace, passing in full view of an apartment which was dignified by the appellation of the Count's study. Studious only in the enjoyment of a cigarette and some kümmel, at the sound of footsteps the Count glanced out of the window and saw him.

"That pestilent priest here again," he exclaimed passionately, bringing his fist down upon the table supporting the liqueur with a crash that made the glass dance. "*Mille tonnerres!* I shall astonish him. We shall have a talk together. Go on, monsieur; madame will be expecting you, and you will receive a welcome from me, I think, to-night."

Louis, in blissful ignorance of the anger his presence aroused, paused to admire the view but a few paces from where the Count sat fuming.

A vast globe of crimson, the sun was preparing to pass out of sight behind successive waves of apparently dense woods. A magnificent expanse of corn land and pasturage was tinged with the warm hue, while, in the immediate foreground, the river flashed and eddied, mirroring in its cool depths the superb colouring of the sky.

Old Pierre Chotard was in the act of ferrying over a boat-load of chattering farm women, and their occasional bursts of shrill laughter, mingling with the low, monotonous cooing of the wood pigeons, alone broke the almost oppressive silence.

Proceeding slowly along the terrace, surveying with delight this charming panorama, Louis encountered Blanche seated before an open window. With her little satin-shod feet resting cosily on a footstool, she was negligently scanning a paper which had just arrived from Paris.

His pulse quickened. Suddenly confronting her without a moment's warning, he felt confused, and was only sufficiently master of himself to touch her hand lightly, and ask, pointing to the paper:

"Is there much news?"

"Next to none. A yacht has been upset, and

someone drowned. There has been another railway accident, and the remainder consists of political quibbles, which don't interest me, and advertisements, which I never read."

A certain curious ring in Blanche's voice caused Louis to survey her inquiringly. He had never remarked it before. Scarcely pausing, she continued irrelevantly:

"The Count has been riding all the morning, and now he has shut himself up in his study."

She paused as though expecting a reply.

Louis made none. He was thinking. What was the matter with Blanche? What new phase of her character was he about to become acquainted with? Had he offended her? By tacit consent, the Count was never alluded to. Blanche was too haughty by nature, to condescend to discuss the unfortunate relations which existed between them. Moreover, she not unnaturally thought that in all probability Louis knew far more than she could tell him. On his part, good sense and right feeling had prevented him from attempting to gain any confidences which did not come of her own free will. Why, then, contrary to this established habit, did she thus pointedly allude to him, as though the way in which he chose to employ his time affected her?

"Yes," she went on, "I think it very selfish of a man to spend his life in amusing himself. Practically, I have been alone all day."

"But had you expressed a wish to the contrary, Monsieur le Comte would not have ridden," replied Louis quietly, watching the effect of his words.

"Oh, you don't understand me a bit," she answered irritably.

This time he fancied he did. Her display of petulance was coupled with a certain nervousness and restraint. Her manner towards him was undoubtedly changed. Did she already regret having spoken so affectionately? Had some kind of reaction set in? He had felt so confident, so joyous, and yet so overcome at meeting her again.

"Don't I?—I thought I did," he replied gently.

"Well, in this case, you won't understand. I am put out—disposed, in fact, to abuse everybody and everything. One reason is, that already I find I miss Amy terribly."

"How could I know that?" he asked mildly, but confident, as he spoke, that Amy was in no way responsible for the alterations he believed he detected.

"True, but seriously, this huge house seems depressingly empty now she has gone, and already I have been saying to myself that I must go away, or get some people to fill it. I have studiously shown so many—who have really wished to be with me—the cold shoulder, and now I fancy I am about to repent it."

Louis was momentarily silent. Each instant he was becoming more confident that this random, almost callous way of speaking, was due to those few rapturous sentences she had uttered on the terrace at the Château de Courcelles. And he was right, for with the calmness which came with time and reflection, Blanche had taken herself to task. An introspective examination had elicited the inquiry, "What is to happen when you two meet again?" And she could not answer it, except by saying to herself, "I must strive not to be so weak. It is wrong. I am frightfully to blame." To this reasoning her conduct was due. Pained beyond measure, Louis at once determined to do his utmost to re-establish matters upon their old footing. Unfortunately, though, he began to remonstrate instead of agree.

"But I have never heard you complain of being dull before. And as for leaving La Jonquières, could you think of such a thing at present?"

"I might."

"That is strange. A little while ago you would not have done so."

Blanche bit her lips. Of course this was a direct allusion to their conversation at the Château de Courcelles. She had compromised herself, she was aware. But what right had he to take advantage of her weakness? Was it generous to do so? Her pride instantly revolted.

"No," she said satirically; "perhaps not. But I am so funny. I don't remember what kind of mood I was in then; I am so impulsive, changeable to a degree. But," she added relentingly, "I have not yet had time to get used to being without Amy, and find myself longing to see her again. Is it not human to covet what one cannot have?"

"You said as much when we talked together last. Then I was discontented; *now*—"

"You would say I am."

"A little."

Blanche shrugged her shoulders. She wanted to appear adamantine. But already she was suffering cruelly. It was clear that she could not deceive this man whom she loved so intensely. But still remembering her resolution to place some restraint upon herself, and vaguely dreading every turn in the conversation, she replied:

"Oh, yes, but you are wrong. As I told you, you don't understand me. But come, this is quibbling. I have a new song I should like to hear you sing."

"The idea of everything *new* seems uppermost with you to-day," he answered, each word ringing with the alarm and sadness he felt, in consequence of what seemed her unreasonable behaviour towards him.

She shuddered at the assertion. How she loved him. How she longed to tell him so. And yet they were to talk to each other like this. What was to become of them? Leaving him standing near the window, she proceeded to search amongst the music, and having found the song, she returned to him, holding it in her hand. Catching a glimpse of his face, she was startled at its pallor.

"What is the matter?" she asked, unable to refrain from doing so.

"Nothing."

"But you seem troubled, or are you ill?"

'Neither."

"Then I was mistaken, and you will come and sing. I like to hear you so much."

He brightened perceptibly.

"Yes, you were mistaken, and I will sing, if it gives you the least pleasure."

It was his turn to become frigid now. She glanced at him. Was he offended—hurt? Well, she would cure him presently by some judicious means. Striking the key-note for him, in a low voice he tried the song over.

"No; let us have one of the old ones," he said; "do you mind? I delight in them. I never cease to love anything I have once loved."

The words thrilled her. She did not dare to speak, but with tremulous fingers she began to play the song he set before her. It was a duetto, and as their voices blended in perfect harmony, the astounding mastery which each possessed over the other asserted itself. For a moment Blanche's sight failed her. She could not see the music; but gradually she became subjugated by the desire to speak the amorous words, as it were, to him. Influenced by the voice of this woman he so worshipped, the same feeling laid hold upon him; and becoming intoxicated, telling each other thus how they loved, they surrendered themselves to the delight, and overcome by the delicious sensation, they imagined themselves like their voices, blended in one.

Thus commingled and enrapt, the Count entered, without either of them being aware of the fact. With his figure erect, his face crimson, and his moustache fiercely pointed, he stationed himself some paces behind them. Unconsciously they had drawn closer together. Louis was now bending over her so that his face brushed her hair. Infuriated, the Count made a horrible grimace at the two; then, as the song ended, he advanced, laid his hand on Louis' shoulder, and almost caressingly, certainly without a symptom of anger, said:

"Charming, charming; but let me entreat you to come with me, my dear Abbé. I seem to see nothing of you. My wife monopolizes you so completely. But she will spare you for a little while perhaps—eh? Ah, yes, for the fact is, I am dying to have a chat with you. I have so much to tell you; you will be astonished. And some funny things, too; but these are for your private ear. Come, this way."

Blanche knew the Count too well to be deceived. On the eve of slaying a man, he was of the sort to speak most calmly. She was suddenly aware that he had made a discovery, and meant mischief. But what could she do? Before she could determine, the two men had left the room, for Louis, suspecting nothing, had followed the Count, having merely murmured the briefest apology for his desertion.

Crossing the great hall, and proceeding to the main entrance, the Count pulled up at the head of the flight of steps which led into the park.

"Now, my dear Abbé," he said, raising his voice and extending his arm, "do you see that fence, that wall, yonder? Well, as you know, it separates the La Jonquières estate from the high road to Mezieres. But look, until now, you have been ignorant of the fact that I should be obliged to you if you will be considerate enough to remain on the other side of it. Oh, you have not got your hat and stick, I see. Félix, attend upon Monsieur l'Abbé Bernard."

The lackey he called, who had heard every word, so loudly had the Count spoken, approached as ordered.

Thunderstruck, Louis partly grasped his meaning and the reason; but as if to clear up all doubt, the Count hissed in his ear:

"I keep my wife for myself, monsieur."

Louis recoiled a step or two. Then drew himself up to his full height, appearing to tower above the Count.

"Monsieur le Comte," he said proudly, steadying his voice, "a man may control his words and actions, alas, he cannot always control his heart. I am thankful I have behaved as a gentleman. With truth you cannot say as much, for before your servants, you have needlessly insulted a man whose cloth alone prevents him from striking you to the earth."

"*Mille tonnerres!* threats, such insolence, such d—d insolence from—"

"You may live to regret your conduct, Monsieur le Comte; but henceforth we are strangers."

Without another word, deaf to a volley of execrations and threats which the now infuriated Count hurled at him, with firm tread Louis passed down the massive stone steps, and crossing the park, disappeared without once turning his head.

CHAPTER XXVI.

HUMILIATED to the dust, Louis continued his course through the La Jonquières' grounds. Having left them behind him, and feeling that no longer was he treading upon soil that scorched him, he became unconscious of where he was going. His head sank upon his chest; he was aware only of having received a crushing blow, the effect of which was such as to rob him of all ideas. His brain felt benumbed. He seemed to have lost the power to think. In this condition he wandered on, his steps instinctively turning in a contrary direction to that in which lay his home. For what comfort could he look for from that quarter, or indeed from any? No one would be likely to sympathize with him.

When at length he began to regain possession of himself, he became aware that he stood within a few paces of the spot where, previous to André's confession, he had rested, reasoned, and attempted so persistently to recall his dream. But now, in place of the sunlight, the fields of grain were silvered by the rising moon. The woods which bounded the fertile champaign, appeared as black as though composed of ink. Flowing placidly between its rich banks, the river pursued its tortuous course, while a family of swans were energetically feeding within the shadow of the old willow, beneath which he had sat. Except that it was night instead of day, all was the same. His circumstances alone had changed. When last he had sat there, he had been so hopeful, and now— Again he seated himself beneath the dome of leaves, endeavouring to analyze and comprehend the position in which he found himself.

His first thought was of Blanche. What would she think? Had he sunk in her estimation? Would she be tempted to turn against him? That was unlikely. But their happiness was destroyed. No longer would they be able to see each other. He could never set foot on soil that was owned by the Count of La Jonquières. All that was over. But neither would she be able to come to him. Worse—he was in the Count's power. His influence with the bishop of the diocese would be sufficient to compel him to leave the place. And then what was to become of him? He could never hope to see this woman, whose existence furnished him with almost his sole wish to live. Certainly death would be sweeter than perpetual banishment from her. And yet this banishment was at hand.

He had thoroughly aroused the Count's enmity. It was unlikely that he would allow him to remain where he was. Besides, people would talk. For at least one servant had witnessed his degradation. His presumption would provoke laughter, and for his weakness he would be despised. Could he endure that? And supposing that for Blanche's sake the Count should exert himself to prevent a scandal —though even in spite of his efforts there was sure to be a leakage somewhere—could he support the anguish of being close to her, of breathing the same atmosphere, and, from his very window, of looking upon the home where she dwelt, without being permitted to approach her?

Such a weight would be more than he could bear. Yet, it would be preferable to quitting La Jonquières.

If the Count chose to be vindictive, he was practically ruined; but he scarcely thought upon that. All misfortunes were dwarfed, completely driven out of his head, when contrasted with such a disaster as separation from Blanche. Reason how he would, no other termination to the affair seemed probable, even possible.

There could be no hope of living the Count's enmity down, and while it lasted, Blanche and he were practically severed. Had they been in Paris they could have contrived to see each other, sometimes, at least; but here, in La Jonquières where a man's cow could not calve without the whole village talking of it, no room existed for such a hope. They would never be able to meet, and moreover, after a fierce fight against the inevitable, he would be compelled to bid farewell to the place.

As this reflection came home to him in all its brutal force, he could no longer restrain his grief; and while the river, urged by the breeze, lapped the far-spreading willow roots, and the swans croaked dismally to each other, this man, utterly undone, wept as though his heart would break. Weakened, his face drenched with tears, at that instant a thought flashed upon him which caused him to leap to his feet. It was as though the tempter, finding him thus enfeebled, seized the opportunity to enter into him. His fears for the Count's safety, in consequence of André's malignity, had undergone this contortion—might it not be as well if the Count were out of the way, might he (Louis) not even expedite matters by some means, because in that case his own prospects would at once become bright again.

So appalled was he by this terrible idea, and

so horrified that he should be capable of conceiving such villainy, that he decided to warn the Count by some means without further delay. He could divulge nothing that had been confided to him, but it was in his power to put the Count on his guard by means of a few simple lines, which he might hope would be understood by this man who had so insulted him. A shudder ran through him. He trembled from head to foot.

Had it come to this, that because he was in despair, he was such a scoundrel that he could contemplate benefiting by a murder. The place seemed fatal to him. Some evil spirit dwelt beneath that dense dome of waving boughs. With a scared glance about him, he quitted the shelter of the tree, and for the instant, forgetting his own cares, set out in the direction of home, engaged in again deliberating how he should apprize the Count of this great danger. No ill-will lurked in his nature. Besides, he was to blame. He had no right to love Blanche. But if he had done harm, here was an opportunity to do good. As though to urge him in his resolution, on passing the Widow Lemaitre's door, who should he see leaning against the wall, smoking his pipe and talking to the old woman, who was knitting briskly, but André Moriseau. Ready to sink into the ground at the sight of anyone who knew him, Louis bent his head, relieved when his own roof hid him from sight. Shutting himself up in his room, he placed pens and paper before him, and seating himself, became thoughtful.

The letter must not contain a syllable which the Count could mistake for an attempt to patch up the rupture. That would be useless, as well as harmful to his pride. This man was powerful, and hated him. Well, though trying to render him a great service, it should be made plain that he asked nothing. Weak he was, because he was poor, but he was not to be trodden under foot. Finally, after much deliberation, he wrote very plainly:

"Monsieur le Comte,—In view of our irreconcilable quarrel, you may deem me presumptuous for addressing you. I am, however, prepared to incur your further displeasure, should these lines awaken it, since I feel compelled to send you this warning, which, I have no doubt will be sufficiently intelligible. It is this. Should you persist in your present conduct, which cannot fail to create a great scandal, I must warn you that your life is in danger. It now remains for you to act as you may think proper. Believe me, Monsieur le Comte, your most humble servant in O.D.L., "Louis Bernard."

After reading this note carefully, he addressed an envelope, sealed it, and, as a relief to his mind, despatched it with his own hand. Having done this, he considered himself free to think over his own grievances. And so, through the long night, with his brain on fire, despairing as he had never thought to despair, the daylight found him, pale and sleepless, tortured and broken-spirited. He recoiled from his own reflection. Such ravages had these few hours made, that his mother held up her hands in amazement on beholding him. Obliged to say something, he asserted that he felt unwell; but it was a trifling indisposition which would pass as quickly as it had come. That was all.

He possessed one hope that morning. It was Sunday, and Blanche usually attended High Mass at ten. She was in the habit of collecting with a little velvet bag, upon which was embroidered the La Jonquières' arms; and of repeating the formula as she passed before the people, "For the poor, if you please." Would she be there? Perhaps she might come alone, and then when she repaired to the sacristy to hand in the accounts, he would be enabled to speak to her for a few moments without provoking criticism, even from the most ill-natured.

An opportunity would thus present itself for a brief interchange of ideas. He would learn from her own lips how she was disposed towards him. Trusting that this might be so, he entered the church earlier than usual. At length the bell began to ring, and singly, or in twos and threes, the sprinkling of well-to-do farmers, their wives, and the customary assemblage of bronzed, hard-featured peasants, streamed into the place.

Louis listened, as in a dream, to the grating of the chairs as they were moved, and to the whispered salutations and discussions. The building, with its arched roof, its stained glass windows, its niches, pictures of saints, and oaken confessional boxes, was not seen by him. A gallery, supported upon four iron pillars, ran across the entire foot of the edifice, and it was beneath that gallery, between those pillars where was the entrance door, that his eyes and attention were fixed. Between the heads and shoulders of the people, a glimpse of the river—blue as the sky, and flashing in the sunlight—was to be had; but his imagination halted before a tall, graceful form, surmounted by a compactly-shaped head, adorning which, wavy golden tresses floated, forming an aureole that no painter could match with his pigment. The fair face, with its clear features and delicate colouring, was conjured before him; he could even see, peeping from beneath the long skirts, two little feet, which, as they advanced up the aisle, made music in his ears.

But suddenly the bell ceased tolling, and the beadle, with silver-headed cane in hand, dispelled his vision as he closed the door.

Blanche had not come. As he realized this, a mist clouded his sight, and a confused mass of objects swam before him. But soon, by a supreme effort of will, and the remembrance that this was no place in which to display his weakness, he went through the service, enduring, throughout, the anguish of imagining that all was known, and that every eye was fixed upon him with varied expressions of scorn and ridicule.

Then, his duty over, in despair he hastened to hide himself, auguring the heaviest misfortune in consequence of the absence of every member of the De la Jonquières family.

CHAPTER XXVII.

HAVING rid himself of Louis, the Count had cooled down, and although there had been a scene between Blanche and himself, summed up, his utterances amounted to this : " Come, we have both been wrong. Let us square matters. I assure you I am more than willing." To do him justice, his reflections having shown him that he was much to blame—at last—he was disposed to admit it ; and the spur which impelled him in this direction most effectually, was jealousy.

This suddenly awakened sensation seemed to have warmed his heart. When Blanche had been so easy to come by, he did not want her. Now that someone else was approaching unpleasantly near, he began to discover in her a host of good qualities, to see in himself a fool, bent upon throwing away happiness by the indulgence of a stupid liaison with a vulgar peasant girl, and to be keenly desirous of effecting a reconciliation.

Louis Bernard despatched to the other side of France—and he would take good care to see to that—what was to prevent Blanche and himself from coming together again? Not Lisette, certainly. He was not disposed to cling too tightly to her. Matters were becoming too serious for trifling, and it was time he set himself to mend them, if mended they were ever to be. Blanche was good, he was sure of that; and, if he were honest, a deuced deal too good for him. In due course she would listen to reason. Lurking in her heart, there must remain the remnants, at least, of her love for him. It certainly had existed, and, to some extent, he was prepared to lay himself out to foster and keep it.

He did not pause to ask himself how long these new ideas of his were likely to last—it never occurred to him. But, with vigorous strokes, he at once set about clearing away the obstacles to their realization; and, as a start, he took steps to secure Louis' removal. Having done this, he exerted himself to pacify his rebellious wife. When Louis' letter came, he instantly grasped its meaning, and was disposed to think less revengefully of him; but he pocketed it, without, of course, saying anything to Blanche. He was disposed to pooh-pooh the danger it was intended to indicate, but he shook hands with himself over the fact that the policy he had determined upon was not opposed to the advice it contained. Then, spending his time as his new desires necessitated, he dismissed the matter from his mind.

In this mental condition, after *déjeuner* one day, he sallied forth, accompanied by his inseparable companions, the two spaniels, intending to scour the country for the sake of exercise, and, if the fit seized him, of fishing in a small mere which lay in a distant corner of the estate. This mere he had, at great cost and trouble, stocked with trout, and, in furtherance of the gentle piscatorial art, upon its mossy banks he had erected a substantial shelter in the form of a summer-house, reared upon a solid stone foundation.

This agreeable retreat which commanded a charming view, was furnished almost as luxuriously as the kiosk, the floor being covered with four large lion-skins, the walls devoted to neatly-contrived cases, in which were rods, tackle, and some few trophies of the chase, which, like the lion-skins, had fallen to the Count's gun during his wanderings abroad, in his earlier days. An admirable kind of stove, ornamented with expensive blue Delft tiles, occupied the centre, and to this comfortable place in which to lounge, two persons alone possessed a key—the Count and his head *garde-chasse*. Laughing at the amusing energy and playfulness of his silky-coated pets, and enjoying the invigorating freshness of the atmosphere, this *grand seigneur* strode through the ferns, beneath his ancestral timber, seeming, in truth, lord of all he surveyed.

He was oppressed with very few cares that afternoon — probably because he was planning to do right. He and Blanche would hit it off after all. He felt as vigorous as a young buck, and after a little while, when De Courcelles' honeymoon was over, and he had moped and made love to his heart's content, together they would issue invitations to a number of mutual friends, charming people, and in the coming glorious autumn weather, they would have the very best of good times. De Courcelles was an excellent fellow after all. They understood each other perfectly, and he was glad that he had married Amy. The little hussy had feathered her nest to some purpose. But he had seen how it would be from the first. Now he had only to wish them luck. Thus amiably disposed, after having made a wide *détour*, the Count reached the mere, discovered that a nice breeze ruffled the surface, and with the excitement of a boy, put his rod together and began to fish. Evidently the finny tribe were voraciously inclined, for they leapt to the bait. The sun was descending westward in saffron and polychromatic hues, which were reproduced with exquisite softness and beauty of effect by the water, which sparkled and flashed as though composed of liquid gold. Some moor-hens clucked and dived amidst the lilies and broad-leaved flags, a woodpecker tapped monotonously upon the trunk of a neighbouring copper beech, while every now and then a rabbit rustled in the undergrowth, or showed its white tail like a flash of light, as the two spaniels, who were enjoying themselves hugely, chased it to its home.

The Count had succeeded in hooking a large fish, and was displaying his skill in handling it. Immediately at his back, a small plantation of silver birch trees reared their delicately tinted stems. A few moments before he had succeeded in hooking his fish, these thin straight trunks had been threaded by a human form and two sharp eyes had scrutinized him through the interlacing boughs. After a while the eyes disappeared, and the foliage was parted by a clouded gun barrel, which quivered and then became steady. There was a flash, a detonation, and, flinging his arms heavenward, the Count sank heavily to the ground. The large fish contrived to swim off triumphantly with rod and line, for a few moments there was a scare amongst the birds, and then, but for the sound of a stealthily retreating footfall in the thick brake, and the whining of the dogs who had returned to their master, the silence was profound.

CHAPTER XXVIII.

THAT night, the *chef* at the Château de la Jonquières was in despair. Dinner had been kept waiting, spoiled in fact. Thinking that probably the Count was somewhere near at hand, Blanche had ordered the big bell to be rung, and then, to keep up appearances, though she could scarcely eat a morsel, she sat down and made a pretence of discussing the gloomy meal. She was not anxious about the Count. He had no place in her mind. It was a relief to her to be alone. And the moment she considered that she had enacted the farce of eating satisfactorily, she hastened to avail herself of the perfect seclusion to be found only in her own room.

With a sigh of supreme relief, she closed the door which protected her from the inquisitive gaze of the servants, and began to indulge in her own painful reflections. She had met the Count's attacks with a coolness, born of the consciousness that whatever her faults were, she was more sinned against than sinning. What right had this man, who had occasioned her so much suffering, to upbraid her? He had himself to thank for whatever had happened. She did not mind his abuse, any more than she desired his advances. Beyond considering that he had behaved brutally to Louis, she even bore him no malice. Her sentiments towards him might be summed up in one word, indifference. Louis absorbed her. Her mind was on the rack. What was to become of their friendship, of their affection for each other? Were they to be separated, and was she to drag out her days, chained to this man whom the law called her husband?

Worse even, though that was sufficient to distract her—was Louis to be ruined by that husband? Poor, and comparatively speaking helpless, who was to deliver him? The Count's influence would undermine him, and he would be regarded by his bishop as a black sheep. Thus weighed down, and with the additional incubus of a father and mother to support, what would become of him? It was not of herself she thought—though if they were torn from each other, she felt that her heart would break—but it was of the misery she had brought upon him. Ever since she had quitted the peaceful shelter of the Convent of the Sacred Heart, she had been the shuttlecock of misfortune. And now this man, whose only sin was the great love he bore her, was to suffer through her. How he had been insulted because of that love which he had never allowed himself to own.

By a comprehensive retrospective glance, she reviewed the main features of her life. Her mother's early death. Her father wedded to his military career, his gaiety perhaps—she did not know—anxious, at any price, to obtain entire freedom from the responsibility of looking after a brace of daughters. Her quiet serenity at the convent, terminating with his unexpected return from abroad. Her marriage to the Count, and fast following upon it, the gradual destruction of her peace of mind. Unfortunate throughout, she had now communicated her ill-luck to the being who had come into her life, at the moment when she had felt weakest and most in need of support.

She could do nothing but blame herself. She ought to have foreseen this ending. And Louis was so placed that she was powerless. She had no children. The Count was not in love with her. Had this man been free, she would have cast in her lot with him in the face of the world, and of all it could do or say. To have made him happy, as she felt she was capable of doing, she would have sacrificed herself without a moment's hesitation. Weighed in the balance, what was name or fame compared with the abandonment, the destruction, of a love such as she knew linked them together? But she was not permitted to do this. Louis was fettered, and there was no hope of breaking the chains which bound him. She had only one comfort. She possessed money, more than a thousand pounds yearly, thanks to the affection of the aunt who had watched over Amy until death had claimed her. Well, with this money, and a clever agent to help her, she could at least contrive so that Louis should not want. This was a great consolation.

When she thought of herself she despaired. Her mind had become benumbed by the contemplation of the cheerlessness of the iron walls within which Fate confined her. She could not go to Louis, and was afraid even to communicate with him, lest such conduct should occasion comment, and injure him. Helpless, there was nothing left for her but to endure her suffering, waiting for she knew not what. Thus, surrounded by every comfort, her heart was lacerated. Sitting there in that condition, her reflections were disturbed by a knock, and with it, a voice, exclaiming excitedly:

"Madame la Comtesse! Madame! For God's sake, come!"

She sprang to the door, and, on opening it, was confronted by old Pépin, the steward of the château, who like his fathers before him, had grown gray in the service of the Counts of La Jonquières.

"What is it, Pépin?" she demanded, with admirable composure, though alarmed at the ashen hue of the man's face.

"Oh, madame, forgive my boldness. But Monsieur le Comte—it is awful. They have carried him home. . . . Think of that. Come, they have him downstairs—oh, dear madame—the master—the dear master."

And, unable to control himself, tears coursed freely down the old fellow's hale but wrinkled cheeks.

Feeling that some calamity had overtaken her, Blanche was half-way down the grand staircase while he was yet talking and gesticulating. At the foot of it, in the hall, a group of the servants were gathered, who, with two tall gamekeepers, dressed in rough shooting attire, were bending over an object, the sight of which made her feel faint. The Count, with the pallid majesty of death stamped upon his face, lay stretched upon his back. On seeing her, the men doffed their caps, while some of the women-servants, who already had their aprons to their eyes, addressed her in frightened accents. Tremulous, but making an heroic effort to be calm, Blanche knelt over the prostrate figure. She raised a hand, and its cold dead weight thrilled her with awe. She attempted to feel for the pulse, but, recognising her own ignorance, and that this was a time to act, and not to give way to childishness, she addressed the men.

"Raise him up, and carry him into the study.

And here, my good girl, run to the stable and tell them to gallop to Mezieres for the doctor."

"The gendarmes should know of this, too, Madame la Comtesse," stammered old Pépin.

"The gendarmes! Why?"

"Because, Madame la Comtesse, the ruffians have shot Monsieur le Comte in the back."

"Shot him. Oh, God!"

"Yes, Madame la Comtesse," began the taller of the keepers; "if you please, as my mate and I were going home by the end of the west mere, we heard the dogs howling, and—"

"Yes, yes, that will do," Blanche interrupted.

It was hideous to her to listen to the horrible details. She could not endure it just then. But she was equal to one more effort in the presence of these people, so touching Pépin on the shoulder she said:

"Tell the man to ride his hardest. Say to him that Monsieur le Comte's life is at stake."

"And the gendarmes, Madame la Comtesse," demanded Pépin tenaciously.

Blanche made no answer, for with her own hands she was endeavouring to pour some brandy between the Count's clenched teeth. Then, as the hopelessness of her task dawned upon her, she broke down, and sobbing, allowed herself to be led from the room.

Towards midnight the doctor arrived, made his examination, and declared that the Count had been dead some hours. The wound he had received must quickly have proved fatal. "But," he added, repeating Pépin's opinion, "the gendarmes must be communicated with at once. I can do nothing. This is a case for them."

Blanche did not see him. What was the use? As she had leant over that rigid form, and gazed upon those pallid features, she had realized that she was in the presence of death. And the expression of that inanimate face had tugged at her heart-strings, stirring within her the dregs of her early love, appealing to all that was womanly in her. One blow upon another seemed to be aimed at her. What was to come next?

In that great silent château she lay prostrate, remembering no longer the wrongs she had sustained, thinking only of all the hard words and unkind acts she had been guilty of, for now, atonement or obliteration was impossible. Unable to close her eyes, she continued to reproach herself unceasingly, dwelling tenaciously upon all the goodness and kindness the Count had ever displayed. She had been woefully to blame. How could she reason otherwise? One, only, could not be guilty. Had she been less exacting, more forgiving, the result would have been different. And whilst she taxed herself thus severely, the sun began to climb upwards, penetrating the thick woods, the rabbits again made their appearance, playing and nibbling the crisp dew-laden grass, and the birds clamoured noisily or carolled sweetly, while a few of the yet hungry ones alighted upon the window-sill within a few paces of the dead man, pecking contentedly some crumbs of biscuit, which the lifeless hand had carelessly scattered but yesterday.

Yes, Count Rudolf, for you the structure of Time has suddenly crumbled. And such a collapse seemed so far off only yesterday. Were you prepared to understand the problem you were so instantaneously called upon to solve?

The moment it was possible, Blanche despatched another mounted messenger, but this one to the Château de Courcelles, entreating Amy to come to her. And with the echoing hoofs, as the excited servant spurred through the roughly-paved street, La Jonquières awoke to turn and twist, to distort and wonder what had happened.

Quite early in the day, Monsieur Loubet, a zealous and ambitious police officer from Mezieres, accompanied by two detectives, disguised as well-to-do farmers, arrived at the château. Having examined the papers and effects found upon the body, and been aided by Blanche's instructions in every way, Loubet locked up the study, put the key in his pocket, and with a grim smile, went off to survey the scene of the tragedy.

Towards four in the afternoon, Blanche had the satisfaction of straining Amy to her bosom. Between her exclamations of horror and expressions of sympathy, she explained that she and the Baron had set off as soon as they had breakfasted and succeeded in putting a few odds and ends together.

And they had come to stay. Leo was so good. He had not hesitated. They had no intention of leaving her, but would remain as long as she might wish. Come, she must be comforted. And when Blanche caught sight of the Baron, grave, but so kind, and echoing with sober satisfaction his young wife's words, she experienced a sensation of profound relief, feeling that instead of being alone, two staunch friends would be with her, and with tears of gratitude she assured them that already her heart began to feel warmer.

T

CHAPTER XXIX.

WITH Blanche's failure to attend mass, Louis had lost heart. He shrank altogether from meeting the public gaze, and, with the exception of the duties his position imposed upon him, went nowhere, until the friendly dusk enabled him to breathe the strong air and cool his heated brow without fear of recognition. His unremitting acts of charity and sympathetic visits were all at once completely abandoned, and those who had grown accustomed to look for him, and set store by his kind words and pleasant smiles, were not the only ones who wondered what had come over the Abbé.

There were those who had always preferred to rank themselves as his enemies, and now, with slander to employ their tongues upon, these people found themselves busy. His friendship with the inmates of the château had from the first been unfavourably commented upon. What did he want there? What good could come of it? An occasional visit, of course, he was bound to pay, but that was no reason why he should be there everlastingly. They had foreseen what would be the upshot, and now that rumours were being circulated, connecting Louis' and Blanche's names, these wiseacres became triumphantly garrulous. There was no longer any reason why they should hold their tongues, since their prognostications were, they contended, established facts. They dwelt upon his changed appearance during the winter, when Madame la Comtesse had betaken herself to Paris. But, *ah, oui!* had he not spread his plumage, like a bird in the sunshine, the moment she returned? At the sight of her petticoats he had grown younger again by ten years. Well, she was lovely enough to turn any man's head. But a priest—and what was she thinking of? Of course, everyone knew what the Count was. He was one of those men who had an eye for every pretty face; so that the poor lady, though she had never been heard to own it—being a deal too proud—was certainly not happy.

When the news of the Count's terrible fate was announced, La Jonquières was shaken to its foundations. The good folk no longer had any time for sleeping and blinking in the sunlight. They had too much to talk about. And it was amongst this babel of tongues—this healthy, sun-tanned ignorance—that Monsieur Loubet, the smart and zealous police-officer, found himself let loose. Here was his chance. And was it not a good one? If he could only succeed in bringing the Count's murderer to justice, his future was assured, he told himself. So, aided by his myrmidons, he was not slow to go to work.

When, in a roundabout way, the news of the Count's death came to Louis, he experienced a painful shock. It was terrible to be told that a man in the prime of life had been stricken down in this deliberate fashion. So his warning had been of no use. It had come too late. But, at all events, he had done his best, and was in no way to blame for the turn affairs had taken. His own gain he forgot in his genuine concern. Of late he had scarcely ventured from his door, but excited and anxious to learn what was being said, he resolved to brave what he knew would at least amount to unkind scrutiny. On making his appearance, some of the people looked askance at him, from others he received a sober " Bon jour, monsieur," and thus threading his way along the narrow street, which had already assumed a bustling aspect, being blocked with chattering farmers in their rough spring-carts, Louis came face to face with Pierre Chotard.

"This is sad news. A terrible calamity, indeed," he remarked.

"Eh, yes, Monsieur l'Abbé," replied the old fellow, with the air of a man who had much rather be let alone.

"Tell me. What have you heard? How did it happen?"

"Monsieur le Comte has been shot, that is all, Monsieur l'Abbé."

"Oh, of course, yes; but by whom?"

"Ah! that is what the gendarmes would like to find out."

"And do they think they will?"

"Ah! what they *think* is a puzzle they'll keep to themselves."

"But you have heard no rumour?" persisted Louis, thinking of André, and as sorry for the handsome young farmer, as he was that the Count was dead.

"Rumours, Monsieur l'Abbé, oh yes, there are plenty going about," replied Chotard, eyeing him slyly, while mopping his face with a red cotton handkerchief.

"Well, but do they throw no light upon the affair?" inquired Louis nervously, and deciding to ask no more questions.

"None, Monsieur l'Abbé. You see, it's like this.

We *think* a good bit, we folks down about the ferry here, but we only *know* what comes from the château, so that all I could tell, monsieur, would be second-hand news."

There was no mistaking the meaning of this cunning remark, and Louis felt himself grow crimson as he turned upon his heel. Shrinking from passing back along the street through the knots of gossiping people, which, unless he made a wide *détour*, was his only way home, Louis walked slowly on midst the thick, white dust, his face turned towards Mezieres. He regretted having come out. Pierre Chotard had as good as said, "Why do you ask me? Why don't you go to the château? They will tell you. Ah, you would like to; but unfortunately you can't, and do you think we don't know it?" Why had he subjected himself to these insinuations? It was foolish in the extreme. He might have known how it would be. And he was disgraced. No one had any respect for him. He was an outcast in the opinion of every member of this little community. Hot tears smeared his cheeks, and fell upon his black coat. Dashing them aside, he defended himself by reflecting that if it had all to come over again, he should do as he had done. Blanche's golden tresses and fair face arose before him, and, clasping his hands together in an agony of spirit, he murmured aloud, "As God hears me, being flesh and blood, I could only love her. And if I have done harm in His sight, I am content to suffer." A carriage approaching enveloped in dust, he stepped aside on to the turf which fringed the road. But when abreast of him the carriage stopped. De Courcelles alighted, bade the coachman drive on to the château, and then joined him.

"My dear Abbé," he began, in his kindest manner,

"notwithstanding everything, I am delighted to see you."

Becoming quite pale, Louis could hardly answer. What did he mean? The Count's untimely end, second thoughts suggested. With a resolute effort he mastered his emotion.

"And I, Monsieur le Baron—I, too, am delighted."

"I have just come from Mezieres, where I have had a long conversation with poor De la Jonquières' solicitor. Who would have imagined that this blow would come upon us when last we met? A fête one day, a funeral the next. That is what happens around one—eh?"

"Alas, it is so, Monsieur le Baron."

"What do you think of it all? Who has done it?"

Louis reflected. What a terrible position was his. To know so much, and yet to be bound by the most solemn oath to keep silence.

"The whole *arrondissement* is discussing that question, Monsieur le Baron," he answered evasively.

"And can make nothing of it. Well, the gendarmes will sift it out, I think. Monsieur Loubet pretends to know a good deal already. They say he is shrewd and believes in himself, which is a good thing if it does not develop into a vice. Clever people sometimes overreach themselves."

"That's true; they are apt to imagine that they can afford to become careless. But, Monsieur le Baron, forgive me. I have been remiss in the extreme. My mind is in such a whirl. Madame la Baronne is, I trust, in good health?"

"Eh, yes, as well as I am. But she is here. Come along with me and satisfy yourself. You are a great favourite, I can assure you."

"Then I have much to be proud of, Monsieur le Baron. But I must entreat you to excuse me, since

I could not present myself before Madame la Baronne in this condition, covered with dust and untidy as I am."

"How ridiculous, my dear Abbé. A little dust must never part old friends. Besides, look at me. I am in precisely the same plight. Come along!"

And already the impulsive Baron linked his arm through Louis', and had drawn him a step or two in the direction of the château. Greatly agitated, Louis resisted, his heart wrung by his intense longing to see Blanche, and his pride, which forbade him to return whence he had been dismissed in the presence of the very servants. Deciding, he replied :

"Indeed, but Monsieur le Baron, I have some few calls to make, and so, for the moment, it is impossible for me to avail myself of the pleasure you offer me."

"Oh, very well," said De Courcelles, disengaging his arm, "if you can't, there's an end of it; but we shall expect you soon, mind."

With a pleasant nod he strode away towards the château, disappearing through the little gate from which the Count had issued, on the night when Blanche had discovered his amour with Lisette. Soon after the *fracas* with the Count, De Courcelles had noticed Louis' absence. It was odd in the extreme, that a man who was always to be found at the château, should have ceased to visit there, and particularly at such a time. His pressing invitation had been made in accordance with these speculations. Louis' refusal, of course, stimulated his curiosity. Something had happened, and he resolved to learn what that something was.

Terribly dejected, Louis turned on his heel, quickened his pace, and, with his cheeks burning, threaded his way amidst the vehicles and groups of people, never once lifting his head until he had gained the shelter of his own roof.

CHAPTER XXX.

ABOUT noon on the following day, La Jonquières became the centre of increased animation. The rumour had spread through the *arrondissement* that Monsieur Loubet had got upon the track of the murderer. The immediate consequence was, that every small farmer or peasant labourer who could lay aside his work, and start for the hamlet, had done so.

The landlord of the "Repos des Artistes," an *auberge* three doors beyond the Chotards' house, was bursting with good spirits. The influx of people was enriching him nicely. He already began to say to himself, "If this continues, I shall soon have enough to live upon. I shall retire." And the weather was simply delightful.

The great cliff in the rear of the village had never seemed more exquisitely tinted with delicate shades of green, pearly gray, and patches of bright-coloured flowers, which helped to impregnate the air with a rich, almost overpowering scent. The red roofs of the houses had never appeared cleaner and brighter, and the smoke ascended in straight blue shafts, for there was not enough wind to ruffle the surface of the river, upon which the sun beat in unobscured splendour.

At two o'clock there was a stir amongst the men and women, who, seated in their carts drawn aside, were laughing, chatting, and, in some cases, indulging in boisterous mirth.

This stir was occasioned by the appearance of Monsieur Loubet, who was seen to emerge from the "Repos des Artistes," cross the street to Louis Bernard's house, knock there, and gain admittance. Louis himself received him.

"Monsieur l'Abbé," Loubet said, when they were alone together, "will you do me the favour to walk with me as far as the Château de la Jonquières?"

"For what purpose, monsieur?" demanded Louis collectedly.

"Because the law requires it, Monsieur l'Abbé," replied Loubet, in dignified tones.

"The law! How so, monsieur?"

"Well, perhaps I had better speak plainly. Monsieur l'Abbé Bernard, it is my duty to arrest you."

Amazed, but not in the least alarmed, Louis inquired upon what charge.

"Upon the charge of having murdered, or conspired to murder, Monsieur le Comte de la Jonquières. The warrant, which has been delayed, is now in my pocket."

"But—" began Louis dumbfounded.

"I assure you, Monsieur l'Abbé, remonstrance is useless. Will you come, or—"

Louis bowed his head. His speech was dried up with astonishment and utter confusion. But was it dignified to argue with this man? He must go. It was enough. To the Château de la Jonquières, though, of all places, and under such circumstances.

Once more he ventured to expostulate.

"Let me entreat you, monsieur, not to compel me

to accompany you to the château. You do not know how strong are my reasons against—"

"Pardon me, Monsieur l'Abbé," interrupted Loubet, with undisguised relish, "but that is exactly what I do happen to know. Your quarrel with Monsieur le Comte, for instance; but there, my time is precious. I am anxious to avoid any noise or scandal. You have only to give me your word that you will make no resistance, and we can walk quietly to the château without anyone understanding why we are together. None but my own men are aware why I am here. But in case of resistance, or a disturbance of any kind, I have some gendarmes—"

Without another word Louis put on his hat, and, strengthened by the knowledge that he was being deeply wronged, quitted his house with the commissary. Their appearance together was the signal for every eye to be levelled at them. Heads were thrust out of windows, and the doorways were filled. People whispered, laughed, or became serious. Louis felt that he was the object of their criticism, while, as though to increase his discomfiture, some ill-bred boys shouted:

"Oh, look at Monsieur l'Abbé."

Pierre Chotard, who had gained some information, rushed from the "Repos des Artistes" to his cottage, and cried excitedly to Lisette:

"What do you think? Loubet has arrested Monsieur l'Abbé Bernard."

Then, without waiting for an answer, anxious to lose none of the fun, he stepped outside to watch.

Lisette ran upstairs and stared through her window, around which the roses again blossomed. Secretly she had done nothing but cry since the Count's death. She had cared for him as much as she was capable of caring for any man. Besides, what had become of all her fine plans for the future? Was it not heart-breaking?

The reason why Louis Bernard and Monsieur Loubet were together, spreading like wild-fire, there was suddenly a clamour of voices, and a rush was made by the mob to close up in the rear of the police-officer and his prisoner. But this manœuvre was at once defeated. A handful of mounted police, who had been stationed near the château gates, bore the disorderly rabble back, and then, in a cloud of dust, the horses champing their bits, the accoutrements glittering in the sunlight, they formed up, and at a walk followed closely behind Louis and his captor.

Monsieur Loubet had acted with such secrecy that even De Courcelles knew nothing of his plans. Blanche had given instructions that all his wishes should be attended to; and then, deciding that her presence was useless, she obtained the perfect seclusion she desired, by retiring to the small drawing-room which adjoined her bedroom. Here the Baron and Amy were sitting with her, when the clattering hoofs of the mounted police attracted their attention. Blanche, who at once went to the window, felt petrified. There at her feet was Louis, approaching with Monsieur Loubet, a formidable array of police acting as a sort of rear-guard. All colour deserting her cheeks, her eyes riveted upon the advancing cortège, she gasped out her feelings.

"What does this mean?"

The Baron and Amy sprang to her side.

"What is it, Countess?" exclaimed De Courcelles. Then, his own eyesight replying to his question, he added, "Deuce take me if I can answer you. The Abbé is evidently arrested."

"Arrested!" screamed Blanche, forgetting that De Courcelles' glance was fixed upon her, and that she was extremely indiscrete. Astonished and alarmed, he saw that the whole expression of her face had changed, and that she had suddenly become perfectly livid. Surveying her searchingly, De Courcelles almost immediately became possessed of her secret. "So you love the Abbé," he at once said to himself. Then, fearing that she might swoon, he hastened to add aloud:

"How foolish of me. Of course, I must be mistaken. What reason could exist for such a step?"

"What reason, indeed!" articulated Blanche feebly, and with an immense effort to control herself. "There must be some mistake."

"Go and see at once, Leo," suggested Amy energetically.

"All right, little one," he replied affectionately, "I'll pop down, see what's up, and be back with you in a moment," and away he went.

Encountering Louis and Loubet entering the château, De Courcelles stepped up to Louis, grasped his hand, and, turning to Loubet, demanded an explanation.

"In the execution of my duty, Monsieur le Baron," the police officer hastened to reply, "I have arrested Monsieur l'Abbé Bernard."

"But there can be no reason for such a step," exclaimed De Courcelles excitedly. "Tell me, my dear Abbé, what does this mean?"

"I know no more than you do, Monsieur le Baron," replied Louis calmly, at that moment more fearful of encountering Blanche, than of the law, for what had an innocent man to be afraid of? He had not grasped the situation, he had not thought.

"Monsieur le Baron," interposed Loubet, "I must ask your pardon, but I have the best of reasons for the step I have taken. Papers are in my possession which, I regret to say, point to Monsieur l'Abbé as having occasioned the death of Monsieur le Comte de la Jonquières. I must proceed with my duty."

In the face of such an assertion, De Courcelles could say no more. But as Louis, obeying a sign from Loubet, followed him, for the first time, so far as his own bodily safety was concerned, he became uneasy. No sooner had Loubet admitted possessing papers, than he recollected the letter of warning which he had despatched to the Count. It occurred to him to ask himself where he was when the murder was committed. The question brought him no consolation. He had been for a long and solitary walk. He had spoken to no one. He could prove nothing. But he was not permitted to think, for the next moment he found himself ushered into the study where the body lay. Loubet perhaps, influenced by the friendship De Courcelles had manifested for Louis, took the opportunity to whisper:

"You are to be confronted with the dead man."

Scarcely paying any attention to the remark, Louis began to examine the faces of several people in whose presence he found himself. His entrance had produced a profound silence, which became painful, as he stood in the darkened room, conscious that all eyes were upon him. Someone drew up the blinds.

"Monsieur l'Abbé Bernard, approach," said a harsh voice. "Can you identify this man?"

The increased light discovered the Count's form stretched upon a narrow iron bed.

Stooping over it, and fixing his gaze upon the pinched features, which were already turning blue Louis answered firmly:

"I can, monsieur."

The magistrate's clerk took the answer.

"Show him the wound," continued the harsh voice.

And Louis was made to look at a ghastly injury which had been inflicted immediately below the left shoulder. Then, turning to a stout gentleman near him, the magistrate continued:

"Will you be good enough to tell us the result of your examination, doctor?"

Thus appealed to, the stout man commenced to relate how he had been summoned to examine the body of the deceased. Then, warming to his work as the love of his profession asserted itself, he poured forth a stream of scientific expressions, from which it seemed that he had discovered a lacerated wound beneath the Count's left shoulder. This, without doubt, had been produced by a gun charged with shot, fired within a few paces of the deceased. That the weapon used had been a shot-gun, was proved by the presence of some of the shot, and the size of the wound, which was about three times as large as that which a bullet fired under the same conditions would have produced. Several of the large blood-vessels in the region of the heart had been injured, and death had been occasioned by hemorrhage.

"Do you admit having been, directly or indirectly, the cause of the death of Monsieur le Comte de la Jonquières, on the evening of the fifteenth of this month?" demanded the magistrate.

"No, monsieur."

"What are you prepared to admit?"

"Nothing, monsieur. I am as ignorant as you are of—"

Louis stopped abruptly. How could he plead ignorance? Though pledged to remain silent, he knew very well that but for André the Count would still have been alive. The magistrate's penetrating gaze was upon him, and his voice became sterner as he said :

"Ah, why do you pause? Tell me what you were about to say. I insist upon it."

"Monsieur, I have nothing to tell," Louis said at length.

"Do you hear that, gentlemen? You have, doubtless, observed the prisoner's strange demeanour?"

A murmur of assent ran round the room, and the magistrate continued with becoming solemnity:

"Monsieur l'Abbé Bernard, will you state what passed between you and the deceased, when you were last together?"

The magistrate paused, and instantly before Louis' mental vision flashed the stormy scene which had ended, as he had then believed, in his farewell to the château. Even in this instance, his tongue was tied. How could he answer such a question, loving Blanche as he did; how could he state the cause of the angry words with which they had parted? His resolution was taken.

"Monsieur, I can only repeat what I have already affirmed—I am innocent."

"In that case," said the magistrate, rising, as a sign that the examination was now at an end, "it is my painful duty to tell you that I must detain you."

"You must do as you think proper, monsieur," was all that Louis could answer.

And that night he found himself incarcerated in the jail at Mezieres.

CHAPTER XXXI.

WHILE this impressive scene was being enacted in the study, Amy was exerting her good sense and gentleness to dissuade Blanche from pursuing a course which at first she seemed determined upon. Amy also had not been behind-hand in arriving at the conclusion which De Courcelles had formed. She could not be deceived. Blanche was in love with the Abbé. She experienced a great shock on making this discovery. For what good could come of such a passion? There was no bright side to it. But now, clearly, was the moment for her to exercise her common-sense and prove her devotion. Blanche, trembling with agitation, insisted upon confronting "those idiots the police," as in her anger she spoke of them.

"I shall go and hear what they are saying. I can find words to defend him," she affirmed recklessly.

"Believe me, you would only do harm," insisted Amy.

"Harm? Absurd. How could I do harm?"

"In many ways."

"No good reason exists why I should remain here, while under this very roof they are perhaps swearing his life away. It is not friendly even. I *shall* go."

"Stay, I tell you," answered Amy, catching her by the wrist. "If I must be plain, there is a good deal more than friendship between you and the Abbé."

"How—how—what right have you to say so?" stammered Blanche, crimsoning.

"A sister's right to speak the truth plainly, that's all. You love the Abbé. Very well, other people know it. Tell me, was there not some quarrel between him and poor Rudolf?"

"Yes."

"And you would complicate matters by giving an additional proof of your interest in this man, whose name is already coupled with yours. Take care what you do."

Thus entreated, Blanche became passive. But she could not sit still. She was distracted. What were they doing to him? He was caught in the toils by unscrupulous enemies, and what would be the result?

She was not kept long in ignorance, for as a closed carriage rolled away through the park, followed by the police, De Courcelles entered the room.

"Well," she exclaimed, "what has been done?"

"As I told you, they have been examining him."

"And their decision?"

"My dear Countess, do be calm. Their decision is, that for the moment they must detain him."

"Where?"

"At Mezieres."

"But how?"

"Well, if I must say it, in the jail."

Covering her face with her hands, Blanche sank into a chair, exclaiming in heart-breaking accents—

"Oh, God!"

U

Exchanging glances with De Courcelles, and gliding to Blanche's side, Amy slipped her arms round her. But as though roused by this contact of flesh and blood, she leaped to her feet.

"Yes," she broke forth passionately, "in the presence of both of you, I am not ashamed to own my love for this man. I am to blame, you will say. This passion of mine amounts to a crime. Judge me as you please. But let me tell you that I have fought against it, and have resisted, only to be conquered. Can one bestow one's heart where one pleases? Is one a mere machine? I choose to think not. From God alone comes the power to love. And the very hopelessness of our position does not affect me. We can never be anything to each other; but in the face of that fact, and of the world; all I possess, my very life itself if need be, shall be sacrificed for him and in his defence."

De Courcelles and Amy were unable to utter a word; they could only look at her and listen, as, borne away by her feelings, she continued—

"It may sound awful, impious almost, to speak as I have done at a time like this; but as God hears me, the man who has gone caused me such suffering that I would rather die than endure it again."

Silence succeeded her avowal.

De Courcelles felt that it was almost impossible to say the right thing, and out of deference to him, Amy, too, remained speechless. At length they discovered that she was weeping, and, unable to endure that, De Courcelles went to her, captured her two hands, and in accents which were touchingly manly and sympathetic said—

"Very well, Countess, the darker the day, the closer I stick to you. Come, you remember what I said once? Well, here I am. Make use of me.

And we can keep secrets, too, my little wife and I. Cheer up, I say. This is just the time to join hands."

Blanche gazed at him with eyes brimful of gratitude. What she felt at that instant was indescribable.

CHAPTER XXXII.

THE Baron was one of those men who say very little and do a great deal. He adored his young wife, and being of the same flesh and blood, he had conceived a sincere affection for Blanche. Besides, he had liked Louis from the first, and his sympathies were completely enlisted in his behalf at this moment when, poor and friendless, he found him accused of a crime of which he had no doubt he was wholly innocent. That Blanche should love him, and that Louis should return that love, as somehow he felt confident was the case, he regarded as a profound misfortune, the magnitude of which it was difficult to gauge. For how in heaven's name was the thing to end? But he set all that aside, arriving at a decision in his peculiarly good-natured way, as he talked it over with himself.

Here were two people in a deuced deep hole. One of them certainly had the best possible claim upon him, he considered; the other was suffering for an iniquitous act, perpetrated by someone as yet unknown. Well, what he had to do very clearly was to find that someone. So, as soon as the Count's burial was over, after discussing the matter in a painstaking way with Amy, he went to Blanche and announced his intention of setting out for Paris.

"But why go to Paris?" demanded Blanche.
"Well, you see, my solicitor is in Paris."
"And you will go to him?"
"I shall go to him."
"And tell him everything?"
"And tell him everything."
"Then you are a dear, good fellow," exclaimed Blanche.

"No, no, Countess; don't say anything about me until I've done something. If you do, you'll spoil me, and I shall get conceited. When I have—if Amy doesn't happen to be looking" (Amy was within a yard of him as he spoke) "you shall give me another kiss."

"Another one," pouted Amy, with a delicious assumption of jealous concern. "What have you two been doing?"

"Why, swearing everlasting friendship," explained De Courcelles.

"But it is not necessary to kiss to be friends."

"No, but it's the nicest way," retorted De Courcelles comically.

"When do you propose to start?" inquired Blanche gravely.

"By the next fast train. A slow one is unendurable. I have looked at the time-table, and if all goes well, I shall be in Paris in time to catch my man before he leaves his office. You will both come with me as far as the station, won't you?"

"No, how can you ask such a thing," replied Amy, thinking of the Count; "we mustn't drive out as though nothing had happened, we must see the last of you here."

"The last of me for a day or so," answered her

husband affectionately. "Ah, it is a great wrench, Countess, I assure you, this undertaking. If it were for anyone else—well, it would be left undone. Why, we have only just come together, Amy and I."

"Therefore I shall thank you the more. She will be safe with me, and," added Blanche sweetly, "we shall both welcome you back, as the flowers welcome the sun."

So De Courcelles drove away amidst the warmth and the bright green verdure, with Amy's kisses upon his lips, and Blanche's last words, "Remember, I am terribly anxious," ringing in his ears. But alas, when he returned he had little to tell. The law seemed so complicated, the lawyer so reticent. And he did not understand one-half of what had been said to him.

Maître Pélisier, his solicitor, after listening most attentively to all he had to relate, had not committed himself so far as to hazard any opinion. He had contented himself with promising to do his utmost. And already the detectives were at work.

De Courcelles' efforts to communicate with the prisoner were ineffectual. He was not permitted to see anyone, or to hold any intercourse with the outside world. The Procureur Général was inflexible on this point. Satisfied that all the legal machinery likely to aid Louis was now in motion, Blanche's kindly heart turned to his parents. Painful though the task was to her, she sought them herself. But Madame Bernard received her advances sternly, almost uncivilly, and she was forced to retire, experiencing the sensation that, in any event, she would not approach them again.

Practically confined to the château, and with a great misfortune overshadowing them, the two young women drew imperceptibly nearer to each other. Before trouble had come, a perfect understanding, a real affection, had been retarded in its growth, owing to Amy's love affair and the reticence, which was a natural consequence of Blanche's peculiar position. Now these obstacles had been removed by the realization of Amy's wishes, and a moment of supreme weakness, in which Blanche had completely betrayed herself.

Decidedly, Amy had been affected by the briefly enjoyed alteration in her existence. No longer was she the light-hearted, thoughtless girl, absorbed in and fascinated by the prospect of becoming a wife. At one bound she had become a woman.

Sorely in need of consolation, Blanche silently recognised and benefited by this change. A prey to anxiety, frightening herself even at times by the vehemence and depth of her feelings, she gladly laid her head upon her sister's breast, like a child who is desperately tired. Delighted to witness this affection, De Courcelles took care to leave them alone together, saying to himself that the sentiment was of the best, and that really, under the circumstances, he would be decidedly *de trop*. He ardently began to desire one thing though, and that was to get back to the Château de Courcelles. Confident that the interests he had espoused were being looked after, he wished to return home. To discover Blanche's opinion on the subject he resorted to probing.

"Don't you think a little change would be good for you, Countess?" he commenced one day after breakfast, while caressing the silky coat of one of the spaniels.

"I have never thought of it," replied Blanche.

"Well, but do. I mean a trifling distance, mind."

"To move at all would be as distressing as a voyage to the Antipodes."

"Oh, but a journey by rail is—"

"True, one has only to sit still."

"But suppose it were only a drive," suggested De Courcelles, approaching his mark.

"It would be a trouble to me. Besides, I can't bear meeting people. No, if I want air and exercise, I can get it in the park here. And there is no one to see me, which is the greatest comfort. Besides, I prefer this scene to any other just now. I think I can bear suspense best in a place I know."

De Courcelles understood her. He knew that she suffered acutely, and he was far too good-natured to press a point, the gaining of which might occasion her additional pain.

"Yes, perhaps you are right. If I were bothered, it would worry me to move about, I'm certain. Well, I shall go and have a look round the stables. I always do at home, you know. The post will be here in half an hour. What blessings the post and the paper are. Come along, Philos," and stepping out on to the terrace, he went away over the smooth lawn amongst the flowers, with the dogs barking and wagging their tails, thus manifesting their unbounded delight at being noticed.

"Perhaps the postman will bring some news," observed Blanche to Amy. "I understand what Leo meant. He wanted to cheer me. He is very kind and thoughtful."

"Well, he is fond of you, and will do all in his power," replied Amy.

"I feel sure of it."

"He is expecting to hear from Maître Pélisier. All I hope is, that when the letter comes, it will contain something that one can understand."

"The law and its windings are certainly very mystifying. But do you know, Amy, the more I think of it, the more terrible does the Abbé's position appear to be. He can offer no explanation, because in all probability his lips are sealed. Otherwise why should he have remained silent. And though he is as innocent as I am, public opinion will go against him. He will be less friendless than any miscreant who is placed in the dock, and mainly through me."

"Through you?"

"Yes. Can you not understand? Oh, it kills me, this suspense. Already the papers say: 'The prisoner is stubbornly reticent.' They abuse him because he is helpless and unfortunate. And can you not see what the spirit of the judges will be? They will show no mercy, for the words, woman and priest, should remain for ever apart. Nothing but hard and fast facts will be dealt with. They will dilate upon our intimacy, upon the quarrel which ensued in consequence. Félix, who heard all, has been gained over to their side. He will exaggerate, I am certain. Then, upon these two facts, they will endeavour to base the motive for the crime he is accused of."

"But that will be terrible.'

"Yes, for him."

"And for you."

"Why?"

"Because they will certainly examine you. Oh, think of it, Blanche. How degrading!"

"I have; but I don't look upon it in that light. What I dread to think, is that my evidence may be distorted and used against him. My conscience would be clear if he were free, but I know that if I had not existed, he would not be where he is. Let us say no more, however. You have listened to these fears and ideas of mine until you must be weary."

"You know better. I am so grieved for you, and—"

"I am utterly wretched."

"Oh, but there is a bright side; let us try to look upon it."

"I can see nothing bright. If you can conceive what your own feelings would be if you realized that you loved Leo one moment, and the next became aware that you were to be separated from him always, you will know what I endure. Yet I have striven so hard to do right. Oh, if his innocence is not established, what will become of me? I should go mad if I stayed in this place. Don't tire of me, dear; bear with me a little. To unburden my feelings to you from time to time, eases me of a load which presses upon me as though it would suffocate me. Think of him, oh, my God, condemned to death, or to serve out a lingering term of years in misery, while I, loving him, could do nothing. There will be no rest this side the grave for either of us. If we had never met, he would have lived in peace and honour, and now, all that can come to him is ruin, and I have occasioned it."

"But why anticipate misfortune?" asked Amy energetically; "it will not come to that. God will not let it, I am confident."

"I feel that too, at times, and one ought to think so; but disasters have come so thick and fast that I am nervous, and frightened to death. I tell you, Amy, as I have told Leo, that the man who shot the Count, must be sought for amongst the lovers of a certain girl in this village. For in what other way could he have awakened such deadly hatred?"

"But Leo agrees with you?"

"Yes; but so far, no discovery has been made."

"Have patience; everything takes time."

"Patience! How can I be patient when he is suffering so cruelly?"

Amy made no answer, and Blanche, with her eyes fixed upon the gay, sunlit garden, and the river winding and flashing amidst the fertile beauty of the scene beyond, began again to revolve all she had said. These outbursts of feeling were not common with her. She was too proud to speak much. Before De Courcelles she was especially reserved, and of the depth and sincerity of her feelings, he judged mainly by the gravity and pallor of her face. She, whose complexion had been so delicately clear and healthful, already gave abundant evidence, that sleepless nights and anxious days could not be endured without leaving their mark. An additional source of regret to her was supplied by the constantly recurring reflection, that her last interview with Louis had been marred by unkind words. She could not forget this, harping upon it perpetually.

De Courcelles came to her with some letters in his hand.

"I have contrived to intercept the *billets doux*," he said jestingly, his remark scattering her ideas.

"Is there anything for me?" she inquired mechanically.

"No, but I can tell you something that will please you."

"And what is it?"

"Maître Pélisier has committed himself so far as to write a long and reassuring letter. He speaks with the utmost confidence."

"That is good news."

"I knew you would think so."

"May I see it?"

"Certainly."

De Courcelles handed the letter while speaking, and

Blanche began to read it with great attention. When he saw that she had finished, he asked:

"Well, what is your opinion?"

"That it is most encouraging. As he says—how could the Abbé have committed the crime? The insinuation that he is not the perpetrator, but the instigator of the outrage, will have to be proved, as he also very pertinently remarks."

"That is true, but the most important suggestion he makes in the fewest words."

"Which—you mean—"

"His allusion to the fact that a really good alibi would enable the Abbé to come off with flying colours."

"But what hope is there of such good fortune?"

"A substantial one, I fancy, if I may read between the lines. I don't think Maître Pélisier would say so much, without some solid knowledge at his back."

"Then, this is a day for rejoicing."

"Ah, but—"

"I know what you would say."

"That we had better not forget that we are lost in a very thick wood, eh, my dear Countess?"

"Precisely. But I shall not attach too much importance to anything, until no doubt remains. Amongst other things, you see, I have learned to be sceptical. Still, one may safely swallow a few grains of consolation."

"Undoubtedly. But now I have a favour to ask. Put on your hat and come for a turn. The air is delightful, and you will get an appetite. Really, you must not shut yourself up in this gloomy old house. Already you are looking pale."

Thus persuaded, Blanche assented, and De Courcelles soon found himself escorting the two young women beneath the refreshing shade of the trees, where, however, before long Monsieur Brunot contrived to surprise them, by rattling up in his barouche, and, before they could make their escape, alighting and greeting them with the utmost effusiveness.

While the purse-proud and egotistical Deputy was making his presence felt, a very different scene was being enacted a few paces beyond the boundary of the park wall.

Lisette, who was recrossing in the ferry, having been on an errand to an outlying farm, was waylaid by André. The two now confronted each other, without the presence of a third party, for the first time since the Count's death.

"Lisette," said the young man, attempting to possess himself of her hand, "why do you avoid me, why are you so cold? Come, my girl, I want a straight answer from you to-day. I can bear this suspense no longer."

"A straight answer," repeated Lisette, her bosom suddenly heaving tempestuously, while her dark eyes glittered dangerously, "a straight answer. Is that what you want?"

"Yes. I love you."

"And I hate you. Yes, hate you—do you hear? Why do I shrink from you? Listen to this. Most people shrink from a murderer, don't they?"

Becoming livid, André recoiled, but promptly recovering himself, he replied:

"Oh, you call it murder, do you, to shoot a man who would rob one of what one loves best in the world? Well, I don't. I would have shot a score of men to come by you. Is this my reward?"

"All you are likely to get from me. Go and ask the gendarmes what they think of you. Oh, I shall not betray you. I am content to hate you, that is all." And without another word, leaving André gazing after her with a white face and wistful eyes, Lisette passed on.

Two of Maître Pélisier's disguised detectives, who were amusing themselves over a game of dominoes at the "Repos des Artistes," would have given their ears to have been a little nearer to Lisette's red lips.

CHAPTER XXXIII.

WHEN the magistrate, on concluding the examination, had said, " It is my painful duty to tell you that I must detain you," Louis thoroughly realized his own helplessness. But even then he did not appreciate the peril in which he stood. The icy chill that pierced his heart was caused by the reflection that he was about to be separated from Blanche. He would not wake in the morning, consoled by the knowledge that she was near, that he breathed the same air, and was at least at liberty to go for a solitary walk over paths they had trodden together.

Approaching the château as a prisoner, he had shrunk from encountering her gaze. When it came to quitting it—the dear home where she dwelt, and where the happiest hours he had ever known had been spent—he experienced a shock which deprived him of speech. For a moment he became blinded with tears, and the sensation as of an invisible hand clutching at his throat, half-choked him. With Loubet's touch upon his arm, and Loubet's voice ringing in his ears, he roused himself. A wild desire for freedom surged through him. It would be sweet to fight for his liberty, and to fall in an attempt to gain it. The mad thought passing, remembering what he was, where he stood, and why he stood there, he bowed his head and followed the police-officer.

One last, wistful glance, and he crossed the great hall, one agonizing pang as he saw no sign of the dear form he sought for, and he was being borne away. Slowly the noise made by the rattling wheels seemed to benumb his senses, he was not conscious of the journey, and in a state of dull despair, he was conducted to the cell which was now to be his home.

From the moment the prison door closed upon him, and he found himself plunged in profound solitude, his mind became the battleground of a series of stormy conflicts. Then began what was to develop into a searching introspective analysis of his love, of his calling, of the life he had led, of the life he was likely to lead. As a man slowly recovers from the effects of a blow that has stunned him, so did he awake to grapple with his thoughts. Again, as before, he commenced to ponder upon this young woman.

He reflected that never since the day on which he had been so ignominiously dismissed from the château, had he seen or heard aught of her. Was this the conduct of a woman in love? His position, it was true, was a peculiarly delicate one. But had she pleased, had she desired to communicate with him, could she not have contrived to send him some message, without compromising herself or injuring him? Decidedly so. Then what construction was he to put upon her silence, upon her complete desertion of him in his hour of need? He had left the very house of which she was mistress without a sign from her. For though the Baron had addressed him kindly, the Baron did not know their secret, and could not be said to represent her.

There was something strange in all this. And was it

difficult to account for it? What more likely than that his quarrel with the Count had led to an explanation and—who could tell?—a reconciliation between husband and wife? Then when this terrible tragedy had so suddenly separated them, might not the slumbering fire of affection have leaped into flame? In the face of this crushing blow, Blanche had become aware that her love for the dead man was not annihilated. Lost to her beyond recall, she would now dwell only upon his goodness, and remembering her own moral faithlessness, would experience a species of disgust for the man who had occasioned this laxity of principle, this neglect of duty. Who could tell, even, but that she might have come to see in him the secret foe who had by some means compassed the Count's ending? Were not the circumstances of the case sufficiently startling, given that the letter had been misconstrued?

A deadly insult had been offered to him—Louis. He had retaliated by a warning; then, despairing of obtaining the redress he sought, and recognising in the Count, an enemy with whom armed neutrality was impossible, he had contrived to strike the fatal blow. But could she think so vilely of him? He could only wring his hands in doubt and bewilderment, though it was almost impossible to conceive her capable of such cruelty and injustice towards him. It might be, too, that she had been silent because she feared exposure. She might deem it wiser to draw back at this critical moment, rather than not at all. Was she—a great lady—to allow her name to be coupled with his—a poor priest? The prospect of such degradation might well appal her. Besides, the fruitlessness of their intimacy, the hopelessness of their love, must be constantly recurring to her. And these insidious reflections must have their effect. The odds against

x

him were so overwhelming, that, sooner or later, he must be vanquished. She would forget him in her happiness with someone else, and he—what was to become of him then?

Hosts of ideas of a like nature occurred to this man, whom silence and solitude had thus condemned to perpetual speculation. After a night spent in weary sleeplessness on his hard and comfortless bed, the dawn would sometimes awaken a revolutionized being. He felt thoroughly ashamed of himself for having entertained such doubts. Was not this woman all that was noble, affectionate, and pure? Wretched man that he was. How had he dared to malign her even in thought? If she had held aloof from him, she had her reasons; but they were not of the order he had evolved and assigned to her. She had not changed. She was not of that sort. If his life depended upon her faithfulness, he would have no occasion to tremble. But, alas, while these sweet thoughts were filling his heart with warmth and restfulness, the opposition would again start up, undermining with cold, hard realities, and inch by inch he would surrender to this irresistible attack, and weakened, spiritless, perhaps slumber would mercifully overtake him.

But in addition to his misgivings on the score of Blanche, these tempestuous nights and days were overcast by the oft-recurring religious doubts and scruples. There was nothing new in this, for ever since becoming vicar of La Jonquières, scales had commenced to fall from his eyes. During the long winter months, when the château blinds had been drawn down, and Blanche had remained in Paris, silent, ignoring him, he had sought to find distraction in the careful perusal of the most able philosophical and theological works. He had attacked these volumes with the whole ardour of his nature, and on many an occasion the lamp—beneath which he turned the abstruse pages—had paled before the grey dawn, the birds beginning to carol happily, while he, shivering and fatigued, would betake himself to bed.

This unremitting study had not borne the fruit he had looked for when he began it, and he had come to think, without any possibility of his decision being altered, that he had taken a most unnatural vow, and that this vow was the one weak point which reduced to a condition of rottenness the whole fabric of which he was but an unworthy particle.

It was to this conviction that he had alluded when, after having laid bare his seminary life, he had said to Blanche: "Some day, when my ideas are clearer, I will come and tell them to you, though, when I do, you are more than likely to say, this man is a depraved monster."

Though he had spoken obscurely then, it was not because he was conscious that his ideas lacked clearness and his judgment soundness. It was because he was not prepared to speak. With the prison walls enclosing him, the loose masses of fact with which he had stored his brain were forming themselves into compact and substantial arguments, upon which he was becoming more and more anxious to speak, more resolutely determined to act.

CHAPTER XXXIV.

The " Repos des Artistes " was the headquarters of the gossips of La Jonquières. There the farmers and the peasantry met, smoked their pipes, sipped their absinthe, anisette, or curaçoa, played dominoes, and expressed their opinions freely. What was said there was retailed to their women folk, and was influential in its effect.

Of course, at this juncture, the habitués of the *auberge*, like the population of the *arrondissement*, were split up into two parties; those who favoured the prosecution, and those who sided with the defence. Latterly, those who were convinced of Louis' guilt had increased numerically, and, in sporting parlance, the odds were against the prisoner. As a matter of fact, some bets were indulged in, and nothing else was talked of but the approaching trial. Reposing in its gardens and park, the château was practically isolated. What went on in the village was not heard of by the inmates of the stately old house; but what the great folks did, and said, penetrated into the little hamlet in a surprisingly short space of time.

The leaves of the centenarian oaks were turning yellow, and crimsoning in the fierce sunlight, the delicate foliage of the silver birches already strewed the ground with patches of gold, the roses were dispersing their perfume and their petals, while, upon the substantial garden walls, peaches and nectarines blushed with ripeness. Amidst the flight of time, Blanche perambulated the pleasant walks in company with Amy, striving to be hopeful, endeavouring to be cheerful, and to summon what fortitude she could command to endure the distracting suspense dictated by the law. It was a terrible ordeal for her, but she bore it bravely. And, since wondering and fretting would not help Louis, she became practical, and laid herself out to increase the comfort and happiness of the two young people who, with such admirable self-denial and patience, had elected to remain with her. They were all breakfasting together, and the open window admitted the refreshing perfume of the flowers. Some letters had arrived for De Courcelles. He was opening them, and Blanche, seated opposite to him, was watching his face with intense interest. Unaware that he was being observed, he made no effort to disguise his annoyance, so that Blanche, who was nervous and upon the alert, found it impossible to remain silent.

"Have you heard from Maître Pélesier?" she asked, point-blank.

"I have, Countess."

"And what does he say?"

"Oh, things are going on all right."

"In that case, why are you annoyed?"

"But how do you know I am?"

"Because I happened to be watching you."

"And you could read my thoughts?"

"Instantly."

De Courcelles looked at her. He knew that she was intensely anxious. The news he had received was not reassuring; but what was the use of increasing her suffering? He resolved to prevaricate for her sake.

"But what if I were to tell you that you are mistaken?" he inquired smilingly.

"I should not believe you."

"Leo, you had better tell Blanche what you know," put in Amy. "You will only vex her if you don't."

"Oh, you little stupid. Am I to fight the two of you, eh?" he asked good-humouredly.

"Yes."

"Then I am vanquished."

"Ah, you are ready to own that together we are too much for you," exclaimed Blanche. "Come, then, tell me what has happened. I have a right to know."

"I admit it, my dear Countess," replied De Courcelles, willing to gain himself time in which to determine what he should say.

"How provoking you are."

"This is the first occasion upon which you have said such a thing. Come, do you really think so ill of me?"

"How dexterously you contrive to change the subject. But no, just now, I am not going to discuss *you*. Let me see the letter. May I?"

"It is marked private and confidential," retorted De Courcelles playfully.

"I have never known you tease me before," asserted Blanche reproachfully.

"That you may not lay such a charge at my door—listen. Maître Pélisier has engaged a renowned Paris barrister to defend Monsieur l'Abbé Bernard."

"Well, so much the better. But that piece of information was not the cause of your annoyance."

"But consider my annoyance as imaginary."

Exasperated, Blanche said sharply:

"Leo, you irritate me. I am not a child, remember."

Driven thus from his guns, all at once the Baron became grave, his eyebrows contracted perceptibly, and he said:

"Well, then, since you will have it, I suppose I must tell you. Maître Pélisier writes that the Deputy Procureur, who is a friend of his, is strangely reserved, and evidently unfavourably impressed, and that other influential men, whose opinions will not go for nothing, are becoming more inclined to the opinion that the Abbé is guilty."

"In Heaven's name, of what?"

"Oh, my dear Countess, have patience. After all, this is but a rumour. Until the trial commences, one cannot say how things will go. But to give you the pith of what Pélisier has to say for himself, he concludes with the curious remark that 'at this moment there can be no doubt that public opinion and justice frown menacingly.' There, read for yourself."

Blanche took the letter, but, struck by the allusion to justice, she remarked bitterly:

"If Monsieur l'Abbé Bernard obtains justice, it is all he will require."

"I am quite of your opinion."

"Then there is nothing to fear."

"Well, I always endeavour to look on the bright side of things, and I strongly recommend you to do the same."

Blanche did not reply to him; already she was immersed in the contents of the note.

Meanwhile, the course events were taking was being watched by a remarkably sharp pair of eyes, and those eyes were set in the sagacious head of Monsieur

Brunot. Ever since Louis' arrest, a brilliant idea, in his opinion, had occurred to him. This idea was the belief that he might make capital out of the complicated fix in which Louis was placed. In his important position as Deputy, he possessed considerable influence, which influence, moreover, had been solidified by his wealth.

He had quietly formed the opinion that Blanche was very much in love with Louis, just as report alleged, but he scouted the further belief that Louis was guilty of the crime with which he was charged. He had always coveted the superb château and estate of La Jonquières, and his ambition, or rather greed, had not rested there, for he had coveted the dead Count's wife. There was now just an outlying chance of obtaining both, he had come to think. At all events, there was no harm in trying for such a prize. He set about his task. He called at the château and condoled, making himself as agreeable as he could ; and, while doing this, he caused rumours to be set afloat supporting the prosecution, and asserting that, above all things, there could be no doubt of Louis' guilt. Then, when matters were ripe, and the session approaching, he set out for the château.

Blanche was alone, De Courcelles and Amy having gone for a drive. But he was refused admittance. Not to be done, he scribbled a few words on his card, and, with a judicious *douceur*, instructed the servant to give it to Madame la Comtesse.

The effect was magical. He was shown into her presence. Now that he found himself actually face to face with this beautiful and dignified woman, Brunot was disposed to wish that he had stayed at home. His heart failed him. How could he say what he wanted? It was monstrous impertinence. But then, audacity had proved so effective in his business.

He had a fair field, too; they were alone. His courage rose. He said to himself: "*Sacrédie*, why should I be afraid? There's nothing like trying. I shall do so. She can't eat me."

Blanche's reception of him was calculated to try his nerves. She was conscious that the ground he had encroached upon was delicate.

"Will you tell me exactly what you know, what you mean, monsieur?" she said, after a brief and ceremonious greeting; "these words upon your card you wrote because you thought they would interest me."

"And was I wrong, Madame la Comtesse?"

"Not altogether. Monsieur l'Abbé Bernard is a friend. He has been constantly with us. I have learned to respect and admire him because of his sterling qualities. Would it be possible for me to know that he is suffering without cause, and to feel uninterested in the issue?"

"Certainly not, Madame la Comtesse. Like you, I am convinced of his innocence, otherwise I should not be here."

Brunot had artfully struck the right chord.

"I am rejoiced to hear you say so, monsieur. He is in need of friends at this moment, if ever he was. But what do you allude to? You speak of 'important news.'

Blanche glanced at the card as she spoke.

"The news that I venture to call important, is that I am willing to aid him. Without boasting, I may say that I am possessed of some influence. I will exert it in his behalf."

"He is indeed fortunate, monsieur. But let me hear in what way you propose to help him. I am, I confess, woefully ignorant on these points."

"I have little hesitation in saying that if I interested myself, the prosecution would collapse. He would be acquitted!"

The prospect of such a blessing caused Blanche to unbend and to become natural.

"Then you *will* exert yourself, monsieur—you will let me entreat you?"

She clasped her hands and leaned towards him; her eyes sparkling with animation, her cheeks deepening perceptibly in colour.

Brunot saw the advantage he had gained. His answer was a cunning one. Fixing his eyes on her, he said:

"Oh, yes, I will listen to your entreaties. It is you who are mistress of the situation."

Blanche instantly remarked his altered manner, his singular assertion, and she at once recoiled upon the defensive.

"I am mistress of the situation! What do you mean? I do not understand you, monsieur. What can I do? Explain yourself," she said coldly.

"I repeat. It is my opinion that if *you* will it so, Monsieur l'Abbé Bernard may become a free man."

"But how, in Heaven's name?"

"Madame, I am willing to work night and day."

"But that rests with you."

"On the contrary, I cannot even begin unless you inspire me, Madame la Comtesse. Unless you set me going, in fact."

"But what have I to do with it? If you choose to render Monsieur l'Abbé Bernard a great, an inestimable service, very well, I shall be glad. As a friend of his, you will have my best thanks."

Monsieur Brunot fidgetted. Was he mistaken? Were Blanche's sentiments for the Abbé purely friendly ones? Had rumour deceived him? If so, he was about to make a fool of himself. He hesitated. But he had gone so far. Then he took the plunge.

"Madame, I must humbly apologize for addressing you on such a subject at such a time. I am in a delicate position. Make allowances for me, I implore you. Your beauty has inspired me with a passion which leaves me no longer master of myself. I am the most—"

"Monsieur, you must be mad," exclaimed Blanche, starting to her feet.

"I am not. Oh, no, I am not mad, unless you have made me so."

"I will not listen to you. How dare you address such language to me?"

"Alas! Madame la Comtesse, it is the language of the heart."

"The effect of which you had better try elsewhere, monsieur."

"Now, you are hard on me, indeed, Madame la Comtesse."

"I have no desire to compel you, but I shall be glad if you will terminate this absurd interview, monsieur," returned Blanche haughtily.

Thus stung, and fearing to lose his cause, Brunot replied:

"And leave Monsieur l'Abbé Bernard to his fate, that—"

"I fail to see what Monsieur l'Abbé Bernard has to do with the matter, and I must decline to discuss it further. Am I to summon my servants?"

"By no means. Be patient with me. He has everything to do with it, dear madame. Let me be plain, but forgive me. He is in trouble, the session is approaching. It is said that the authorities are inclined to make an example of him, to be terribly severe, as you are doubtless aware. You may not grasp the full significance of this condition of things. But I know very well that if they are *anxious* to find him guilty, they will probably do so. Now, I will undertake to rescue him from their clutches—"

"On what terms?" demanded Blanche, in desperation.

"If I succeed, I would entreat you to bestow your hand upon me. Oh, I know you despise me, and think me a plebian *now;* but once married, I should endeavour to win your affection by my devotion. You would forget my birth, for, after all, a man is but a man, and the greatest amongst the aristocracy of the earth have, in many instances, sprung from obscure origin. My position is at least a respectable one. I am a Deputy. I am rich. My own efforts have placed me in the position I now occupy. Fate seemed against me when I began. I have conquered Fate. In all I have attempted I have succeeded, because I have believed, and acted upon the belief, that all obstacles may be surmounted by an indomitable will. Madame, I entreat you to remember that the man who can wear smooth the rough rocks of difficulty, because he assails them as untiringly as the sea its boundaries, is not altogether unworthy of some slight consideration."

M. Brunot had never been so eloquent before. He even imagined that he felt the fine things he had said. But he was breathless.

"Monsieur, I must remind you to stick to your text. The transaction you have proposed to me is purely a business one. You are a business man. You have not forgotten the training which made you one—"

"But, madame, if my tongue has misled me—"

"Not in the least, monsieur. We understand each other."

Blanche fixed her eyes on him as the incisive remarks dropped from her lips. This man had guessed her secret. Gossip had set him on the track. And in the position in which she found herself, what disguise was she capable of assuming? Had she anything to hope for from such a person? Undoubtedly not. The small, piercing eyes — cruel expression — and massive, almost brutal jaw, told their tale. He had named his price. She could accept it or not, as she liked. But certainly he would remain inexorable. If he possessed the power to help Louis, it would be agonizing to her to decline his assistance. But the price. How could she pay it? She became pallid, and her teeth met as though between them writhed some malignant foe. Such a terrible expression of despair distorted her features, that Brunot, who caught the look, started. During the brief pause in the conversation, he had employed himself in recalling the sensation of intense nervousness, which had once so nearly deprived him of speech in that very room. Before him again stood the Count — rigid, proudly severe; by his side, De Courcelles, the perfection of quiet, well-bred authority; behind them both, Louis Bernard — tall, kindly, but dignified. Ah, well, he reflected, what a transformation. The Count, who had regarded him as an impertinent interloper, was dead, and he, Brunot, was actually proposing to his wife. Monsieur l'Abbé Bernard was in jail, powerless to help himself. And the irreproachable Baron — well, they might become relations by marriage. But, *en verité*, what did he behold? Madame la Comtesse's face fairly frightened him. He might win a game which he would live to regret having played. A woman certainly could be the very devil when she liked. Yet, what was there to be afraid of? Pshaw, he would tame her. He could hold his own. Blanche scattered his cogitations.

"Monsieur," she remarked calmly, "I will consider your proposition. Have the goodness to come to-morrow at this time. You shall then receive my answer."

The result of this interview was that M. Brunot re-entered his carriage and drove back to Mezieres, satisfied that he was a lucky fellow, and that the battle was as good as won. The château and estate of La Jonquières, not to speak of its brilliant and beautiful mistress, were in a fair way to become his.

Returning from their drive, De Courcelles and his young wife discovered Blanche seated where she had sunk when Brunot had left her. She had not thought of hiding her feelings, for her reflections were too bitter. Suddenly aroused from them by the entrance of the young people, the expression and pallor of her face told them at once that something unpleasant had transpired during their absence. With a great effort, she chatted pleasantly during dinner, but as soon as she could reasonably do so, she retired to her own room.

Slipping his arm through that of his wife's, De Courcelles descended the terrace steps, and when in the garden inquired what had happened.

"To Blanche?" asked Amy.

"Of course."

"That is more than I can say. She is certainly very much upset. But she has not confided in me. Monsieur Brunot has called, I am told. The horrid creature! Could he be the cause?"

"Perhaps. He may have been entertaining her by repeating all the absurd rumours that are afloat. The silly fool. If he has, I should like to treat him to a piece of my mind for his trouble. But what the deuce is to be done? She has received some crushing blow. I asked her if she felt unwell."

"And what did she say?"

"Oh, she smiled unnaturally, and declared that she had seldom felt better. Go and talk to her, and find out what has happened."

"Very well; but I have my own opinion on the subject, and I'm pretty certain I'm not far wrong."

"And what is it?"

"She is simply distressed about the Abbé, Leo. You don't know how she loves him—I do. I am confident of this, that she will be unhappy all her life unless something can be done."

"What do you mean, dear? Extricate him from this fix?"

"More than that."

"More than that? But what, and in what way? Speak plainly."

"Well, if they are prevented from seeing each other, from coming together—Blanche—"

"The deuce! Just think of what you are saying. How is such a thing to be brought about?"

"Well, all the same, it must be."

"Amy, darling, you are talking nonsense."

"Indeed, I am not."

"Indeed, you are. Since he is a priest, what can be done? Besides, they should not have fallen in love. They must have felt it coming on."

"You goose. As if one can help oneself."

"Certainly, I could not have helped loving you, and—"

"There, don't. I feel too serious to joke. Blanche has suffered frightfully already. Rudolf made her life unbearable, as she has admitted, and now this calamity has come upon her. Seriously, Leo, for my sake, you must do what you can to help her."

"Do what I can? Good heavens, as if I am not doing all I can."

"Well, think. Come, I'll light a cigarette for you, and then I must go to Blanche. She must not be left alone. Her looks have frightened me."

With her fresh rosy lips, Amy did as she had proposed, and then she reascended the steps to the terrace and disappeared, leaving De Courcelles to lapse into a brown study.

That night was one of indescribable torture to Blanche. She never closed her eyes. Brunot's face haunted her, and Brunot's words rang in her ears like a death-knell. She seemed to realize that she had become his wife, to feel his hateful touch, his loathsome caresses. And it had come to this, after all she had attempted, all she had endured. She shuddered in agony, and rendered desperate, expelled the revolting ideas. But she was instantly confronted by a picture of Louis. Dread and phantasmal arose before her the image of this dear one she loved so fondly, being severed from her and life by the knife—the awful guillotine; or, escaping that, sentenced to a long and cruel imprisonment, and for this crime which he had never committed.

He was enduring the degradation of imprisonment, for her, as it were. He would stand in the dock, an object of contempt and execration, all for her. Could she reason otherwise? But for her intimacy with him, could he have come to be placed in the situation in which he now was? And could she desert him under such circumstances? Had she the power to do so, loving him as she did? Decidedly not. Then it had come to this. She dare not refuse Brunot's offer. To gain one chance for Louis was worth the payment of any price. And here was an opportunity of saving him. For the understanding was to be, in return for Louis' freedom, no matter how gained, her hand. In her excitement, on hearing that Louis had been taken to the jail at Mezieres, had she not told the Baron that her wealth, anything—life itself—she would sacrifice for him? She had now to prove her words and her love, and though to yield her person, her existence, into the keeping of such a man as Brunot, seemed, to her refined nature, a worse alternative than death, she did not flinch or hesitate. Since he (Louis) could never be anything to her, it would be sweet to feel that she did this great thing for him. She could never love anyone else. So, since one man was no better than another, what did it matter? The knowledge that she was doing all this for him, the memory of past joys, innocent, but yet so ineffably sweet, would enable her to play her part, would nerve and give her strength sufficient for her need. And thus the poor martyr reasoned with herself all night through. Though pale and wearied, the morning found her calm, determined. And when in the afternoon M. Brunot presented himself, though De Courcelles and Amy were present, she stepped up to him, and without being overheard, said:

"Monsieur, I have decided. If Monsieur l'Abbé Bernard is liberated through your influence—and you can take steps to prove this to me—I am prepared to grant your request. Beyond desiring you to be silent, I have nothing more to say to you."

M. Brunot had a good deal to talk about, however. In a few rapid sentences he avowed his affection and devotion. But Blanche never heard him. She *awoke*, as it were, only when he had gone, for she had spoken the words, acted the whole scene, benumbed into a kind of stupor. She was as a bird robbed of its senses by the appalling presence of a destructive and poisonous serpent. She told no one what she had done, and, striving to forget herself, became composed, as she reflected that Brunot's powerful influence would now assuredly be exerted on Louis' behalf.

CHAPTER XXXV.

MINDFUL of all that Amy had said, and more anxious than ever to be of service to Blanche in her trouble, De Courcelles good-naturedly redoubled his efforts to help Louis. He wrote most urgently to his solicitor in Paris, he secretly exerted his great influence to correct the ill-natured rumours which were afloat, he renewed his efforts to see Louis, and, as a result of his energetic attitude, coupled with the respect and esteem he commanded, at length came the permission he sought. Availing himself of this concession, he set out for Mezieres without an hour's delay, but possessing certain ideas, the substance of which he regarded as a kind of forlorn hope. For was not the situation one of extreme difficulty and obscurity?

He found Louis much changed; very pale, subdued, and tearful at the sight of a friendly face

"You see, I have succeeded in making my way to you at last, my dear Abbé," De Courcelles remarked affably, and really glad in his heart to see the poor fellow.

"And, Monsieur le Baron, I can assure you I do not know how to thank you enough."

"But do not thank me at all. Why should you? You would do the same for me, eh?"

"Yes; but, indeed, you are so kind, Monsieur le Baron."

"Because I like you, my dear Abbé. You see, selfishness is the mainspring of every motive."

"Is it so, alas? But, nevertheless, you honour me much, Monsieur le Baron. Ah! I never thought I could have longed so intensely for the sight of a friendly face, for the pressure of a hand I have once touched. But I am, indeed, fortunate to meet with so much kindness."

"Do you think so? Ah! very well; but really it has been one's misfortune that one could do so little. There has been but poor scope, with these thick walls and inexorable guards. But you see what it is to have friends. And you have many, my dear Abbé, I assure you."

Louis regarded him wistfully. He had tutored himself into believing that Blanche was completely changed towards him. He had forced himself to swallow this bitter pill, and had striven to accustom himself to the sensation of utter hopelessness which it had occasioned him. When the Baron spoke of friends, was he alluding to her? His flesh tingled with the desire to know this, to ask, to say at least something which might evoke a direct allusion to this woman whom he had taught himself to look upon as lost to him, but whom he felt he loved unalterably.

The Baron fancied he understood that swift, searching, and yet anxious glance. He was perfectly certain in his own mind that Blanche's love was returned. And the good-hearted fellow longed to smooth the road for these luckless people. Had he not gained his own ends; was he not absurdly happy with his young girl-wife? Besides, in his opinion, Louis was a clever, amiable, and cultivated gentleman. Ancestry, in his eyes, was of less importance than the possession of ability, united to an admirable disposition. There was only one obstacle, he said to himself, "What a pity he is a priest. But we shall see." Then, in pursuance of his ideas, after having discussed the burning question of his captivity, De Courcelles began, with some dexterity, as he thought, to probe.

"You must have felt intensely lonely," he suggested.

Louis rose to the bait. He was in that condition when a word of kindness seemed the key to his soul.

"I, Monsieur le Baron? Indeed, I have been reduced to the depths of despair."

"And what has comforted you? Your religion, eh?"

Louis reflected for a moment with his eyes upon the ground, then he raised his face suddenly, and with the hot blood surging into it, and evidently labouring under much excitement, for he was in reality very weak owing to his close confinement, he said:

"Monsieur le Baron, I am longing to confide in someone. These grim and silent walls have witnessed the growth of a great and irresistible longing to speak —to tell the thoughts which press upon me. You have been so kind. But ah! you may think ill of me."

De Courcelles experienced a sense of surprise. What was he about to hear? Eagerly he said:

"Try me. Have confidence. I shall consider whatever you relate to me as sacred, my dear Abbé."

"Do you say so? then I will. It would be such a relief to me, Monsieur le Baron; and I have an idea, somehow, that you are not bigoted. I have never exchanged religious opinions with you, but left to myself, and, indeed, for a long while past, I have been absorbed in them. I mean restlessly, unduly so. And what could be more natural, placed as I am?

Accused of a brutal crime of which I am as innocent as an unborn child, I have reflected as though the shadow of death hung over me."

De Courcelles' expression became slightly suspicious. It was strange that Louis should touch upon the very subject upon which he had determined to speak—his forlorn hope. It at once occurred to him to wonder whether this allusion to religion had anything to do with Blanche. But he replied mildly:

"Alas, my dear Abbé, I feel myself a terrible delinquent when I hear you speak with so much gravity and feeling. But we Frenchmen are not what we should be, I fear. Madame la Baronne who, as you know, has been brought up as a Protestant, is completely shocked at us. Having lived with a worthy but religious aunt, she has been accustomed to think the Sunday attendance at church a necessity, nay, an absolute duty."

"And so it should be, Monsieur le Baron."

"Yes; but what she has remarked in your parish of La Jonquières, I do not hesitate to say is the case throughout France. The men are ashamed to attend church. Out of every parish of five hundred souls, fifty women or so may be regular attendants. There are in addition, perhaps, two or three old men, one of which is probably your own sacristan."

"Ah, how forcibly that has struck me. But why is it so, Monsieur le Baron?"

"Well, will you forgive me if I speak plainly? I think it is entirely due to a general want of confidence in the clergy."

"And to what is this due, Monsieur le Baron?" demanded Louis, with growing excitement.

"Again, if I may speak with the same straightforwardness, as an educated man, I should say that it is a natural consequence of the failure, on the part of the priests, to keep inviolate the solemn vow they have taken."

"Ah! now I see that I may speak plainly with you, Monsieur le Baron. You have struck at the very root of the evil. But first, let me consider this vow in relation to myself. How did I come to take it? In the hands of clever men, whose existence was spent in obtaining converts to their doctrines, I know *now* that I was but a tool. My ignorance and innocence was a splendid soil in which to rear the theory of damnation. If I did not become a priest, I was lost. In the strong hands which were fashioning me, alas, I was malleable enough. Having done what was required of me, what do I find on taking charge of a parish? Have I joined a body of men who are respected throughout the country? On the contrary. Doubts quickly entering my mind, I lay myself out to examine critically the position in which I find myself, and aided by one in whose years and experience I rely, I arrive at the conclusion, that of every hundred priests, there are perhaps twenty-five good and holy men, twenty-five who manage to conceal their faults, though not enjoying the esteem of their bishops, and that the remaining fifty have failed hopelessly to keep their oath, and are the cause of the scandals with which every village in France is from time to time visited. What is the result of this misconduct? The people say of us, 'He preaches what he fails to practice. He is worse than ourselves, for we make no professions. We no longer believe in him.' And is it not natural that they should reason thus?"

"Perfectly so, my dear Abbé. But I do not blame the men; I blame the vow, and I am not altogether ignorant of the subject."

"The knowledge that you have been so good to me, and that I may have implicit trust in your discretion, Monsieur le Baron, impels me to unburden myself, and to discuss these formidable questions with you. Besides, your kind interest more than warrants my confidence."

"In return for which, that interest shall be lasting. Yes, I can conceive no situation in which human sympathies are more powerfully appealed to than in yours. So you see," added De Courcelles, "you may safely number me amongst the friends to whom I alluded. But to return to our subject."

"Monsieur le Baron, to return as you say to our subject. Describing this vow, let me recall the famous Dr. Raspail's clever remark: 'Nothing makes one more dishonest than a position contrary to nature,' and there can be no doubt that it is in direct opposition both to nature and common sense. When I took it, I have no hesitation in saying that I meant absolutely nothing by it, since I did not understand it. Above human laws, there certainly exists a natural law, which dictates that promises based on a material error are null and void."

De Courcelles, convinced that Louis' principles were heartfelt and genuine, now took the opposing side, the better to develop them.

"But, my dear Abbé, let me argue with you. I should say that it was the wish of Christ that His disciples should imitate His own life of solitude and celibacy."

"Monsieur le Baron, I answer you that it has never been the wish of Christ to impose an unbearable burden."

"But the Church has been practising celibacy for, let us say, seven or eight hundred years with fair results, so the burden is not unbearable."

"Monsieur le Baron, when you affirm so much, you forget the scandals of the monasteries—scandals which have worked reform in England and all over Germany, from the Pope downwards. I have studied the question as thoroughly as the means at my disposal would permit. One must judge of the beneficial effects of a policy by the results. The decayed and decaying condition of the Roman Catholic Church is such that it will not bear comparison with the vigorous condition of the Protestant Church. And doubtless this, as you say, is due to the bad conduct on the part of the priests."

"And you would add that this is an evil resulting from the nature of the vow?"

"And you could not possibly dispute the contention, Monsieur le Baron," exclaimed Louis excitedly.

"No, perhaps not," replied De Courcelles, very willing to retire before' Louis clear and substantial arguments, which to his delight cleared the road which he had despaired of cutting. Pausing momentarily, he suddenly added, as though a brilliant thought had occurred to him : " I am willing even to support your opinions with the aid of this idea, which seems to me to be very strong. Why does the Church allow a certain class of priests to marry? This is certainly so. For although Roman Catholics, although performing the tremendous duty of confession, in the East priests are married men. I think you will also bear me out when I say that the first bishops consecrated by the Apostles were also married men. Why this concession to some and not to all? Why should a French priest, on ground of marriage, be doomed to hell, and a married Bulgarian priest, for instance—over whom Rome considers she holds sway —find rest in paradise? Why—"

"I know what you are going to say, Monsieur le Baron, and it is conclusive," exclaimed Louis, in intensely interested tones. 'Why has Rome two sets of weights and measures? Is Rome, like a monarch, who, being pressed hard by a hot-headed and impetuous party, grants them the reforms and concessions demanded, but continues to be severe to his more timid and better-disposed subjects?

"Is *that* illustrative of the dignity and splendour of a Church which claims to be infallible? Is it not rather illustrative of the expedients of a supremely human institution which blows hot and cold, is severe or indulgent, according to the requirements of time and circumstance? I would end my life as I have begun it, with the desire, the aim, to leave behind me a track of good as the course of my earthly pilgrimage; but I cannot even begin, placed as I am upon this basis of hypocrisy. After a searching investigation I have arrived at this decision. The Protestant religion is consolation for a Christian, Romanism is despair. For a Protestant, heaven is so easy to reach. It is only necessary to be a good and honest man; but with us the complication of duties to fulfil, frequent confessions to a priest, frequent communion, daily meditation, daily mass, fasting, and, after all this, the near prospect of eternal punishment, makes life a perfect burden. And how is this burden to be tolerated when immorality shows itself? It is notorious that there is not a single prison in France, that has not sheltered some French priest sentenced for immorality, and her colonial penitentiaries keep many of them for life. And is this to be wondered at? I think not. Doctor Raspail's words ought to be written in golden letters over the gate of every seminary, 'Nothing makes one so dishonest as a position contrary to nature.' And, again, how can men come to us priests, when we preach that of one hundred people dying, five only are saved, ninety-five lost? Is fright the way to conquer their hearts?

They prefer to laugh at us and at God's pretended cruelty. They prefer to become utter unbelievers."

"Then, my dear Abbé, you think with the talented preacher of Notre Dame, Father Hyacinthe Loyson, eh?"

"On many points, yes."

"Well, I, for one, certainly agree with you."

"Monsieur le Baron, my thoughts, my belief at this moment have, I am confident, been shared by thousands who have gone before me. We leave the seminary as innocent, as desirous of good and uprightness as young St. Louis de Gonzaga, whose religious zeal would not permit him to lift his eyes to his own mother's face, when she visited him during his noviciate at the Jesuits. Suddenly we are sent forth amongst mankind, and upon our astonished gaze bursts the spectacle of the world in its myriad phases and manifold conditions. Our eyes are opened, gradually we comprehend the mummery which surrounds us, we become alive to the hollowness of the religious structure which has been erected by those sufferers who have long since passed away, and then I imagine that, like myself, many a man recoils with horror from the hypocrisy he is called upon to enact. The weak, and those who are so placed that they cannot help themselves, sink further and further into the mire, and consent to play out the farce their position demands ; but for the young and strong there is another course, and that course, Monsieur le Baron, should I be released from the position I am placed in, I am determined to follow, for I am a man *now*, and am capable of judging according to my conscience and with the sense which the Almighty has given me. But I must weary you."

"Not in the least, I am profoundly interested."

"Let me make this one remark, then. If God

permits this Protestantism to thrive, if He allows the clergy, as a body, to be respected and loved, while Catholicism languishes, and in languishing develops Atheism, which Church does He favour? Which Church has evidently, in His opinion, best interpreted the wish of Christ? Is it Catholicism, which is diffusing widespread indifference and disgust, or Protestantism, with its clergy so respected, and in the majority of cases, I have reason to believe, so respectable? Now, Monsieur le Baron, I will say no more. It is so good and kind of you to come to me, and, if I have abused your time and patience, I can only plead the sorrow which is in my heart, the solitude to which I have been condemned."

"I know, I understand well. You must have felt very wretched; but, my dear fellow, just try and forget all you have suffered. I am going to do everything that a man can, to extricate you from this absurd charge which the Public Prosecutor ought to have known better than to make; and then, don't think that I shall desert you; you shall not be friendless while Leo de Courcelles is alive to help you. So cheer up, have a good heart, and believe me, happier days are in store for you. Now, I have said all I have to say; besides, here is someone coming, I think. Ah, so it is. Come, have you any message for Madame la Comtesse?"

Louis was too weak to conceal the agitation he felt, at this sudden allusion to this woman. Pretending not to notice the effect his words had produced, De Courcelles stood without speaking. With an effort to appear calm, Louis said:

"Please convey my best compliments to Madame la Comtesse de la Jonquières, and—"

The jailor entered, escorting a gentleman who proved to be the barrister whom Paris credited with possessing one of the sharpest of tongues, and whose services Maître Pélisier had been so glad to secure.

De Courcelles, having exchanged a few courteous remarks with this new-comer, and pressed Louis' hand with much warmth, left the prison to return to La Jonquières.

On the terrace of the château he found Amy. In the cool evening air, amidst the last gleams of sunlight, and the faint odour of late autumn flowers and fallen leaves, she stood, awaiting his home-coming with impatience and curiosity. She flung herself into his arms with all the affectionate *abandon* of her nature, and then, almost immediately, she began to question him. But to all her entreaties to relate his interview with Louis, De Courcelles would make but one reply.

"Come, come, the Abbé is well enough, I tell you. The turn affairs have taken has pleased me much, and all I can say is, that I shall be deucedly astonished if I don't contrive to surprise you yet. No, I shall not explain what I mean. Not now, at least. My dear Amy, I am adamant, I assure you, just for the present, so—"

"Well, I call it horrid of you," retorted Amy, with the most delicious little pout. "What am I to say to Blanche?"

"Oh, so she has sent you to pump me. Is that it?"

"I never said so."

"No, only I guessed as much. Well, say nothing. You must be discreet. Conceal the—"

"Conceal, indeed! At least, a husband has no right to conceal anything from his wife."

Laughing merrily, De Courcelles slipped away to change his coat, and Amy looked after him admiringly, wondering what he could mean, and determining to get it out of him when once they were really alone.

CHAPTER XXXVI.

As the session drew nearer, Blanche's excitement and anxiety increased. She would not suffer herself to dwell upon the misery which would await her as Brunot's wife. She repeatedly said to herself, "If Louis is spared further humiliation through this act of mine, I shall find means to endure the detestable advances of this creature, who is unscrupulous enough to obtain possession of me through a weakness he has discovered.

"But I shall be supported. My consolation will be derived from the knowledge that I, who have occasioned Louis so much misfortune, have at least been the means of extricating him from his difficulties. I shall have it in my power to be his guardian angel, to advance his interests, to take care that he wants for nothing, and if possible to more than atone for the injury our intimacy has done him. He shall never know whose hand is helping him, and it will be such a comfort that in the sight of God I shall be making reparation for the evil I have been guilty of. The peace which He can give will then take possession of me, and I shall find strength because I shall be doing right."

But try as she would, the poor martyr could not divest herself of doubts—doubts which wrenched at her heart and set her brain working. She kept asking herself: "What if Brunot's boasted power comes to naught? He probably thinks he has more influence than he really possesses. There can be no doubt that he will do his utmost. The desire to gratify his passion at my expense guarantees that. But try as he will, he may fail, and then—"

It was this uncertainty, this constantly recurring dread, that made her writhe and shudder as though in torment. She knew that she loved Louis so devotedly, that to save him physical or mental pain she would have bared her own shoulders to the lash, she would have stood in place of him in the dock, been arraigned as a criminal, and accepted the sentence passed, if only he might be spared. But what if the greatest sacrifice it was in her power to make should miscarry through some blunder! There was something so agonizing to her in this reflection, and the consideration of the consequences which must attend its realization, that as she lay awake, in the blackness and silence, she could barely refrain from screaming forth her fears. Night after night these hours of torture were endured by her, each one as it came seeming the more completely to lay under subjection and undermine her nervous system.

The truth was, that physically she was becoming weaker, while pitilessly, resistlessly, came the slow approach of the great day from which she had so much to hope, so much to fear. It was as though some Titan advanced upon her with huge strides, before which she all the while must be content to retreat and cower. Then, after these distracting periods, when through her brain tore endless, distorted, and distressing thoughts, would come the whitening dawn, the tumultuous twitter of the rejoicing birds, and she would admit the light, and gaze at her own reflection, horrified at the ravages with which these appalling moments had marked their flight.

"God is merciful," she would say to herself. "He will not torment me long. He is incapable of such cruelty. It will end soon, and I shall be in a position to recall these harrowing reflections with calmness. To say to myself—how foolish you were, could you not trust? You were fighting for the right, had you no faith? You might have known that you would triumph."

And then, having dressed with the care and neatness which was a part of her nature, she would sink upon her knees, and tearfully address to the Deity an earnest appeal for pardon, pity, and help for Louis; Louis, who could never belong to her, and whom it was a sin even to think of. Comforted, outwardly calm at least, and even more beautiful with the impress of sorrow upon her sympathetic face, she would then descend to breakfast, where to spare those who were so kind and good to her, she would force herself to be cheerful, even gay, and so it would go on through the sultry hours, while to her heart, even the sun seemed to shine in mockery of the anguish which lacerated and left it bleeding.

During this season, Monsieur Brunot, as might have been expected of him, displayed the bad taste to present himself at the château from time to time, as though to assure himself that the treasures which were to be his, were safe, and in no danger of taking wings to themselves. And on these occasions—vulgar man that he was—he would devour Blanche with his eyes, whenever he thought no one was looking. With volubility, and in loud tones, too, he would discuss the approaching trial, and with a shudder, her flesh becoming cold, as though the marrow were frozen within her, Blanche would listen, while his coarse lips formed the name which had become so dear to her.

Sometimes her pent-up indignation and loathing for the overweening and vulgar Deputy would summon the blood to her cheeks. Her blue eyes would flash dangerously, while she would clench her hands tightly, as though she felt her fingers closing about the neck of this callous, unprincipled brute.

When she looked like that, Brunot generally came to the conclusion that he had better make himself scarce. Yet, as he drove away amidst the stately timber of the park, and feasted his eyes upon the old château, and the delightful prospect which it commanded, he would say to himself, "Yes, she has a devil of a temper, I can see that; but once let her become my wife, and we shall quickly see who is master. Ah! she will become as docile as a dog one has beaten. Women are like that." And he would loll back in his carriage and fold his arms deliberately, as though he could already feel Blanche within their grip.

Those visits always annoyed Amy, and elicited from De Courcelles some irritable comment.

"Why the deuce does that fellow choose a time like this to present himself, eh, Countess?" he would inquire of Blanche. "Upon my word, I call it distinctly bad taste."

"Oh, he means well enough," Blanche would feel constrained to reply, while wondering what De Courcelles would say if he knew what she had done.

"I hate him more every time I see him," Amy would exclaim passionately.

And at the outburst of genuine wrath on the part of his pretty wife, De Courcelles would open his eyes and remark:

"That's right, little one. Upon my word, what

you do feel, you feel thoroughly. Nothing half and half about you. Now, just say the word, Countess, and we'll kick the fellow out."

"You forget, Leo, how dangerous Monsieur Brunot might make himself."

"Oh, ah! well, after the trial we can really square up with him, if you like. A good many people will be surprised, I fancy, if all goes as I intend it to, but—" and he would make a significant pause, and move away as though to leave the room.

"Now have the goodness to explain what you mean by that remark," Amy would insist, stepping up to him with a threatening air.

"Mean! why, nothing, little one," he would provokingly retort.

"I believe you really are telling us the truth now. But don't persist in throwing out those meaningless innuendoes, or I shall get cross, for you know I can."

"But not with me."

Whereupon he would kiss her, and Blanche would smile, for it cheered her to witness the unalloyed happiness of these two, who were daily becoming more and more dear to her. She had overheard similar remarks, however, from De Courcelles' lips more than once, and she could not help wondering what he meant, though pride forbade her to ask.

In this way—while the leaves lay thick upon the ground, and cold blasts swept through the boughs they had clothed, changing from gold to bronze the bracken amidst which the rabbits sported—the time passed.

De Courcelles visited Louis with the same unvarying kindness and good-nature, the same manifestations of unalterable friendship. For, really, the heart of this amiable young fellow was touched. And as he had frankly told Louis, he could conceive no situation in which human sympathies were more powerfully appealed to than in his own. How could a sadder picture present itself than the spectacle of this young, upright, and talented man, beginning his life journey, pledged to bear the burdens of others, joyless, himself a prey to perplexing, nay, agonizing doubt, profoundly solitary, his whole existence at variance with the great fundamental laws of nature? Truly, De Courcelles felt that Louis Bernard stood in need of his assistance and pity. The more he saw of him, too, the more he liked, nay, admired him. As for the discussions they indulged in, their truth had laid hold upon his mind.

And so the day of the trial at length dawned.

Blanche, Amy, and De Courcelles set out for Mezieres by an early train, and towards three o'clock found themselves in the Assize Court, occupying a corner of the first row of seats, where, sheltered from the gaze of the curious, Blanche wrestled with her feelings and strove to appear unconcerned, remembering that all she did was for Louis' sake.

The court and approaches to it were thronged, the public even cramming themselves into the spaces reserved for the barristers and reporters.

Immediately before Blanche lay the empty space, in the middle of which was the bar; beyond this again, the table upon which was laid the incriminating letter Louis had addressed to the Count.

At the far end of the hall sat the judges, imperturbably grave, dignified, and awe-inspiring. On the left was the jury-box, and upon the opposite side, the dock, where stood Louis, guarded by two gendarmes; while within easy reach of his client sat the eminent Paris barrister engaged by Maître Pélisier.

Amongst the crowd of spectators were to be seen the

familiar faces of Pierre Chotard; Lisette, looking as radiant and impudently pretty as ever; Félix, who had witnessed the quarrel between Louis and the Count; and in a corner alone, and apparently convinced that she had but come to witness her son's discomfiture—Louis' mother.

The proceedings commenced, and soon the defence and the prosecution were engaged in exchanging sharp blows.

Louis, to whom the moments were supremely painful, stood in dignified silence, humility and resolution marking his face. He kept his eyes persistently fixed upon the judges, for he had caught a glimpse of Blanche, and had felt a wave of emotion thrill through him which threatened to unman him. He at once told himself that unless he wished to wear the face of a criminal, he must not dare to encounter her gaze again. There was no longer any coughing, whispering, or shuffling of feet; the people were becoming thoroughly interested, for the examination of the prisoner had, it was considered, gone against him. This was enough to make this collection of peasantry pay marked attention, for in all likelihood was not their superior, their preceptor, their earthly pattern, about to be handed over to the guillotine? Of course, there was no saying what wonders might be worked by the lawyer from Paris, yet somehow they had little faith in him; besides, the facts against Louis were too strong to be upset by volleys of words, no matter how cunningly strung together.

This was the state of affairs when the Paris barrister began to urge the existence of a few astonishing facts, in a voice of great power and sweetness.

Suddenly the attention he had attracted was diverted by some confusion near one of the entrances. There was evidently an angry altercation between the gendarmes and someone who wished to gain admission. Then while people were craning their necks, and wondering what the fuss could be about, a young man was seen to force his way past all obstacles, and heard to exclaim in a loud, clear voice which commanded silence:

"Monsieur le President, the man who killed Monsieur le Comte de la Jonquières stands before you. I repeat, I, André Moriseau, shot him. And it was because he robbed me of the woman who was to have been my wife."

As these words rang forth, M. Brunot, who had contrived to seat himself quite near to Blanche, became intensely agitated. He looked as though he could have slain André with his eyes alone.

Blanche, upon whose delighted ears the announcement fell at a moment when her anxiety was becoming unendurable, received such a shock that her senses swam.

She was conscious of fixing her eyes upon Louis, and of trying to read his thoughts, while controlling an intense desire to give audible expression to her own feelings of joy, conscious also that De Courcelles addressed her and supported her with his arm; then the whole scene became a blank. The confusion in the court, and the proceedings which followed, passed without her knowing, and she became completely mistress of herself again only when the four walls of the Hotel Mont D'Or, which was near at hand, sheltered her, and De Courcelles in his kindly tones was saying:

"Come, come, Countess, joy never kills; you must pull yourself together. You have given us a fright, I assure you. I said that everything would go right from the first, though deuce take me if I thought of this dénouement. Now that you are better again,

I'll get back to the court, and Amy will look after you until I return. I shall not be long."

And away sped De Courcelles at the best speed of his long legs, leaving the two young women to discuss events, Amy taking upon herself the task her husband had assigned her with an affection and good grace that was comforting as well as irresistibly charming.

It was now becoming late, and many of the good people who had driven miles to satisfy their curiosity, were setting off homewards, having delivered themselves of their opinions as freely as they had imbibed their liquor.

De Courcelles found the authorities not over anxious to part with their prisoner, but after some delay Louis again stepped into the fresh air. The good-hearted young Baron, who had poured forth a torrent of congratulations, and had even embraced him, now conducted him across to the Mont D'Or with this one remark:

"Come with me, my dear fellow; I wish it. There is plenty of time. You can rest here a little while, and then decide what you intend to do."

Following his kind conductor, with his heart overflowing with gratitude and thankfulness, Louis traversed the hotel until, pausing before a door, with a merry twinkle in his eyes, De Courcelles flung it open, and Louis found himself in the presence of the two young women.

"The hero of the hour has come to pay you a visit, Countess," remarked the Baron delightedly. "Those confounded fellows yonder tried hard to keep him, but I would not hear of it. I assure you I had my work cut out for me, though. They hummed and hawed, until I became exasperated, and felt like telling them to hang themselves with their red tape. However, here we are, and no bones broken. Now, Monsieur l'Abbé, you shall relate your own story to Madame la Comtesse, and if you will excuse me for a few moments, I will attend to some little commissions which must not be forgotten. Come, my dear," he added to his wife, accompanying his words with a look and a significant gesture.

Amy took the hint, and Louis, who was too much agitated to deliver himself of more than a confused greeting, found himself in another moment alone with Blanche.

Turning to his wife, as they traversed a corridor, De Courcelles remarked:

"Now, do you understand? Things have gone precisely as I wanted. Leave those two together, and if they don't succeed in arriving at an understanding—well, don't blame me."

"But—" began Amy.

De Courcelles laid his finger on her lips.

"Hush," he said; "I like people to be happy, if possible. Have patience." And the two walked away together.

By a powerful effort of will, Louis collected himself. Had he been given time to think, he might have gleaned something from De Courcelles' conduct; but so much was compressed into those few seconds in which he stood before Blanche without words to express himself, that he could base his conduct only upon these ideas.

Before him was a woman who was his superior in rank, whom he loved, it was true, devotedly, but who, he had taught himself to believe, could not be anything to him, and, moreover, did not wish to be. So many times had he said to himself, "She does not love me," that he had come to believe it sufficiently to appear cold and dignified.

Blanche, her good resolutions flying before the feelings which the mere sight of him awakened, striving to stay the beating of her heart, attempting to guide her tongue even, could only falter forth a confession of her love in the brief sentence:

"Thank God, you are safe!"

Telling himself that this warmth of sentiment towards him was probably assumed, Louis replied icily:

"Madame la Comtesse, I can only assure you that I am deeply grateful for the good feeling your words convey."

The moment he opened his mouth she became aware of the existence of a difference between them. What was it? what had happened? Why did he speak to her in such tones, and with such words—she who had endured, and been willing to endure, so much for him? "Ah, if he only knew!" she thought. Her pride asserted itself. Drawing herself up haughtily, she said:

"No gratitude is needed. But if you are at liberty to do so, will you answer me this question? Have you known all along who was guilty of this crime?"

"Yes."

"And the seal of the confessional prevented you from speaking?"

"Precisely."

"Then you wrote that letter as—"

"A warning."

"Who do you think ought to be grateful, then?' she exclaimed warmly, overjoyed in the same breath to think that Brunot had no hold upon her, and now longing to beat down the barrier which seemed to divide them.

"It was simply my duty," he murmured.

"To return good for evil. To write a generous letter in return for an unnecessary insult. That may be, but—"

"Do not speak of all this, I implore you. The dead rest; let it sleep, as he does."

"But why?"

Louis glance at this woman, and felt his courage, his goodness, fail him. Her cheeks were flushed with excitement, her dear eyes sparkled with animation. She had never seemed so beautiful. An agonizing thought flashed through his mind. "You must leave her," it said. "This may be one of your last interviews."

"Why?" she repeated.

"Oh," he replied, in confusion, "because I have other things to talk about. You see I cannot count upon the future. You will be in La Jonquières or in Paris—I shall not."

"But again, why?" she demanded, repressing the eagerness and interest, the love which was consuming her.

"Well, you will understand how impossible it is for me to go near La Jonquières, at least."

"What, when in everyone's eyes you are innocent and a martyr to an unfortunate mistake. I see no earthly reason why you should leave it."

Every gesture, every word as it fell from her lips, vibrated through him. The sound of her voice, the light in her eyes that seemed to him as the eyes of an angel, shook his resolves, his doubts of her, and fairly unmanned him.

"I cannot explain all I feel—why I have decided to go, fully. But it would be too painful to me to have any further dealings with people who have gossiped about me for weeks. Let them think and say what they like, but I must part company with them."

"But you forget what that means, surely?"

He understood her. It meant separation; the simple idea coming from her lips obscured his sight, and made his tongue so dry that it would hardly frame the reply which rose to his lips.

"Perhaps Monsieur le Baron has supplied you with reasons why I should no longer remain at La Jonquières," he faltered.

"He has told me nothing."

"Well, I have suffered so much, in one way or another, and the suffering has made me think. I have long had misgivings, long had doubts. What will you say of me when I tell you that this dress, this religion, no longer becomes me? A long while ago, I remember saying to you that you would deem me a monster of depravity if I told you my convictions. Well, now they can no longer be hidden. In some quiet spot where I am unknown, I shall go and preach what I believe to be right. Only when I am gone, because I am a changed man, do not think of me as an apostate."

He glanced up at her, where, with wildly beating pulse, she sat combating the anguish which half-choked her.

"You are a changed man, you say; but why are you so changed to me?" she entreated almost in a whisper.

"I am not," he found strength to reply.

"You are not? Then why should I think you so? No, don't interrupt me, I mistake nothing. You speak calmly of my being in La Jonquières or in Paris, while you—you are elsewhere."

"And can I help that? Am I to blame?"

"Can you help it? Are you to blame?"

"Yes."

"Shall I reply to you as I think?"

"I ask it."

"Then would you have come and told me this once, in the days gone by? Would you have informed me that you were about to quit the spot where we met, and where we have spent days which I own were happy to me, without a sigh, without any apparent regret? Would you have done this? I think not."

"You misjudge me. But what is there left for me to do? When I bid farewell to La Jonquières, in the opinion of the world I shall be degraded, for I shall be destitute. In the opinion of the Church I shall be an outcast, an object of loathing, a heretic. In God's sight alone shall I have done right, for the conscience He has given me tells me so. Better be anything than a hypocrite."

"When you leave La Jonquières, you may be all that you have said in the estimation of those who don't know you; but—" she broke off, abruptly, startled by sounds, as of someone approaching the door. Then remembering that the Baron and Amy might return at any moment, she continued boldly—"but have you thought of me? If you cannot forget, can I?"

"You?" Louis faltered, for this direct appeal was more than he could bear.

"Yes," she retorted. Then no longer able to control her feelings, she added with rapid utterance, "Have we not always understood each other? And at such a moment as this, shall we fail to do so? Oh! I cannot endure this any longer. There shall be no misunderstanding if I can help it. No false pride shall silence me. Wherever you go, whatever you do, let the world and the Church frown upon you as they may, my place is beside you, for God has given me but one heart, and it is yours."

Leaping to his feet, his pale face radiant with joy, one word only escaped him :

"Blanche!"

His knees seemed to knock together. With outstretched arms, his soul in his eyes, and those eyes encountering the look which had made them one at heart before, he stood for an instant irresolute, as though his very senses lied to him in that he was unable to comprehend this great joy. Then the lips he loved, and yet had never dared to touch, replied softly :

"Louis."

There was no longer a veil between them, and they sank into each other's arms.

In through the open windows came the soft evening air, strong with the odour of the country, and bearing upon it the faint hum of distant traffic. Awakening as from a dream, they again became conscious of these sounds of life. They lived, and lived now for God and each other.

CHAPTER XXXVII.

THE superabundance of bliss into which Louis had been so suddenly plunged, had had the very natural effect of partly depriving him of speech, so that throughout the whole of the drive back to La Jonquières, through the quiet of that marvellous evening, he could barely do more than look—his eyes occasionally bright with tears—and try to understand, to grasp the fact that he was actually free, and breathing an atmosphere of devoted love and genuine kindness.

Had he been asked, he would have contended that mere words would fail to describe his ineffable happiness, but that his silence was understood and appreciated—for were not Blanche and he henceforth one in thought and aim, and were not Amy and De Courcelles intensely sympathetic and his devoted friends? For once in his life he failed to notice the sights and sounds of the delightful country district through which he was being driven, and for which, under ordinary circumstances, he had so quick an eye and ear.

Years after, it all came back to him, and he could feel the loving pressure of Blanche's hand as he bade her good-night—could hear De Courcelles' and his young girl-wife's cheery farewell—and on the threshold of his own door, could again see, as though in life, his mother's face, stern and unsympathetic in proportion to the need of the moment, and seeing that he had returned from what had looked very like death.

Though steeped in this languor of love, this delicious stupor, after the immense fatigue, the frightful anxiety he had endured, it was not long before he became alive to the fact that he was still in the thick of the fight. The peasantry, his own parishioners, would have gone wild over him—would have worshipped him as a hero, seeing that one of their number had occasioned him such suffering, and that he was their priest; but, then, was he not the friend of the great people at the château? According to M. Brunot, was he not—they could scarce believe their ears—the chosen, the accepted lover of Madame la Comtesse?

There could be no doubt that M. Brunot held strong cards, and no less could have been expected of him and his wealthy vulgarity, than that he should play them for all they were worth.

Black looks were therefore soon lavished upon Louis, and but scant courtesy met him on all sides. Then came a communication from his bishop, as outcome of the dead Count's action, ordering him to move, within a certain period, to another parish; and then, too, came the decisive moment for Louis.

Blanche and De Courcelles were consulted, and after hearing all he had to say, Blanche approved, and De Courcelles supported with his usual staunchness, the result being a simple reply to the bishop, in which Louis explained his feelings and opinions clearly, and as he understood them.

Prior to all this, though, and within forty-eight hours of his return to La Jonquières, Louis' big, kind heart had overflowed with pity, and a certain sense of sympathy, for poor, passionate André, and he had set out for Mezieres, driven by De Courcelles, and had gained admittance to the doomed man, for, as his priest, he had a right to be there.

André was brutal at first, resented the visit, and became sullenly silent; then, when pressed to speak, in Louis' most gentle and persuasive tones, fiercely affirmed that his admission of the crime was due to Lisette's conduct. She had fooled him, the heartless coquette. He had nothing to live for; that was why he was in jail. No pity for Louis, no sense of guilt, had influenced him. He was not so womanish, not he. Saddened, distressed beyond measure, fearful that this man should meet death in such a mood, Louis decided to remain at Mezieres until he had reasoned with him, tried to soften his heart.

So, almost within the shadow of the Hotel Mont D'or, where he and Blanche had spent such sweet moments, he engaged lodgings; and there, in the silence of those four walls, prayed with his whole heart, his face bathed in tears, that God might pardon and take André into His keeping. Each day he visited and reasoned with him; the result being, that touched, changed by the display of so much tenderness and sympathy, when the day came to step to the guillotine, André met death calmly, and blessing him.

All that remains to be told now, unfolds itself in a few words, a few brief sentences. Rather less than one year from the date of that evening at the Hotel Mont D'or, Louis' life was crowned with happiness. The devoted woman, who, in the face of all things, loved him so sincerely, waited only until the customary period of one year's mourning had passed, and then she became his. And these two, into whose existence at once stole the calm that comes to those who have striven and won their life's desire, removed to Paris, where Louis proceeded to develop the ideas he had conceived.

Backed by De Courcelles' influence, he began to teach with a vigour and ability that daily increased in the light of Blanche's loving smiles, the principles he had come to believe in, and as though fortune had done her worst and had now nothing but the sunlit side of her fickle face to turn towards him, not only was he soon recognised as a powerful, though original, preacher, but a man in whose heart God dwelt.

THE END.

Printed by Cowan & Co., Limited, Perth.

www.ingramcontent.com/pod-product-compliance
Lightning Source LLC
Chambersburg PA
CBHW020226240426
43672CB00006B/430